WEiRD N.J.
VOL.2

Sterling Publishing Co., Inc.
New York

Weird N.J.

Vol. 2

Your Travel Guide to New Jersey's Local Legends and Best Kept Secrets

by
MARK MORAN
and
MARK SCEURMAN

WEIRD N.J. VOL.2

Published by Sterling Publishing Co., Inc.
387 Park Avenue South, New York, NY 10016
© 2006 Mark Sceurman and Mark Moran
Distributed in Canada by Sterling Publishing
c/o Canadian Manda Group, 165 Dufferin Street
Toronto, Ontario, Canada M6K 3H6
Distributed in Great Britain by Chrysalis Books Group PLC
The Chrysalis Building, Bramley Road, London W10 6SP, England
Distributed in Australia by Capricorn Link (Australia) Pty. Ltd.
P. O. Box 704, Windsor, NSW 2756, Australia

10 9 8 7 6 5 4 3 2 1

Photography and illustration credits are found on page 302
and constitute an extension of this copyright page.

Sterling ISBN 13: 978-1-4027-3941-5
Sterling ISBN 10: 1-4027-3941-9

For information about custom editions, special sales, premium
and corporate purchases, please contact Sterling Special Sales
Department at 800-805-5489 or specialsales@sterlingpub.com.

Design: Richard J. Berenson
Berenson Design & Books, LLC, New York, NY

CONTENTS

Introduction

It's often said that you can never go home again. Well, folks, we're here to let you all know that not only CAN you go home again, but there is no better feeling in the world! After a couple of years spent traveling around this great country of ours in search of weirdness in every corner of the United States, we can safely say that there is no place like home—and none weirder, that's for sure!

But how do we introduce *Weird N.J.* to our fellow New Jerseyans, many of whom have known us for several years already? That's the question we asked ourselves when it came to writing the introduction for this, our second *Weird N.J.* book. We've been research-ing and reporting on all the strange and previously undocumented aspects of the Garden State for more than a decade now. So long, in fact, that our readers seem more like old traveling buddies to us than anony-mous page-turners. So friends, we thought that for this next leg of our journey together, we'd reintroduce ourselves by taking you back to where it all began. And, to do that, Mark S. will now tell you a little tale from his formative years. . . .

I remember the excitement of my first night being able to drive a car by myself. I was just seventeen and had convinced my old man to let me borrow his 1965 Ford Galaxy XL 500 (a classic that had been passed down through the family a few times). After getting the fifty-minute lecture and a promise to him that nothing would happen, I was on the road, sailing off to unknown adventures and feeling the freedom of the road for the very first time.

In actuality, I just picked up my friend Pete and two girlfriends, and proceeded to drive around town, looking cool.

We somehow ended up riding around the Cedar Grove Reservoir, next to Mill's Reservation. It was dark, and Pete and I decided to scare the girls. I drove along the gravel road and started to tell a spooky story. Then I would suddenly shut the headlights off for a few seconds, turning everything into total darkness. Each time I did that, the girls would scream, and Pete and I would laugh and howl out the window, "The Hook-armed Man is outside the car! The Boogeyman's behind us!"

The more they screamed, the more we would taunt them with stories of ghosts, serial killers in the woods, and Jersey Devils, and all the while I turned the head-lights on and off as we drove around the reservoir.

Then it happened.

I looked in the rearview mirror, and racing up behind us was a police car—red lights flashing and siren wailing.

The adrenaline rush suddenly sank to the depths of fear much more real than any legendary maniac in the woods: I was going to get a ticket, and worse, my old man would never let me drive again. Everyone in the car was white as a sheet and silent—like they really did see a ghost.

The officer walked over to the car and looked in the window and said, "Do you know it's illegal to drive a vehicle at night with the lights off?"

"Honest, officer," I replied. "This is my first night driving, and today is my birthday."

"What are you doing here?" he said.

And the first words out of my mouth were, "Telling ghost stories!"

The officer gave me a stern look and rolled his eyes,

This is the sort of recollection that *Weird N.J.* is all about--the thrills, both great and small, that are waiting to be experienced right in our own backyard. It is a journey of discovery of our surroundings and of ourselves that takes us to places that are sometimes talked about but seldom explored firsthand. It is folklore, mythology, and yes, even history, melded together with pride. It is our voice, echoed by the resounding voices of thousands of our fellow Jerseyites, celebrating our home state's eccentricities. It is a love affair with New Jersey and everything about it that is left of center and outside the norm.

Whether all the stories we tell about odd places in the state are true or not is not really important. What is important is that while we read and retell them, our minds are open to the possibility that they might be true. The sites we visit are noteworthy because they are catalysts that inspire our imagination and blur our all-too-well-defined perceptions of what is real, and what we'd like to believe just MIGHT be real. For what would life be without a sense of mystery, adventure, and curiosity about the unknown? We know that we wouldn't want to live in a world like that!

then shined his flashlight at the two girls in the back seat, who both gave the officer a sheepish smile.

After looking over my license and registration, he handed them back and said, "Get out of here and grow up."

That was my first encounter with what would become known years later as a Weird N.J. *experience.*

So we visit the places and people that might offer us something out of the ordinary, and we share what we find out about them with you. Fortunately, the state of New Jersey seems to have an inexhaustible supply of weird stories for us to investigate and document.

Just one more reason why there's no place like home!
—*Mark and Mark*

HIGH SCHOOL, LAMBERTVILLE, N.J.

SPEED
LIMIT
35

Local Legends
(of Your Garden State Variety)

New Jersey possesses an incredibly rich and complex fabric of modern folklore and localized legends, perhaps more so than any other state in the country. But still, in these rapidly changing times and fast disappearing Garden State landscapes, some of our mythology gets transformed, overlooked, or worst of all, forgotten forever.

Some sites that once lured carloads of midnight legend trippers have, for one reason or another, fallen out of favor with younger generations of adventurers. Other once popular destinations have sadly become victims of the ever advancing bulldozer of progress.

On the other hand, some New Jersey myths seem impervious to the fickle trends that might squelch a lesser legend. These stories live on and even grow more potent, surviving long after the physical site that first inspired them has disappeared. Perhaps there is something more to these tales than meets the eye. Or perhaps it's just that a good story never dies.

In this chapter, we'll visit some of the locations that have inspired the coming-of-age stories of generations of New Jerseyans. They tell of the places we once went, and in some cases still go, for our rites of passage. Some can be visited to this day. Others live on only in the memories of people who were indelibly marked by the experiences they had there once upon a time.

The Legend of Bud's Grave

Many versions of the legend of Bud's Grave have been told over the years, and most contain some elements of truth. The story is this: An old man lived in a bungalow he called Hollywood in the Highlands of Monmouth County. It's located on a lonely bay shore road at the bottom of a wooded hillside. The man's son, Bud, wandered away from home one day, never to be seen again, and was presumed dead. The old man, consumed by grief, began constructing a monument to his son's memory. Over time, the shrine became a mass collection of toys, dolls, and colorful decorations that seemed designed to lure the boy back home from the netherworld.

Before long, the curious began making late-night jaunts to the monument. Many claimed they saw a strange, misty apparition at the site, which by this time had become known in local lore as Bud's Grave. Some believe that the apparition was the ghost of Bud himself, who would return to the playground on moonlit nights to play with the toys set out for him by his heartbroken father, only to disappear when midnight visitors came.

It's a good story, and we know that some of it is even factual. There was indeed a site on a lonely road in the Highlands where an old man had built a structure festooned with toys, dolls, and decorative signs. We had in our possession a picture of the site in its heyday. The old man lived in a bungalow across the street, which bore a sign saying HOLLYWOOD. We also know that the location was indeed a popular late-night destination for carloads of youthful ghost hunters. And we know that the entire site had been dismantled by the time we first visited there in the early '90s.

Yet people's memories of Bud's Grave would not let the story fade quietly into the night. Years after the destruction of the shrine, *Weird N.J.* continues to receive letters from readers telling us about it.

So imagine our surprise when one day, at a magazine-signing party in Red Bank, a man in a suede fringe jacket, cowboy boots, and a western-style belt buckle moseyed on up to us, pointed to a picture of Bud's Grave featured in issue number 10 of *Weird N.J.*, and said, "Hi, I'm Bud—of Bud's Grave."

Mind you, although the story was always one of our favorites, we never really believed that there was ever an actual flesh and blood BUD! But there he was, big as life, a tall, rugged-looking man, in his mid to late fifties. He had a wistful grin and a kind of mischievous twinkle in his eye, which at first made us suspicious of his claim to the Bud identity. But when he produced his business card and we read the name Buddy Rodgers and the address, which we knew to be the location of the bungalow, we knew he was the real deal.

Of course we set up an appointment to interview this walking, talking icon of New Jersey folklore.

Dead Man Talking

We met with Buddy on a hot sunny morning at the bayside cottage given the moniker of Hollywood by his late father, Buddy senior. An easygoing man with a playful sense of humor, Bud invited us in to meet his ninety-year-old mother. He told us that he'd been living on the West Coast for many years—acting, writing, and taking photographs—but had recently returned to New Jersey to look after his mother.

After Buddy showed us a couple of video clips of Bud's Grave in its prime, we walked across the street to a soggy plot of land.

WNJ: So we're standing on the site where the original . . . umm, what would you call it?

This is the site where the legend began, from the seeds of collectibles gathered by a gruff, rugged man—my father. Statues of little angels, girls, dogs, wagon wheels—anything one might collect, my father collected.

In the pictures we've seen, there was a hut of some kind. What was that?

That was a shower house, before it became my father's toolshed. Everybody used to come up from the beach, and they'd go into the shower house. The water came out of the spring, so it was freezing!

What made your father start putting together the monument?

Originally there was this big open area. Then us kids came along. My father was really great with his hands, and with all these little canals that run by here, he built miniature piers and marinas. I had my boats and stuff in there. Then as we abandoned it during our teenage years and when we went off to the service, he started collecting things. It was decades in the making.

When do you first remember hearing the site referred to as Bud's Grave?

I was in Corpus Christi, Texas, when my father phoned and asked if I'd heard the rumor that I was buried over in this lot! I said, "Dad, that's the last thing I would have heard!" That was 1963. It kind of aggravated me to even hear something like that.

One of the rumors was that I was killed in Vietnam; another, that I had drowned at a young age.

I'd be down in Manasquan at a bar or in the navy or in college or even in New York City, and I'd mention the Highlands, and people would go, "You ever hear of Bud's Grave?" I started realizing how big this had grown, especially when I saw pictures of the grave in restaurants in Red Bank. Look at me, I'm calling it the Grave.

That's the power of myth. You've seen the album cover that the site appeared on.

Right. I really got a kick out of that. It was a local band, In Between Dreams. Meanwhile, this thing's growing and growing. So, of course, people start coming around here. My mother would call me and say, "I wish your father would get rid of all that stuff, because two, three in the morning there's cars lined all the way up the street. Beer cans, the neighbors are complaining. . . ." And there was a rumor that if you took anything from the grave, before you got a hundred yards away, you'd be struck dead.

Your father maintained this site until he died, right?

Right. Just before he died, he had a dump truck come here and take care of everything. So this is what remains (pointing to a handmade cross). What else remains is what's in people's minds, memories, and fantasies.

How does it feel to be a walking dead–living legend?

I have my good days and my bad days!

Buddy, when you die, where would you like to be buried?

I think about bringing authenticity to this place. I'm an East Coast man and a West Coast man. I love the nautical which is out here, and I love the cowboy life which is out in California. Maybe I'll have my ashes spread a little on each. Looking ahead, there's a good chance that someday Bud's Grave will really be Bud's Grave.

The True Tale of Bud

I grew up near Sandy Hook and I have the real story of Bud's grave. Here it is:

When I was 17, I remember hearing that a child had recently been reported missing—that was Bud. They never found him. His parents were bereft so the father left toys out there, hoping Bud would return home. Well, he never did. Later on, teens would use that place to hangout and leave stuff, mostly their old toys. Now all that is left is a statue of the Virgin Mary. I have heard from my friends that a ghost appears there on some nights in a glowing white haze.—*Brad Cherney*

Bud: A Dead Dog?

As a native New Jerseyan, I made many a trip to Bud's Grave.

On one such occasion, I met an old gentleman rearranging some of the "offerings." He lived across the street and I inquired if he knew anything about the place's origins. He suddenly produced a set of keys and opened the door to the shed on the site. The inside of the door was lined with newspaper clippings written about the site over the years. He chuckled as he related the story of how this all started.

It seems an old man (never got his name) had a dog named Bud. After a long and fruitful life, Bud left for that great fire hydrant in the sky. The old man felt obliged to give old Bud a proper funeral. He took Bud's remains across the street and buried him on the side of the road, marking the site with a sign that read BUD. He also placed some flowers, and some of Bud's favorite dog toys.

The next day the old man noticed that someone had added some dolls and knick-knacks, and over the following weeks, more and more items were added.

Kids hanging out started adding items and concocting tales about the mysterious origins of the place. This made its way into numerous college papers, changed into the story of Bud, a young boy who died of various means.—*Mike Nocks*

Bud's Grave, spelled here with two Ds

Ringoes' Skeleton Beneath the Floorboards

When I was a kid growing up in Ringoes, there was a local myth that there was a skeleton kept in the old Case house next to the church. As a matter of fact, two older friends of mine got into a fistfight over the one teen trespassing in the house to see the skeleton. The other teen worked for the Case family and did not take kindly to town kids fooling around with property that belonged to the Cases, who had been part of the community since the 1700s. As time went on, most of us forgot about the skeleton. That is, until we were teens.

One summer afternoon when we were all about 14, our friend Mark (who was working for the Cases) told my friend Scott and I that there actually was a skeleton in the old house. He offered to show us. Well, this was an opportunity we would have been crazy to pass up! The old house was definitely off limits, but since Mark worked for the family we felt relatively safe. As we entered the old dwelling, the first thing we noticed was all the old furniture, boxes, and assorted dusty crap that filled the downstairs. Mark led us up the stairwell. At the top was a small room containing some tables, a cabinet, and a strange sight on the floor. Mark walked over to a hatch of some kind. He picked up a metal bar, stuck it in a small hole in the hatch, pried it open, and there it was—a small wooden coffin that appeared to be for a small adult or large child. Inside the coffin was an actual honest-to-God skeleton that was wired down to the back of the coffin! Why it was there, I still don't know.

As we left the house Mark told us that when he got off work later that day he would show our friends Rob and Brad. He warned us not to go there without him because if we got caught, the consequences could be quite serious. Of course, as soon as the guys arrived, along with a couple of girls we hung out with, we took them up to see the skeleton right away.

Then, the wheels started turning. Rob suggested that it would be really funny if someone hid in the hatch, lying on the coffin, and jumped out at Mark when he was showing us the coffin later that day. Of course, we all thought this was brilliant. Rob got in the hatch and Scott hid in the cabinet in case Rob needed any help. The girls and I greeted Mark out on the sidewalk and told him Rob had been grounded, so he couldn't be there. As Mark led us up the stairs he turned to the girls and with a macho smirk said, "This is gonna scare the crap outta you!"

We got to the creepy foyer and I proceeded to pick up the metal bar to open the hatch. As I slowly opened it, Mark bent over to open the coffin lid. Suddenly Rob leapt out and grabbed Mark's leg with a ghostly shriek! Mark then shrieked and almost jumped into Brad's arms. He turned white as a ghost with his hair actually standing on end—I swear to God! We left the house pissing our pants we were laughing so hard. Mark tried to get on his bike to ride home but he was still shaking so hard he couldn't balance himself to ride. He had to walk his bike home.

Over the next few years we made a few more skeleton episodes, the funniest being when we snuck up and took pictures of the skeleton with us posing next to it. We put cigarettes in its mouth, sunglasses on its head, and generally acted like typical teenagers. I brought the pictures into school and showed them to a bunch of my classmates. Before long, Ringoes was being deluged with kids who wanted to see the skeleton. These thrill seekers were not as careful as we had been and many got caught. Eventually, I heard that the Cases moved the coffin or boarded it up or something. To this day I have no idea what the hell it was doing there under the floorboards, but it is one of the weirdest stories to come out of Ringoes.—*John Hedgepeth*

Case Family Claims No Skeletons in Their Closet

Curious about the story of the skeleton, *Weird N.J.* decided to do a little more digging. We paid a visit to the house, which is located on John Ringo Road. The house sits in front of the Case Nursery, a small family farm that sells fruit tree saplings and berry plants. The farm has been operated for the past hundred years by five generations of Cases. Though nobody was around to speak with us about the skeleton, we did manage to contact a family member via telephone. When asked if the family had heard the rumors about the coffin, they said they had but that the story had been misconstrued. According to them, the skeleton was never in the house, which is still occupied, but rather in the ramshackle Odd Fellows lodge that is located right next door.

They presumed that the skeleton was a replica and went on to speculate that it was most likely used by the Odd Fellows as a prop during initiation rites. The old lodge is now used for storage by the Case farm, and the skeleton is no longer there—though they did not say what had become of it.

So we did a little research into the Independent Order of Odd Fellows and the Cases' theory that the skeleton might have been employed in some sort of ceremonial lodge ritual. As it turns out, they might just be on to something! The following is an excerpt from an article by Dennis McCann that appeared in the *Milwaukee Journal Sentinel* that tells of a Wisconsin museum's exhibit dedicated to the strange ritual props used by fraternal orders in their initiation rites:

It's too bad that for so long so many fraternal organizations were thought of as secret societies, because some of their secret rituals were pretty wild.

In the new American Museum of Fraternal Studies that opened a few weeks ago in Berlin's [WI] historic Masonic Lodge, there is a coffin once used in Masonic initiation ceremonies. It looks harmless enough in the light of day but imagine it in a fog-filled room lighted only by candles, where an unsuspecting initiate wearing eye shades would be led to view the dearly departed—in reality a mechanical skeleton whose teeth could chatter on command. Though probably not as loud as the initiate's own teeth. . . .

Fraternal groups, most of which modeled their organizations along the lines of Freemasonry, were involved in more than ritual ceremonies and strange initiations. . . .

The Independent Order of Odd Fellows, the onetime organization of "Honorable, Frugal, Humble and Poor Laborers" whose symbolism was all taken from the Old Testament—at its peak claimed 1.5 million members in more than 22,000 lodges.

Tales of Berry's Chapel

In the nineteenth century, a thriving African-American community was developing in the tiny township of Quinton, NJ. Located deep in the piney woods of Salem County, this community was spread out and disparate.

John Berry, a Quinton resident who lived in the woods off Harmersville-Pecks Corner Road, decided to unify the local community by constructing a Methodist church on his property. Known as Berry's Chapel, it was originally just a log cabin with a small adjoining cemetery. African American Methodists came from miles around to worship at the small chapel in the woods. Legend has it that the chapel was a stop on the Underground Railroad, a safe haven for slaves fleeing bondage in the South.

At the same time, there are stories about the chapel's being continually terrorized by the K.K.K. It was abandoned in 1923, not because of the K.K.K. but because of progress. A new house of worship, the Haven M. E. Church, was built on the Bridgeton Pike, or Route 49. This new, more accessible house of worship was embraced by congregants of Berry's Chapel, who abandoned their old church. Eventually, the old chapel burned down, leaving only the overgrown cemetery as a reminder of the past.

In 2002, the Reverend Chuck Coblentz, a Quinton resident and Pennington School teacher, led an effort to restore the cemetery. Residents and students teamed up to begin the slow process of repairing the toppled gravestones. Once the cemetery is restored, locals would like to have the former location of Berry's Chapel recognized as a historic site due to its past importance to the local community and because of its ties to the Underground Railroad.

Burning down the House of Worship

There is a site in Quinton that was home to an African-American Church when slavery was still intact. The church was built in the woods by a pastor named Berry. It was burned down twice. The first time no harm was done to anyone; the second time the entire congregation died, including Berry. The remaining graveyard became a teenage drinking spot and was a supposed cult meeting ground.

They say on many nights if you go out there, you can see the church fully intact and burning and you can see and hear the parishioners dancing and praising. They also say you can hear metal scraping and people screaming. Berry is buried here but his grave is so far in the woods no one can ever seem to find his gravesite.*—Shannon*

Hanging Out at the Hanging Tree

I live in Salem County. There's a place about 5 miles from me called Berry's Chapel. It was supposedly burnt down by the Klan in the 20s and they were supposed to have hanged a bunch of people in the cemetery there.

That would explain "The Hanging Tree" as it's called. It's a huge tree—I can't tell what kind because it has no bark and never has leaves on it, but it is alive! There's a bulge on one of the branches where it looks like the tree grew around a rope that may have been tied around it. An old local man told me there used to be a piece of rope there when he was a boy back in the 30s.

I've heard countless stories of ghosts and devil worship and grave robbing. I have seen the dug up graves there. It's definitely a weird and scary place.*—Chris*

Crematory Hill

There is, or once was, a legendary place off a dirt road called Disbrow Hill in Monroe Township (Middlesex County) known as Crematory Hill. Back in the 1970s it was one of those scary places where at night anything could happen. It was supposed to be a structure where bodies were cremated, with the remains either shipped out or buried in the graveyard near the building. It was abandoned long ago due to the presence of ghosts and spirits.

It was a great place to go with friends to get a good scare. There was usually clothing and stuff hanging off the trees at the start of the road, and on several trips, we saw a large wooden sign on the side of the road with the warning: WELCOME TO HELL. Screaming sounds were often heard from the woods, but we drove on, excited and expecting anything!

The Crematory was down the road a while, on the right side. We got out and walked the path, adrenaline pumping. In the beams of the flashlights we saw the structure looming up on a hill. It was made out of bricks, stone, and cement. There were openings for windows and doors. In the basement there were some pipes through the floor, which were supposed to be part of the crematory equipment.

After exploring the Crematory, more courage was mustered to walk the grounds and find the cemetery. The walk back seemed longer and scarier. When you got closer to the road and your car came into view, you breathed a sigh of relief.

One time when we got out of the car at the Crematory, from the dark came howling voices and figures trying to attack us. We piled back in the car and I got out of there like a bat out of hell. Who they were and why they were there is a mystery.

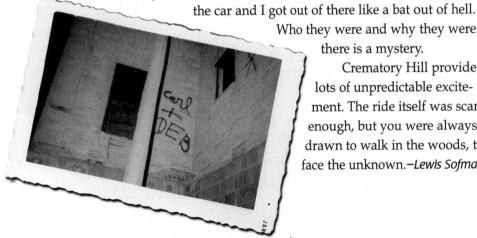

Crematory Hill provided lots of unpredictable excitement. The ride itself was scary enough, but you were always drawn to walk in the woods, to face the unknown. –*Lewis Sofman*

Memories of Crematory Hill

I lived in South River and I remember stories of all the "older kids" going to Crematory Hill, my brother included.

One night a lot of kids in the neighborhood went in about five cars, and they decided to scare the girls. A few hours later they came back racing down the street and some of the girls were crying and really shaken up. From what I heard they had been shot at and almost didn't make it out alive. When I asked my brother what had happened, he was white as a ghost and said I don't want to know.

They eventually bulldozed and built condos and stuff there, so I never got a chance to check it out. Too bad they took it away from us. And they wonder why kids get into trouble all the time, and why they have nothing to do. –*Grafxchik*

The Man on the Roof

Casting a watchful eye on the residents of Huber Street in Secaucus is what the locals call the Man on the Roof, a silhouette of a man standing on a rooftop. It is apparent only at night.

The "man" is a double chimney on a two-story house that strikes a remarkably manlike pose. Over the years, the figure has turned into an enigmatic icon for the neighborhood and is continually repaired and retarred for new generations of sightseers. The silhouette is viewed to its most dramatic effect from one block north of Huber, on Franklin Street.

The legend is that a lonely man keeps a silent vigil as he waits for his long-lost family to return. Another story says he's a sea captain waiting for his sailors to arrive in town. The most dramatic scenario is that the man is waiting to exact revenge on a burglar who brutally killed his family and kidnapped his young daughter many years ago.

The Man on the Roof legend is well known outside New Jersey. Visitors are known to honk their car horns as they drive by. Neighbors asked the owner of the building to paint the chimney white or take it down, but the owner just laughs off the whole issue.

"People come because it is an attraction," said former mayor Anthony Just in a *New York Times* article about the legend. "It gives the town a new twist."

Al Capone's Summer Home

On one Weird N.J. excursion we went to Beechwood, just north of Bayville. We had heard reports over the years of "Al Capone's Summer Home" somewhere in the Bayville area, so we decided to see what we could dig up on the Chicago crime boss's travels in New Jersey. The only information we had was that the place was now called the Bayview Convalescent Home and was located near Double Trouble Road. (Hmmm, sounded like gangster lingo to us.)

We inquired at a deli about the convalescent home's alleged Capone connection. "Oh, yes," said the girl behind the counter, "I've heard that for years. The place is just down the road."

A man standing by the magazines chimed in with ". . . and his mother was there too! I heard that he actually built the place for her, as a kind of retirement home."

We headed to the diner next door and asked our waitress if she had heard the legend.

"Oh, that's old news, honey," she snorted. "Al Capone built the hospital for his mother, who was a patient there."

After she left our table, we discussed how strange it

was that everyone we encountered seemed not only to know the story but took it as a matter of fact. We know that when we get two similar leads, a local legend, like Prohibition hooch, is brewing.

We drove to the Bayview Convalescent Home and right away noticed that certain architectural features, such as Corinthian columns and reliefs depicting sailing and hunting scenes, gave the place an odd appearance for a hospital. Nearby was Crystal Lake, which was overgrown with reeds and had a long-forgotten cement deck overlooking the water.

We inquired at the admitting desk about the date of the building, and the woman told us she had a brochure that described the place in the 1920s. We then told her we had heard a legend about Al "Scarface" Capone's visiting the hospital.

"Well, I can't vouch for that," she replied, "but if he did, he came when it was a hotel. That story has been circulating for a long time."

It was then that one of the administrators showed us an old brochure that had ROYAL PINES HOTEL on the front and boasted "fine dining and dancing." There were many pictures of the hotel in its art deco splendor, including a grand view of the "Indian Room," the Mediterranean-style solarium, and tiled outdoor patio. The pictures also showed Crystal Lake in its heyday, with guests swimming and gondolas gliding across the water.

"Would you like to see the Indian Room?" the administrator asked, and of course we said yes. He walked us into what is now used as a TV room for the elderly residents. Looking at the intricately designed

rafters in the ceiling, we could see that at one time this had been a beautiful dining hall that could have easily attracted high-profile members of society. We also suspected that due to the location of this hotel, just on the outskirts of the Pine Barrens, Prohibition laws might have been somewhat less strictly enforced here than elsewhere.

We asked our guide if he had ever heard stories about the appearance of Scarface at the hotel.

"Oh, yeah, I've even tried to find the hidden tunnel entrances that are supposed to be all through this place, but I've yet to discover them."

Whether or not the Royal Pines was ever a favorite hideout of Al Capone is still unknown. But two things are certain: In its prime, this place must have been one hell of a joint, and if you ask anyone you meet in Beechwood or Bayville about Al Capone, they will undoubtedly point you in the direction of the Bayview Convalescent Home.

Capone Drank in the Tunnels

There is a huge building in Bayville that was, at different times, a prosperous hotel and an insane asylum. Also, Al Capone supposedly once owned and lived in the property. Now it's a convalescent center for old folks.

I used to live within a mile of the place. There's a small lake in front of the building, and it's rumored that there are a series of tunnels running underneath the property and even a secret hatch in the middle of the lake. At first I had heard that the tunnels were used by Capone to hide from the cops, but a more likely story (which was told by one of my teachers at high school) is that the tunnels were used by servants who brought food and booze to Capone and his men, who would drink and gamble down there. —*Rob Thayer*

Al Capone at Royal Pines

In the 1920s, Pinehaven Sanitarium was a hotel. It was also a famous hangout for Al Capone. During prohibition, the hotel would charge $1.90 per glass of whatever they had, and Al and his gang would sit (heavily armed) and drink.

There are also, I believe, two tunnels—one supposedly goes underneath the lake and is either an escape route or it leads to a wine cellar. On the edge of the lake is a boathouse that is said to be where Capone's men would keep a lookout. After the Great Depression, they turned the hotel into a hospital, then into a rehabilitation center. There are at least two ghosts there—a girl named Gracie and one they call "the bell boy." Oh, and down the street is the Spanish Castle, or what is left of it, and it is said that this is where the mobsters used to take out the trash (if you know what I mean)! And there used to be an old stove where they would burn their "garbage," and there was a path to a stream where they would dispose of whatever was left. —*angelkisses*

Bullet Holes and Cold Storage Corpse Tunnels

A friend of the family was a nurse who worked in Bayview when it was being renovated. She told me that the construction workers found bullet holes in the wall while removing wallpaper on the 5th floor. These were documented in a book that was written about the Pine Barrens. I have not been able to locate the book yet, but I am looking.

When I turned 15 I began volunteering on a local first aid squad. I became very good friends with one member in particular and she told me that one of the first contracts the ambulance service got was Bayview. One winter during a blizzard she and her partner received a call to go there for an emergency involving someone having trouble breathing. When they finally arrived they were told that the patient had already passed on, and they were asked to go downstairs and pick up the body. They went down a freight elevator and were led to a tunnel that went under the lake adjoining the building. My friend said it was freezing cold and damp. There was moss growing on the walls and a dirt floor.

They were led further back to a table where the recently deceased was placed. The old man that led them in there said this was the coldest place and the best place that they could think of to put the body. He said they weren't expecting the ambulance for a while due to the weather. My friend told me that they quickly transferred their cold patient and were on their way. She said she never went back to the place after that day. —*Heather Irons*

Holy Holy Holy Holds the Jersey Devil

There is a legend that the Jersey Devil is sealed inside a stone altar on top of a mountain. The altar is up on the woodsy hill after which the town of Mt. Holly was named. It is a big stone sucker with the words Holy Holy Holy inscribed on the front.

When I was a kid, back in the early 70s, there was a story that the Jersey Devil was chained up inside that altar, and if you put your ear to it, you could hear his chains clanking against the stone. It was also said that the altar was the capstone for a deep shaft that went all the way to Hell.

There's an old graveyard, Mt. Holly Cemetery, right down the hill from it on Ridgeway St. with a gravestone of a young woman. It reads something like, "Thus is the fate of all who turn from God," and it was said that this was the woman who summoned the Jersey Devil. He killed her, and was caught and chained up inside that altar.–*Ken N.*

The Mount and the Witches' Well of Mt. Holly

There is a place located in Mount Holly called the Mount where there is an altar called the Holy, Holy, Holy. This site is where they hung people that the town believed were witches. The altar is actually an old judgment table. You can still see where the gallows pole was. The pole was cut down, but there is a piece remaining.

Off to the left of the Holy, Holy, Holy is the Witches' Well. Supposedly, before the gallows were put up, a witch was thrown down this well. The witch wasn't killed instantly. She screamed and banged on the inside of the well walls until her hands were bloody, begging to be helped. After she died, the townspeople used to hear her cries for help, and the sound of her knuckles rapping on the walls. They later built a shed over the top of the well to end the haunting. It is said that if you go there at night and knock on the walls of the shed, you can hear her knock back for help.–*Ghsthntr1978*

Lambertville High and the Legend of "Buckeye"

The town of Lambertville was a great place to grow up, especially in the 80s. All my friends and I ran around in leather and plaid, harassing tourists who came to town to go antique shopping, and with mohawks high in the air, we would proudly march across the bridge to New Hope and terrorize everything that moved. Since then, I have lived in a number of places (currently, I reside in a correctional facility), but of all of the places I have seen, my childhood times in L-ville were by far the weirdest. Here's a story that I'd like to share with the rest of my fellow New Jerseyans:

High atop a hill sits the ruins of the old Lambertville High School. It closed down around 1955, and then a fire destroyed much of it around 1984. About 50 feet behind the school, through some tall weeds and brush, sits the old football field, still marked clearly by the rusty old goal posts. This is where the weirdness begins.

It was a cold day in November 1935. Lambertville High was getting ready for the big game against archrival New Hope. The marching band was practicing, banners hung in the hallways, and there was a pep rally in the gymnasium. At 4:00, the New Hope buses rolled up the hill and by 4:30, the game had started.

Both teams went scoreless the first quarter, but by the time the half rolled around, the score was 21–21. You could feel the tension in the air. The Eagles (L-ville) and the Buckeyes (New Hope) both did their best with the halftime show, and then the third quarter began. New Hope had the ball and was running for a touchdown when the wide receiver from New Hope was tackled. To everyone's surprise, he didn't get up. The coaches rushed the field but by the time they got there, the boy was dead, his neck broken, and his head turned almost completely around. The game was forfeited.

The parents of the boy who was killed petitioned that football was too dangerous and that New Hope should give it up. (This is why New Hope doesn't have a football team to this day.) But as the years went on, the memory of the poor Buckeye who lost his life faded from memory.

1955—L.H.S. closed down and the place soon became a hangout for greaser gangs. Many fights between L-ville and Flemington or New Hope took place there. One night, a group of 4 or 5 guys was hanging out on the back steps when one of them told the story about the Buckeye who had died there.

The guys were a bit drunk. They started joking about the death and one of them stood up and proclaimed, "I challenge Buckeye to a race across the football field!" Everyone laughed and continued drinking. Pretty soon, a cold wind started to blow and everyone became silent.

From the far end of where the football field once was, a pair of evil red eyes appeared in the darkness and a voice whispered through the wind and told the boys, "Run across

the football field from end to end or die!" One of the boys turned and started to run when he fell to the concrete, cold and blue. The remaining boys heard the voice again, so they all lined up on one side of the field and began to run to the other side. They ran with all they had and when they finally reached the other side, another one of the boys was missing. They all ran home and locked the doors behind them, not saying a word about what had just happened.

The next day the two bodies were discovered up at the old high school, their heads turned almost completely around.

I have been to the old high school many times and I can attest that there is a strange presence there. If you decide to visit the old school, take my advice: don't go there alone, and definitely don't go there at night! –*Johnny K.*

Challenging Billy, Not Buckeye

"Buckeye" isn't the name of the dead football player that most of the Lambertville kids remember. The ghost is "Billy." The legend connected with Billy is that you go inside and face the front window of the school while standing between the first and second floor stairway and utter the words "I challenge Billy to a game of football." Then Billy will throw a football from the top of the staircase, breaking your neck in two! Just like what happened to Billy almost 75 years ago!

Another story is that kids who challenge Billy to a game of football will be enveloped by a strange mist and then will disappear. A guy I know named Lem actually tried to summon Billy on the football field once after a kid he and his friends had just met brought them up there to try it. The mist arose along with a strong gust of wind and something came charging across the field. They all ran and nobody ever saw the mysterious kid again! I asked my grandmother, who attended the school. She assured me that the legend of the boy being killed during the game was true, but his name was Jimmy Cavallo, not Billy or Buckeye.–*Richard Scurti*

The Crukker (or is it Kruker?) of Indian Cabin Road

I went to school at Stockton State College and there are a ton of great scary dirt roads down that way. My friends and I heard about Indian Cabin Road and decided to drive down it.

There is some freaky stuff on this road. It's very narrow and long with tons of pine trees surrounding it. At some points your car barely fits through. First we came across a house that had some type of devil shrine. Very scary and bizarre. We chose not to stop since there was a light on in the house. We kept going and a good distance up we came across a shallow grave and gravestone that had appeared to be there for many years. I later found out the tale about it. Apparently in the late 1800s a young girl was assaulted by some man who was only known as the Crukker. Her family buried her in the backyard of their home, which burned down in the early 1900s. The grave is the only thing left.

This Crukker is supposedly a rapist/child molester who lives off of Indian Cabin Road deep in the Pine Barrens. I've heard that on dark foggy nights the cries of young children can be heard as you stand by the grave of the girl and face east. I've ventured down that desolate road many nights but have never come across him or anyone else. This road is quite scary and the fact that people still live back there is perhaps even scarier.
–J. Magliaro

Chased on Indian Cabin Road

Around five years ago my brother attended Stockton State College. Whenever I visited him we would inevitably end up on some road adventure deep in the Pine Barrens. One time we went down Indian Cabin Road, which stretches far back into the woods where strange cults and deranged mental patients are known to live. As we were driving on it, we reached something truly bizarre.

Off in the distance stood what appeared to be the remnants of a house or an old church. In front was a statue of the Virgin Mary and her eyes had been covered in blood or red paint. Strange symbols and the body of a skinned dog were left on the ground near it. As my friends and I stepped out of the car to take pictures we noticed a light on in the church. A few minutes went by and my brother commented, "Hey, the light went out." With that, the headlights of a pickup truck went on! We scrambled back in the car as the truck came at us. It chased us going 80 mph down a bumpy dirt road while the driver waved a shotgun out the window. We managed to speed away and narrowly escaped.

There is also a grave known as the Shaler grave located near a little bridge on this road. I have heard stories of this grave being inhabited by a homeless child molester by the name of "The Kruker" although this may well be folklore, because I have heard similar stories of this guy living in both Tuckerton and Bordentown. They are incredibly scary!
–Ryan L.

Weird Travels on Indian Cabin Road

When we as *Weird N.J.* get a lead on a local legend, we usually file it in hopes that we can compare notes, do some snooping, and possibly shed light on some new weirdness for everyone. A letter recently came in describing a lonely stretch of road in the middle of the Pine Barrens called Indian Cabin Road. Filing it under ROADS LESS TRAVELED, we looked for similar entries and found a file called PINE BARRENS CHURCH; its location was Indian Cabin Road. When a third letter arrived saying

Indian Cabin Road is a must-see site among the student body at Stockton State College, we were on our way.

Finding the road on a map is not easy. Finding it in your car is even tougher. The map tells you it goes straight through the Pine Barrens, but the locals who live along the road will tell you, "It don't, so stay off it!" We encountered a not-so-friendly Piney who definitely didn't want us traveling on "her" road. So much for southern hospitality and the kindness of strangers.

Forging ahead, we decided to make the full run on Indian Cabin Road—from the beginning until we hit the town of Sweetwater. The scraggly scrub pines that crowd the road make it look extremely foreboding, even in the daylight. We had our checklist from our leads: a lone gravestone, a satanic church, a bloody Virgin Mary statue, and crazy Pineys who chase you in trucks. What more could you ask for?

The desolation of the road seemed to swallow us up as we four-wheeled it through the sporadic potholes that lined the trail. The road splits; other roads cross it, all with no street signs to guide you; then it narrows to the size of a goat path.

We found the lone Shaler grave about fifty feet from the road. Nothing was around it but remnants of a cement foundation and a small, stagnant stream. We recalled one of the legends that recounted that Mrs. Shaler and her three children were massacred by local Indians while her husband was out to sea. Though the inscription on the tombstone confirmed that Mrs. Shaler was indeed interred with three of her infant children, it offered no clue as to whether the family had really been massacred. It reads:

SACRED

TO THE MEMORY OF

MRS. SIBBEL SHALER

CONSORT OF THE LATE TIMOTHY SHALER

WHO DEPARTED THIS LIFE

ON THE 2ND DAY OF APRIL 1785

IN THE 34TH YEAR OF HER AGE

AND WHOSE MORTAL REMAINS REPOSE

HERE TOGETHER WITH THOSE OF THREE

OF HER INFANT CHILDREN

Continuing on, we came to a fork, where we had to make a decision: Do we go left or right? At this point, we were totally lost and decided to take the road that literally looked less traveled. We proceeded on, and after about a quarter mile, we saw a cement statue of Jesus on the side of the road. A dilapidated churchlike structure lay beyond it, as did a few other buildings that we could not quite make out through the trees. Just as we began to take a few photos, we turned around to see a pickup truck emerge from behind the church and start toward us.

"Can you tell us how to get to Sweetwater?" we asked the teenage driver, looking hopelessly lost, map unfolded on the hood of our Jeep. He pointed in the direction we had just come from, without saying a word.

"Is this Indian Cabin Road?" we inquired.

At that point, he turned the truck around and went back behind the church. A moment later a woman with a dog emerged and started toward us. She was a large, heavy woman with unruly gray hair.

"Do you know you're on my property?" she squawked, puffing on a cigarette.

"We don't know where we are," we replied. "We just stopped to ask if this road continues on to Sweetwater."

"Oh, come on," she snapped back angrily. "You can't see the NO TRESPASSING SIGNS all over here?" We were sort of stunned by her unprovoked aggression. For the last ten minutes, we hadn't seen a sign of any kind, and believe us, we were looking. At this point, we were perhaps ten feet in from the road on a barren patch of sand, perhaps fifty yards from the nearest building on the property.

"We're on a public road," we told her. "We have a map. It tells us we can follow this road until we get to Sweetwater. Is that right or is it wrong?" I was getting a little agitated.

She seemed to think we were lying to her (which, of course, was partially true, but she had no way of knowing that). Then she gave us directions that seemed to be way off course, according to our map. We turned around and backtracked (with the pickup truck right behind us as an escort) until we came to the first paved road, then stopped the car. At that point the pickup turned around and headed off back to the weird compound in the woods.

We gathered our thoughts. We had managed to find two of the legendary sites we'd set out in search of: the

Shaler grave and the dilapidated religious retreat with its unfriendly guardians. But there was still one story of Indian Cabin Road, told among the Stockton State crowd, that we had not found any sign of. So, tossing our map aside, off we went, heading deeper into the weird south Jersey wilderness in search of the infamous Kruker (or is it Crukker?).

The Kruker's Soda Pop Shrine

I have traveled Indian Cabin Road on many an occasion. I have seen the Shaler grave and also been chased by the Pineys that seem to inhabit the macabre house/church/compound at the end of the road. However, none of this even comes close to the experience I had a few years ago while riding my bike on this road.

I was on a comfortable afternoon bike ride one Sunday when I got brave and decided to venture down Indian Cabin Road. As I drove further down the dirt trail I began to notice an unusual amount of garbage on the road. At first it seemed like nothing out of the ordinary, a few old softballs, some soda bottles, an old Philly's hat—nothing that shocking. However, as I continued on, I noticed that the garbage seemed to be getting more abundant and I saw more and more bottles of Dr. Pepper. Literally piles of Dr. Pepper bottles everywhere!

As I followed this trail further into the woods it eventually led to an old sign that read ICE COLD SODA. Beyond that was some type of shrine or sculpture made entirely of bottles of soda—it formed a large triangle that had been glued or taped together, and was supported by softball bats duct taped together. In the middle was one word, Candyman. I don't know what it meant, but it freaked me out! Anyone who could have drank this much D.P. has to be slightly deranged!

When I got home I talked to several friends about what I had seen. Some said they had heard of a local man known as The Kruker who is supposed to live in the woods behind Indian Cabin Road. They said that he was a child molester who used to live in the area and that he would sometimes try to tempt children with candy and soda. I don't know if what I saw was the work of him or just some thirsty campers, but it was weird, that's for sure!–Seth F.

Weirdness is not a recent phenomenon here in New Jersey. We actually have quite a long history of strangeness and a very storied, if not checkered, past. Odd occurrences and curious events have taken place in our state over the years that, while they might not have seemed so bizarre at the time, today strike us as almost impossible to have happened here.

It's undeniable that our history offers a great deal to be proud of. On the other hand, some of it is nothing to crow about. A number of those incidents simply reflected questionable judgment, while other events were far more covert and even sinister. There are those of us who would rather sweep those parts of our history under the carpet. But as the saying goes, those who forget the mistakes of the past are doomed to repeat them.

Mystery History

So let's now take an unflinching look back with our 20/20 hindsight into the annals of NJ history—to places that many of our textbooks have overlooked (or conveniently forgotten). These are the shadowy corridors of time, where history becomes mystery—and vice versa. If you're one of those people who like to think that "it could never happen here," then think again—because it can, and it did.

The Castle, near Plainfield, N.J.

WEST JERSEY BRIDGE. NEW YORK CITY.

19693

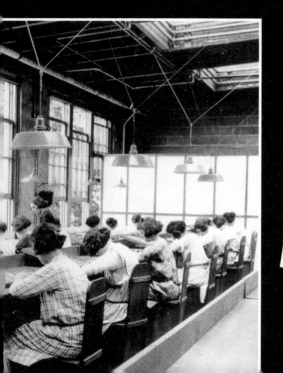

U.S.S. "ATLANTUS"

REMAINS OF EXPERIMENTAL
CONCRETE SHIP, ONE OF TWELVE
BUILT DURING WORLD WAR I.
PROVED IMPRACTICAL AFTER
SEVERAL TRANS-ATLANTIC TRIPS
BECAUSE OF WEIGHT. TOWED AND
SUNK HERE AS WHARF IN 1926.

The Mount Holly Witch Trials

On October 22, 1730, an article appeared in the *Pennsylvania Gazette* chronicling a recent witch trial that had occurred in Mount Holly. The story explained why those accused were suspected of practicing witchcraft as well as the actions undertaken to determine if they were truly tapping into dark powers.

According to the *Gazette,* locals began fearing the worst when their animals started acting strangely: "The Accused had been charged with making their Neighbours Sheep dance in an uncommon Manner, and with causing Hogs to speak and sing Psalms."

The ability to control the actions of animals had long been considered a surefire sign of witchery, and the citizens of Mount Holly would not stand for it. A rowdy mob of three hundred rounded up the witch and wizard they held responsible and proceeded to test their innocence. To validate the results, two members of the rabble also underwent these tests as a sort of litmus.

First the accused were weighed against copies of the Bible, which were placed on a gallows constructed near the courthouse. It was believed that anyone who gave in to such dark tendencies would be lighter than a weighty copy of the Good Book. All four people were tested, and all four weighed more than the Bible. The crowd didn't give up there—they proceeded to a local millpond, where the real scientific testing began.

The four were stripped down and checked to make sure they weren't hiding any heavy objects on their bodies. Then their hands and feet were bound with rope and they were put into the pond. It was thought that anyone who was a witch would float on the surface, while an innocent would sink. Only one man, a member of the mob, sank. The other three floated on the surface of the water. This baffled and discontented the crowd.

The article ends ambiguously, without telling of any final decisions made regarding the accused.

Many have long speculated that the article was merely a joke. This seems to be based on the fact that a young, well-known prankster named Benjamin Franklin wrote the piece. According to those who doubt the validity of the article, it was a way for Franklin to poke fun at folk beliefs, as well as to have a joke at the expense of Burlington County residents, whom Philadelphians saw as rustic yokels.

It may be too convenient to dismiss the account as a joke, though. After all, the events allegedly took place a mere forty years after the infamous Salem witch trials in which twenty innocent men and women were tortured and brutally executed on the basis of superstitious beliefs.

BURLINGTON, Oct. 12. Saturday last at *Mount-Holly,* about 8 Miles from this Place, near 300 People were gathered together to see an Experiment or two tried on some Persons accused of Witchcraft. It seems the Accused had been charged with making their Neighbours Sheep dance in an uncommon Manner, and with causing Hogs to speak, and sing Psalms, &c. to the great Terror and Amazement of the King's good and peaceable Subjects in this Province; and the Accusers being very positive that if the Accused were weighed in Scales against a Bible, the Bible would prove too heavy for them; or that, if they were bound and put into the River, they would swim; the said Accused desirous to make their Innocence appear, voluntarily offered to undergo the said Trials, if 2 of the most violent of their Accusers would be tried with them. Accordingly the Time and Place was agreed on, and advertised about the Country; The Accusers were 1 Man and 1 Woman; and the Accused the same. The Parties being met, and the People got together, a grand Consultation was held, before they proceeded to Trial; in which it was agreed to use the Scales first; and a Committee of Men were appointed to search the Men, and a

Digging for History in Sybil's Cave

It was a hot, steamy summer afternoon on July 28, 1841, when James Boulard and Henry Mallin saw what appeared to be a body floating in the Hudson River near Hoboken. The two men, who had been relaxing near the river at a quiet retreat called Sybil's Cave, raced to a nearby boat and retrieved the floating object. It was the body of a young woman, later identified as Mary Cecilia Rogers, who had been missing from her New York City home for three days. The discovery brought national attention to a site already locally famous.

At the time, the Hoboken shoreline was an area for relaxation for the stressed urbanites of nearby cities. A tree-lined path along the river, dubbed River Walk, served as a respite to the crowds of city life. Businesses had cropped up to accommodate the day-trippers, who would ferry across the Hudson from New York. These new establishments included taverns and inns, among which was the renowned Sybil's Cave and Spring. It was located between Eighth and Ninth streets at the foot of Stevens Institute of Technology on what is today Frank Sinatra Drive.

Sybil's Cave was not a natural formation: It was dug out of the cliff to reach a natural spring in 1832, as the River Walk gained in popularity. Glasses of water were sold to thirsty hikers for one cent a glass, an outrageous amount for that time, but people were willing to pay because of the medicinal properties the water supposedly held. Tables were set outside the cave, and a building was erected to serve the growing clientele.

In the 1880s, with the advent of the board of health, the spring water of Sybil's Cave was declared unfit for human consumption. However, this was not the end of the cave. A new tavern was established on the site by a man

SYBIL'S CAVE, AT HOBOKEN, N. J.

named Fred Eckstein; it served food and had an Old World ambience. The cave, accessible by a sliding metal door in the tavern, was used for storage.

The area continued to be popular with visitors, but eventually, the commercial shipping industry encroached, blocking out the views of the river and New York City. Eckstein's tavern began to decline and became a gin mill for dockworkers. In time, it closed, and the building was torn down in 1937. The cave was filled in, and today there is very little evidence of its existence.

The Mary Rogers Tragedy

The discovery of the body of Mary Cecilia Rogers in the shallow waters near Sybil's Cave provoked outrage. Mary, a young and beautiful twenty-year-old, ran a boarding house on Nassau Street with her aging mother. On the morning of July 25, she left her house, telling her boyfriend and boarder, Donald Payne, that she would be visiting her aunt uptown. She would never return.

The Hoboken coroner said her death was caused by strangulation and that she had been sexually assaulted and beaten. More than a month later remnants of her clothing and some personal items were found in a wooded area near the river in Weehawken, just north of Hoboken. It was assumed she was killed there by a man, or a gang of men, and then thrown into the river.

Since Mary had also worked as a salesgirl in a Broadway tobacco shop, the media soon dubbed the story the Case of the Beautiful Cigar Girl, and dozens of reporters and writers followed up on every aspect of the case. The murder brought a burst of publicity and tourism to Sybil's Cave and to Hoboken, as thousands flocked to the area to view the scene of the crime.

Watching and reading all of this was an out-of-work writer living in Philadelphia named Edgar Allan Poe. He later transformed this story into the pioneering detective tale "The Mystery of Marie Roget," changing the location of the saga to Paris, France, but leaving other important facts intact.

Despite endless speculation in the press, the case was never solved. Every one of Mary's former suitors was charged and then cleared. The constant publicity was blamed for the apparent suicide of Donald Payne, who was distraught over the loss of Mary and the suspicions of his involvement in her death. His body was found outside Sybil's Cave in early October of the year she died, a bottle of poison nearby.

Today New Jersey is attempting to return the Hoboken shoreline to its past glory as a recreation area for nearby city dwellers. Hopefully, these plans will include an acknowledgment of the area's rich past, including Sybil's Cave and Mary Rogers.—*Michael J. Launay*

According to a March 9, 2006, article by Dylan Archilla in the *Hudson Reporter*, "One of the people who remembered the stories of Sybil's Cave is Hoboken mayor David Roberts, who has taken a personal (and financial) interest in unearthing the cave. He recently succeeded this past December when the cave's entrance was discovered. Sybil's Cave has become something of a *cause célèbre* in Hoboken, and no one is more excited about it than Roberts. 'This is going to be such a fun project,' Roberts said. 'Being from Hoboken and growing up in the '60s and '70s, you couldn't help but hear old-timers tell stories about Sybil's Cave. This is all very exciting.'

"Roberts said he plans to have the cave refurbished and opened to the public in time for Hoboken's 150th anniversary celebration this year."

PRICE, 10 CENTS.

THE

BEAUTIFUL CIGAR GIRL;

OR,

The Mysteries of Broadway.

BY

J. H. INGRAHAM, Esq.,

Inside Sybil's Cave

I was in Sybil's Cave several times when I was a student at Stevens Tech, '57–'61. The cave is just below and to the right of Castle Point on the Hoboken waterfront, directly below where the Stevens Student Center is now. When I was there, the entrance was just a small crawl space at the base of the bluff at about the level of the road.

The "cave" is obviously man-made, as you can see the tool marks on the wall. It was filled with rubble, and you could just about stand up. There were two rooms, the entrance room was about 12 to 15 feet in diameter with a small carved stone structure in the center that might have had four columns which I guess might have had something to do with the spring.

To the left of the entry was a second, smaller room, about 8 to 10 feet. The cave was obviously a hangout, judging from the mattress, beer bottles, cigarette butts, etc. littering the floor.—*Gary Fitton*

The Mexican Lindbergh Goes Down

A bright October day found me driving through the Pine Barrens. I was out to find the Carranza Monument in Burlington County. It was marked in red on my map as a point of interest, but I had no clue what it was. Some forgotten settlement? A Catholic shrine? It would turn out to be more interesting than that.

The turnoff for Route 206 had the only marker for CARRANZA MONUMENT. Carranza Road cut through the village of Tabernacle and into Wharton State Forest. The trees flanking the road turned from oak to pine, and white sandy "roads" veered off to the left and right, snaking through the scrubby brush.

I passed no hikers, no other cars, saw no animals. Eventually, I saw signs for BATONA CAMP SITE and BATONA TRAIL. Then the pavement ended and I was headed down a washboard road of packed dirt. After a mile or two of bouncing, I turned around, figuring I had missed a turn.

After passing the Batona Camp, I glanced to the left and saw a wooden barrier along the road, bordering a sandy clearing. There, standing in the middle of this space, surrounded by yucca plants, was the Carranza Monument.

The face of the stone depicted a dying bird, with footsteps leading away, and the back had a cleanly incised arrow that pointed to the heavens. Pennies were laid out along the edge of the monument, and there were inscriptions on both sides—one in

Spanish, the other in English. The English inscription reported that the monument was erected in 1930 to the memory of Captain Emilio Carranza. A metal historical marker on the road informed me that Emilio Carranza was "returning from a goodwill flight, back to Mexico, when he fell to his death in 1928." The pennies of Mexican children financed the monument to their hero; the stone had been quarried in Coahuila, his birthplace.

Captain Emilio Carranza, age twenty-three and the grandnephew of a Mexican president, was considered the Lindbergh of Mexico; he was befriended by Lindbergh and is regarded as Mexico's greatest aviation hero. He had come to America in the summer of 1928 on a goodwill flight in response to Lindbergh's flight to Mexico City. During his visit, he was greeted in Washington by President Coolidge.

Carranza was to return to Mexico in July, but several bad storms kept him grounded. Then, on July 12, while dining at the Waldorf-Astoria in New York City, he was called away by a telegram. Immediately after reading it, he contacted the airport and told them to ready his plane.

Captain Carranza's *Excelsior-Mexico* left Roosevelt Field, Long Island, at 7:18 p.m., in the middle of a terrible electrical storm, against warnings by the

weather bureau and airport officials. Residents of the Pine Barrens, near Sandy Ridge, recalled hearing the sputtering of an airplane engine during the storm. The next afternoon the wreckage of his plane was discovered by a family out picking blueberries. Soon after, Emilio's body was found, his hand clutching a flashlight. It was believed he had been flying low, looking for a place to land, when he hit the treetops, causing the plane to flip.

In the pocket of his jacket was found the telegram that had prompted his ill-fated departure. It was from his superior officer, General Joaquin Amaro, who reportedly wrote, "Leave immediately without excuse or pretext, or the quality of your manhood will be in doubt."

The Carranza Monument marks the place where the pilot's body was found. Every year on the anniversary of his death, representatives from the Mexican consulate in New York come out to honor him, and on the weekend closest to the date, members of American Legion Post 11 hold a small ceremony. It was Post 11 that took charge of Carranza's remains until they were returned to Mexico.

The uniqueness of the monument and the tragic tale it tells is worth the long trip deep into the Pine Barrens, where Captain Emilio Carranza crash-landed into New Jersey history.—*Kate Philbrick*

Carranza's Ghost Will Get You

Local lore goes that if you park your car at the gate, flash the headlights on the memorial three times and yell "Emilio" out the window, you will see his plane. Of course we had to try it.

We followed the instructions and about 10 minutes later my friend's car stalled for no reason. We got it started again and began rolling out of there. She kept asking us what the lights were behind us. My other friend and I turned around and saw nothing! She swore she saw lights in the rearview mirror! We figured she was just trying to scare us, but suddenly we saw them too. They were too high to be car lights and too low to be a plane. Needless to say, we got out of there as fast as possible.—*LokoKitty*

A Bridge Abridged

Today, one backyard along Twelfth Street in Hoboken is five feet wider than it was a few years ago. That's when Hoboken's "Phantom Bridge" mysteriously disappeared, thanks to the need for "a little more space."

In the backyard of 1200 Garden Street, there once was a massive eight-foot-tall block of concrete. Cut into its side was the inscription FOUNDATION LAID—NORTH RIVER BRIDGE CO.—1895. It was to be the 57th Street Bridge, linking Hoboken and Manhattan, and one of the grandest projects in the history of American engineering.

The brainchild of Gustav Lindenthal, an Austrian-born bridge builder, the 57th Street Bridge was to be nearly twice the size of the yet to be constructed George Washington Bridge. It would be six thousand feet long,

two hundred feet above the Hudson River, and two hundred feet wide. It was to carry twelve railroads, twenty-four lanes of traffic, and two promenades. Lindenthal envisioned a single span, anchored on both side by cables, soaring across the waterway.

Although the cornerstone was laid, the 1898 depression, followed by the coming of World War I, halted construction. After the war, Lindenthal revised his plan to suit the automobile, adding a second layer to accommodate the anticipated traffic jams of the 1920s.

There was opposition to the plan, however. The Port Authority, formed in 1921, claimed the span would hinder navigation; then the railroads decided to tunnel under the Hudson. And local businessmen and chambers of commerce were not in favor of the project. Finally, in 1933, the Secretary of Transportation rejected the bridge plans because they would have competed with the Lincoln Tunnel, which opened four years later.

Lindenthal continued to fight to build the bridge; even on his deathbed in 1935, he still discussed the span.

He died a wealthy man on his two hundred and fifty-acre farm in Metuchen. His victories were the bridges in New York that he designed and were erected—the Hell Gate, Manhattan, Queensboro, and Williamsburg. His defeat was the abandoned 57th Street Bridge project.

Walking Hoboken's narrow Twelfth Street today, one can only imagine what the town would have looked like if the bridge had been built. The neighborhood would have been destroyed, and more than likely, Hoboken would have become covered with exit and entrance ramps.

When we asked a neighbor what happened to the cornerstone, she replied, "They were just tired of it. They needed a little more space for the kids to play in the backyard." We were told that the stone had been demolished.

And so it would seem that this curious reminder of one man's grand vision, like so many of our state's great landmarks, has passed into forgotten history like so much water under the bridge—that nearly was.

Cornerstone Comeback

A couple years back I was telling a friend about an inscribed stone I had found along the Hoboken waterfront, and we realized it was the cornerstone to the phantom bridge.

About a year ago, I could tell that the stone was in imminent danger of falling into the Hudson River, as the pier it was located on was rapidly collapsing. Using a long steel bar, three pipes as rollers and a whole lot of brute force, I was able to pry the stone out of the hole it was falling into, up onto the rollers, and move it to a resting place above a relieving wall.—*Joe Wasielewski*

Final Resting Place

The cornerstone is alive and well. It is situated on the campus of the Stevens Institute of Technology, in Hoboken, in front of the S. C. Williams Library, between the entrance and the southeast corner of the building.
—*Lou Nunez*

If you're a fan of mysteries and foreign intrigue, you don't have to read a Ken Follett novel to get your fix of espionage stories. Some of the most secretive cloak-and-dagger dramas in our nation's history have played out right here on the New Jersey home front. So make sure you've committed your secret password to memory and that your cyanide capsule is securely tucked beneath your tongue, because we're about to administer a mind-altering dose of truth serum.

Black Tom and the Dark Invader

It was two a.m., July 30, 1916, and all was quiet in Jersey City. Despite a war raging throughout Europe, most residents of the New York metropolitan area, along with the rest of the nation, lay in their beds secure in the knowledge of America's isolation and neutrality. All of that was about to change, however, and the belief that most Americans held of their country's invulnerability was about to be shaken to its very foundations.

The Black Tom warehouse in Jersey City operated as the main overseas shipping depot for munitions destined for Great Britain, France, and Russia. Seventy-five percent of the nation's armaments left the Black Tom dock. Named for its shape, which was said to resemble a monstrous cat's head and neck, Black Tom was a twenty-five-acre, windswept outcropping of rock that jutted out into New York harbor from the swampy shores of Jersey

City, near the Statue of Liberty. Although the United States was still neutral, its sympathies were with the Allied powers against imperial Germany. This made Black Tom a prime target for sabotage.

German intelligence was sent to the New York area to infiltrate the docks and set up an operation to destroy munitions cargo ships bound for Europe. One person, an aristocratic German army reservist named Captain Franz von Rintelen, entered the country under an assumed name, but preferred to be known to his co-conspiritors as the Dark Invader. He employed men from New Jersey to make what were known as "cigar bombs," a proto-

type of the modern pipe bomb. The shop was set up in a German vessel along the docks, and the bombs were placed in the hulls of the ships. Cigar bombs often took about five days to ignite, causing many ships to burn at sea.

On May 7, 1915, the British liner *Lusitania* was hit by German torpedoes off the coast of Ireland, killing over twelve hundred passengers. This act of aggression heightened security in our own country. Soon the Dark Invader ceased his operations after a bomb squad (the first of its kind) was formed to investigate the sabotage being done along the docks. When one of the cigar bombs was found in a hull, and authorities started asking a lot of questions, the Dark Invader left for Europe, but was apprehended by the British. He surrendered as a prisoner of war.

There still is a cloak of secrecy about what happened on July 30, 1916. It is believed that three men seen making their way along the Black Tom docks at midnight had set timed fuses and then fled. At 2:08 a.m., five million people were awakened by an explosion that was heard as

far away as Maryland. The shock threw people from their beds in Deal and shattered skyscraper windows in New York City. Thousands of ammunition shells shot across New York and New Jersey, lodging in buildings and trains. The Brooklyn Bridge swayed. Every window in Jersey City's town hall was destroyed, along with many churches, businesses, and homes. Disoriented men, women, and children ran out into the streets in their nightclothes to witness a huge red fireball rise up from Black Tom. A ten-week-old Jersey City boy named Arthur Tosson was killed when the force of the explosion threw him from his crib.

In April of 1917, the United States entered the war in Europe, but the first American blood had been spilled right here in New Jersey nearly a year earlier. After twenty years of investigations and charges, Germany was found responsible for the explosion, though final reparations were not settled until 1979.

Today Liberty State Park is located at the site of the explosion, though few of the park's visitors realize the his-toric impact of this powder keg once known as Black Tom.

Tuckerton Tower Says, "Get Lucy!"

The square blocks on Mystic Island were once the concrete anchors of the Tuckerton Tower. These anchors are twenty feet high and extend twenty feet underground. The Tuckerton Tower was eight hundred and twenty feet high and built in 1912 by the German government to communicate with an identical tower in Germany, as well as with ships and submarines in the Atlantic Ocean. It was one of the first and most powerful transatlantic radio stations ever constructed.

Mystic Island (then Hickory Island) was chosen because the ground was level and the island was in a desolate location. All the parts were built in Germany, then shipped to the United States. Early in World War I, while America was still neutral, the government kept a close watch on the tower to ensure it was not broadcasting any military messages in violation of the Neutrality Act. This censorship was ineffective, however, as seemingly harmless messages could be delivered in code. It is believed by many that the station sent out the order, "Get Lucy," to a German submarine as code for the order to sink the *Lusitania*.

When America entered the war, the U.S. military took over the tower and used it until the war ended. Later, RCA operated it until World War II, when the military took it over again. On December 28, 1955, the tower was torn down and cut up for scrap.

—Michael J. Launay

Clockwise from left: The base of the tower about 1913; the tower in 1916; one of the guy anchors

Nazis and the KKK Bund Together

During the years prior to World War II, America was in the grips of the worst economic depression that the nation had ever experienced. Unemployment was at a record high, and soup lines were a common sight. Fringe ideologies like the Communist Party and the Ku Klux Klan were enjoying record recruitment in the United States.

Overseas in Germany, Adolph Hitler rose to power, creating a time of great uncertainty and mistrust. Here at home, that mistrust was aimed squarely at German Americans.

In the 1930s, there were 112,000 German-born immigrants living in New Jersey. Generally, they and other citizens of German descent dealt with the political climate by ascribing to one of three different viewpoints: Many embraced their Americanism and rejected Germany altogether; others recognized Germany as their homeland, but did not condone the actions of the new government there; and still others proudly embraced Nazi ideals and pledged their allegiance to them. This faction would come to be known as the Bund (which means federation); it was the American equivalent of the Nazi Party and boasted over 10,000 members. Its history is intricately tied to New Jersey.

The Bund started out as a group known as the Friends of the New Germany. It had regional chapters scattered throughout the nation and was given funds by the Nazi Party in Germany. In 1935, a Munich-born German army veteran of World War I named Fritz Kuhn, who had become an American citizen, was chosen as the organization's leader, and the group was renamed the German-American Bund. Kuhn even traveled to Berlin to meet with Hitler and get his blessing and official recognition as the "American Führer."

The Bund's headquarters were located in Manhattan, and New Jersey had chapters in Clifton, Hackensack, Union City, Fairfield, North Bergen, Passaic, and Newark.

Incredibly, the Bund promoted itself as a pro-American organization, preaching the values of isolationism, while conveniently slipping anti-Semitic and racist rhetoric into its message. The antiwar stance was, of course, merely an endeavor to keep the United States out of the war.

The Bund promoted solidarity among its members by running camps all across the nation. The camps provided weekend retreats where German Americans could drink beer, sing songs of the fatherland, converse in their native tongue, and take comfort in the belief in their own racial superiority.

Three such camps existed in New Jersey—one in Bloomingdale, one in Griggstown, and most importantly, Camp Nordland in Andover. Camp Nordland opened on July 18, 1937, and its opening festivities drew 10,000 German Americans to Andover, a town with a population of 479 people at the time. These out-of-towners patronized local businesses, and the flood of money led most locals to tolerate the Bund—despite their wearing of swastikas and military uniforms, the large portrait of Hitler they displayed in their recreation hall, and the parade they held with their

Bund camp head August Klapprott speaking, 1940

guests, a group of Italian Americans dressed as Mussolini's Blackshirts. In a short time, though, this tolerance would disappear.

Local newspapers and town leaders began to condemn the Bund, and spread the word that the organization was promoting violence, denouncing Jews, and bashing Franklin Roosevelt's New Deal. The state government warned the organizers of Camp Nordland that they were violating a New Jersey law that forbade the promotion of race hatred and race hostility. Undaunted, the Bund simply toned down its public visibility.

The camp still hosted large gatherings, including weekend getaways for children. To the outside observer, these events may have looked like nothing more than Boy Scout jamborees or church retreats, but in actuality they were much more sinister. In the woods of Andover, ten- to fourteen-year-old boys and girls were marching around in Nazi garb, and being formed into ranks reminiscent of the infamous Hitler Youth. "Our camp," Bundesleiter Kuhn proclaimed, "is designed principally to be a place which breathes the spirit of the New Germany . . . [where young people] shall be strengthened and confirmed in National Socialism so that they will be conscious of the role which has been assigned to them as the future carriers of German racial ideals to America."

By 1939, as news of Nazi atrocities began to filter back to the States, any illusions of the Bund as a benign social fraternity evaporated. Not only did Jewish groups often protest at Camp Nordland, but New Jerseyans of German descent were also in the ranks of the demonstrators.

In addition to their ideologies, certain Bund activities at Camp Nordland also garnered bad publicity. One Bund leader was arrested for sexually molesting two high school girls at the camp, and a seventeen-year-old girl testified that she and her friends were served liquor at the camp's bar, leading the town to deny renewal of the camp's liquor

Camp Nordland

license. Fritz Kuhn was under investigation for misappropriating funds from the organization. With that charge as well as several DWI convictions and scandals involving extramarital flings with underage girls, Kuhn stepped down from his post, and Gerhard Kunze of Union City became the new Bundesführer.

Around this time, Sussex County sheriff Denton Quick began a personal crusade against the Bund. He would attend meetings at Nordland, where he recorded the license plates of every car in the parking lot. His work interested both the FBI and the IRS, and eventually nine leaders of the camp were indicted. They were convicted, but after several appeals, the convictions were overturned. Fritz Kuhn was not so lucky. He was convicted of grand larceny for embezzling $14,000 from the Bund and was sent to Sing Sing prison.

By 1940, the Bund desperately wanted to rebuild its all-American German image of years past. Its solution (definitely not the smartest) was to invite the Ku Klux Klan (who claimed some 60,000 New Jerseyans as members) to Camp Nordland for a joint rally. The gathering was described in a book published in 1943 by an author who went undercover to infiltrate the Bund. He wrote:

Flames from the wooden cross, forty feet high, crackled into the night throwing lurid shadows on the participants below, some of whom were dressed in hooded white robes, others in the gray uniforms of the German-American Bund. The scene took place at Bund Camp Nordland in New Jersey on August 18, 1940, when the Klan staged a monster anti-war, pro-American mass meeting jointly with the Bund. . . .

August Klapprott, the vice-president of the Bund, speaking with a thick German accent, shouted: "When Arthur Bell, your Grand Giant, asked us about using Camp Nordland for this patriotic meeting, we decided to let them have it because of the common bond between us. The principles of the Bund and the principles of the Klan are the same."

The merry racists spent the rest of the day burning crosses and ranting about minorities, until incensed local residents attacked the camp, causing the frightened leaders to again call the police.

That same year terrorist attacks began occurring in the area and were attributed to the Bund. One of these incidents was when the Hercules Powder Company of Kenvil, in Morris County, exploded. Forty-eight people died, but the cause of the explosion was never uncovered.

In his 1999 self-published pamphlet, "Warren County Chronicles: The Undercover Boys," author Frank T. Dale describes the final days of Camp Nordland:

The year 1941 was a bad one for the German-American Bund. In the spring, a bill came before the New Jersey legislature revoking the charter of the German-

American Bund Auxiliary, the owner of Camp Nordland. It wasn't passed in time to legally stop the big May Day opening at the camp, but Sheriff Quick acted anyway. On April 30, he and 10 deputized American Legionaries struck. Quick dispersed the Bundists he found, confiscated some material he thought the FBI would like to see, permitted the press to photograph Hitler's portrait and the huge swastikas affixed to the roofs, and then he padlocked the place as a public nuisance. Camp Nordland would never open again. . . .

In mid-summer the final betrayal occurred: the Ku Klux Klan met in Central Jersey—even the horses wore hoods for the occasion—and burned a cross to celebrate the demise of the Bund in New Jersey.

In December 1941, the United States entered the war with Japan and Germany. This made all investigations of the Bund moot, as Nazis in America were now officially enemies of the state. The German-American Bund disbanded.

After being paroled from Sing Sing in 1943, Fritz Kuhn was sent to an enemy alien internment camp in Crystal City, Texas. When the war ended, he was deported to Germany, where he died in 1951.

Today, the 205 acres on the banks of Lake Iliff that Camp Nordland once occupied are used as recreational fields. The buildings stand within Hillside Park in Andover. One would never guess that this peaceful setting, where children are now encouraged to play together, was once the ground used to instruct children how to hate one another.

Sheriffs investigating swastika on the ceiling of one of the assembly halls at the camp in 1941

Stealing the Would-be Emperor's Throne

Back in 1945, my father, Sgt. Ragnvald C. Borch T-4 U.S. Army MPC 1180th Co., was asked to go along with a few officers to observe the French Army assault Hitler's home at Berchtesgaden. My father spoke fluent German, and the officers thought he might be handy if they should run into Hitler. Well, they didn't find Hitler, only a bombed out shell of a building. The French Army began to loot and my father decided to join in. He took a number of items, one of which was Hitler's toilet seat. He would say, "Well, this is where he used to do his thinking."

This toilet seat has been a joke in our house for years. *–Michael C. Borch*

Concrete Ship and Lead Balloon

For eighty years, the weather-beaten remains of a ship have lain just a few hundred feet beyond the breaking surf of Sunset Beach in historic Cape May. It's the S.S. *Atlantus*, a concrete ship—a poignant monument to dubious engineering and ill-conceived ideas in general.

Toward the end of World War I, shortages of steel made it necessary to find low-cost alternative materials for ships that could serve as troop and supply transports. The federal government invited Norseman N. K. Fougner to head a study into the feasibility of concrete ships. After numerous prototypes, in 1918 the United States Shipping Board rolled out the S.S. *Atlantus*, the first of twelve concrete ships. The freighter weighed three thousand tons, measured two hundred and fifty feet long, and was built with a five-inch-thick hull of special concrete aggregate. The freighter was launched on November 21, in Wilmington, North Carolina.

Sadly, the concrete fleet was too slow and not actually cost-effective, and with steel once again available when the war ended, the fleet was decommissioned and the S.S. *Atlantus* sent to a ship graveyard in Virginia.

Then, in 1926, Colonel Desse Rosenfeld, an entrepreneurial-minded man of Baltimore, decided to give the *Atlantus* another chance. He had always dreamed of a ferry service between Cape May and Lewes, Delaware. He had the *Atlantus* towed up from Virginia to be used as the ferry landing. But during a storm while she was awaiting positioning, the ship broke loose of her offshore moorings and ran aground, where she rests today. In 1937, a seam ripped open in the ship's hull, and in 1961, she split into two parts. At that time, her stern disappeared beneath the water's surface forever.

The seamen who once served on the ships of the concrete fleet had an apt nickname for these vessels—they called them "floating tombstones." Today one of these tombstones can still be seen just beyond the crashing surf of Cape May Point—it just isn't floating anymore.

S.S. ATLANTUS

REMAINS OF EXPERIMENTAL CONCRETE SHIP. ONE OF TWELVE BUILT DURING WORLD WAR 1. PROVEN IMPRACTICAL AFTER SEVERAL TRANS-ATLANTIC TRIPS BECAUSE OF WEIGHT.
BROKE LOOSE DURING STORM (JUNE 1926) WENT AGROUND. ATTEMPTS TO FREE HER WERE FUTILE.

Castles of New Jersey

Once upon a time in a kingdom not so far away there stood medieval castles replete with turreted towers, burial tombs, and even one with a great iron cannon aimed out over its stony ramparts. Castles invoke a rich imagery of romance and drama, as well as an inherent sense of history. The mere sight of them conjures thoughts of mystery and a storied past. Of course the stories that most of us equate with such fortresses are usually associated with far-off lands like the Scottish Highlands and the Carpathian Mountains and not the humble state of New Jersey. But there have been a few feudal lords in our state's past who have built grand monuments to themselves that would rival the most egocentric dwellings of European monarchy. Here are some reminders of the unusual historic dramas that have taken place in our state, which were set in, of all places, a castle. . . .

The Castle, Watchung, N.J.

Moldenke's Castle

It kept a solemn and stoic vigil over the Watchung Mountain range for nearly seventy years until a mysterious fire brought Castle Elsinore on Washington Valley Road down to the ground in 1969.

More familiarly known as Moldenke's Castle, the structure was built in 1900 and was fashioned after the Moldenke family castle in Denmark. It took over thirty years to complete and was the home of Dr. Richard Moldenke, a metallurgist, who decorated the estate with many historic artifacts from his family. Moldenke's father was a world-famous Egyptologist, and the Moldenke heritage could be traced back to the Third Crusade of Europe in 1189.

The castle had thirty-five to forty rooms. There was a huge entry hall that had two chandeliers, each made up of eight Civil War muskets. Suits of armor, helmets, guns, and trophies adorned every wall. The library held thousands of books, and the basement housed a machine shop, foundry, and the laboratory Moldenke used for scientific studies. There was also a mausoleum with twenty-one crypts.

A naval cannon perched on one of the ramparts had been on a Union gunboat during the battle of Vicksburg. Legend has it that Moldenke aimed the cannon at his neighbor, Representative Charles A. Eaton, with whom he didn't see eye-to-eye on the United States's entry into World War I. (Moldenke was against it, and his sympathies allegedly were with the Kaiser.)

Moldenke died in 1930, and most of his artifacts were sold off, save the family keepsakes. The castle was sold in 1945 to Dr. Jerome Herrick, a biological researcher, and eventually resold to a land development agency.

By the late 1960s, the castle had fallen into disarray. Vandals had stripped it of its ornate woodwork and copper piping, broken all of its leaded-glass diamond-shaped windows, and pushed the grand piano down the main corridor. The Delft tile work was torn off the walls and smashed. The developers offered the castle to the town of Watchung, but the town wanted the developer to renovate before they would take it over. In 1969, it was decided to raze the "obsolete and dilapidated" landmark.

The castle was slated for demolition, but on October 26, 1969, a fire broke out and gutted most of the building. Firefighters reported a strong smell of kerosene, and arson was suspected. When the blaze was over, it was discovered that four large tanks of fuel oil stored on the property had been opened prior to the blaze.

The castle was bulldozed and most of the four-foot-thick stonework was buried in nearby ravines and valleys to make way for new developments on the property.

Moldenke Castle is now just a footnote in the borough's history.

The Mad Scientist

The castle was brought over block by block from Europe. It stood for years, until it suspiciously burned down back in the mid-seventies. Word has it that a man named Hirsch purchased it from Moldenke, and he was a scientist instrumental in the development of the atom bomb. He, like others associated with the bomb, lost it after he realized how many people it killed in Japan.

He became a recluse and gave credence to the term mad scientist. When we would go up there the place was in ruins but still intact. One of the wings was loaded with broken beakers and row after row of laboratory equipment. The basement was said to be a dungeon.

On the property there was a family crypt, which had signs all over the doors reading RADIOACTIVE KEEP OUT. Today, where the castle used to stand, are upscale houses . . . what a shame. If Moldenke knew, he'd turn over in his radioactive grave.–*Dave Coriell*

Nightride to the Castle

One place that had many stories back in the late 60s and early 70s was the Watchung Reservation area. My favorite was the castle. The story was that a rich family had the castle moved from Scotland, stone by stone, and reassembled in Watchung. They hated visitors and would release their vicious guard dogs on any trespassers or shoot at them from a small cannon mounted on the walls. We would drive up the dirt road at night with our lights out until the castle was in view. Then we would park and see if we were brave enough to walk up to the walls.

Usually someone would hear a dog bark or think they saw a light. This would be enough for the rest of us to run back to the car and out to the main road as fast as we could.–*John Suzansky*

Mysterious Cult of Monk's Castle

Located on the ridge of First Mountain in Montclair is the Klasztor Salvatorian Fathers Monastery. This is an actual monastery, where a cloistered order of priests live, pray, and even take confessions. Their home, however, is not the building that is known in local legend as Monk's Castle. That building is next door to the monastery, and it sits on a fifteen-acre piece of property known as the Kip estate.

Perched on the highest point of the estate is a Rhineland-style castle. Built for Frederick Kip, a textile industry magnate, and his wife, the home was originally known as Kipsburg, or simply the Castle. It was transported stone by stone to this country from Europe in 1902, including its stained glass windows, oak-paneled rooms, hand-carved banisters, and a small chapel. When the thirty-room mansion was completed in 1905, it lay entirely within the town of Montclair. However, due to a realignment of town borders, the western portion of the building and estate is now located in Verona.

In 1980, the estate was purchased by Bhagwan Shree Rajneesh, an Indian swami who had recently wriggled his way out of tax evasion charges abroad and into this country under the pretense of a medical visa. In India, the forty-nine-year-old guru's ashram at Poona had over ten thousand disciples. There were four hundred centers worldwide, with two hundred thousand followers.

The Bhagwan (which means "God"), a self-proclaimed "rich man's guru," had accepted the worldly goods of his faithful (known as Sannyasins or Rajneeshees) to the tune of several million dollars. Believing that their surrender to Bhagwan must be total, followers would give up their belongings, their pasts, and even their names.

To announce his arrival in the United States, Bhagwan had placed ads in *Time* magazine preaching spirituality through sex. "SEX," one of the ads proclaimed, "Never Repress It! Search all of the nooks and corners of your sexuality. It will be more fun."

Naturally, rumors of a "Sex and Drugs" cult soon began to fly around Montclair, where followers began pouring in from London and Bombay, grabbing up any available living quarters to be nearer to their spiritual master. Nervous locals spread stories of red and orange dye (the colors worn at all times by the Rajneeshees) being planted in the washing machines at local Laundromats.

Bhagwan's chief administrator was Ma Anand Sheela (formerly Sheela Silverman), who convinced him to buy the castle after falling in love with the area during her thirteen years of study at Montclair State College. The castle's new owners promptly covered the walls with Sheetrock, the floors with linoleum, and smashed the stained glass windows to keep followers from becoming too attached to the house's materialistic trappings. Bhagwan, meanwhile, kept himself occupied by driving on the back roads of Montclair in one of his eighty-three Rolls-Royces.

By the end of the summer of 1981, Rajneesh was in the process of moving on to greener pastures. With $6 million generated from sales of his books and tapes, Bhagwan purchased a 64,228-acre ranch in Wasco County, Oregon. Before long, the settlement, known as Rajneeshpurum, boasted its own airport, shopping mall, restaurant chain, beauty salons, police force, discos, and Bhagwan-made lake.

Each day legions of the faithful would line the roads to catch a glimpse of their leader during his daily drive to one of the tiny neighboring towns of Wasco County. One such town, the minute hamlet of Antelope, was soon incorporated into the city of Rajneesh when its newest residents, far outnumbering the local citizenry, elected Rajneeshees to six of the seven town counsel seats.

A slew of legal battles were soon under way as Bhagwan's number two in command, Sheela, was brought up on charges, including burning down the Wasco County planning office. She fled the country and was arrested in West Germany and extradited to the United States to stand trial for the attempted murder of Rajneesh's personal physician.

Bhagwan was arrested in 1985 in Charlotte, NC, while en route to Bermuda, and charged with thirty-five counts of felony immigration violation and unlawful flight to avoid prosecution. Ma Anand Sheela was found guilty of attempted murder, assault, arson, and wiretapping, and was sentenced to twenty years in federal prison, of which she served four and one-half. Bhagwan received a ten-year suspended sentence, a $400,000 fine, and five years probation to be served outside the United States.

Bhagwan returned to his native India and died there of heart failure a few years later. The city of Rajneesh, Oregon, has once again become Antelope, and back in Montclair, the Kip estate now houses the law offices of Schwartz, Tobia & Stanziale. Next door the Salvatorian monks still occupy the monastery, taking confession from visitors and maintaining their piously low profile.

Getting Shot at by the Cult of Kip's Castle

I'm from Cedar Grove and as a grade school kid we always talked about the horror stories of Kip's Castle. It was said that a Satanic Cult lived there (full of Black Masses and Sacrifices). My mother worked for a local food store, and she states that they were part of some religious cult. They would shop, wearing their red hooded cloaks and religious or sacrilegious medallions on chains. They would hand shopping lists to the department managers without speaking and the managers would prepare their orders for them. These creeps scared the hell out of the employees.

One day we worked up the courage to interact with this clan. The castle was set back from the road. Stone walls blocked off the property. There was a type of stone structure (guard house) that had rusted chains, so we worked our way through the woods, instead of walking up the driveway. When we made it to the top of the driveway, you could see a beautiful view of Manhattan. There were no people, no cars.

We talked one kid into going into the castle through the front door, as the rest of us stood guard in the driveway. As he entered, the door closed behind him. I started to walk to the side of the castle to look out. I caught sight of a figure in a ceremonial cloak on the top of the roof/steeple/tower.

The next thing I know, he raises his arms and takes aim at me with some sort of rifle (BB-Gun or Salt Pellet Gun). Now, I'm not fleet of foot, but I busted my ass out of there. The kid who entered came running out and screaming. They let the dogs loose on us. We all ran away like a bunch of sissies. I can still hear the dogs barking and the shots being fired. Due to the distance, the shots that hit us only made a little pinch. We continued running, two miles until we were home. I never found out what they did up there or why they left. The building is now a law office. I think they were a cult from Utah. I also think the castle was owned by a king from India. —*Dean*

The Tragic Toxic Tale of the Radium Girls

In this day and age, radioactivity is recognized as a serious health threat. We were not always this wise, however. A particularly gruesome tale that illustrates this lesson originates in our own home state. This is the sad tale of the Radium Girls.

In the early part of the twentieth century, the United States Radium Corporation ran a small watch factory at the corner of Alden and High streets in the city of Orange, Essex County. These were no average watches, however. These timepieces boasted luminous dials that glowed in the dark, a true novelty at that time. The watches glowed thanks to a staff of young women who worked at the factory, tirelessly applying numbers onto the watch faces with a special iridescent paint.

Warning bells go off for residents of the twenty-first century, who know that anything that glows and involves something called "radium" is probably harmful. Unfortunately for the working girls at the U.S. Radium Corporation, this knowledge would be gained only at a great cost.

Watching Time Run Out

In the early '20s, the results of this unwitting radiation exposure began manifesting itself. Women all across Essex County were visiting doctors and dentists with the same symptoms: tooth loss, aches, ulcers of the gum, anemia, pneumonia, and angina. The most common problem was a malady termed "jaw rot," which was the painful decay of the tissue and bone in the mouth.

It wasn't long before people noted that all the women afflicted either worked for, or had once been employed by, the watch factory in Orange. The reason that their illnesses centered around the mouth, it would later be determined, was because the workers licked the tips of their paintbrushes to get a sharp point.

Blaming the Victims

In spite of the public outcry, the watch company denied that the paint was at fault. In an attempt to discredit the women, the factory owners brought in an expert who said the women were suffering from syphilis. The disease spread among them because they worked in close contact with each other. Although it was an act of unmitigated corporate gall, it is not surprising that in an era before workers' rights existed, state investigations of the plant found no industrial hazard present.

While the corporation was denying blame, the problem was taking a severe toll. By 1924, fifty women had fallen seriously ill and a dozen had died. When word of the epidemic spread, many doctors began voicing their opinions that radium was somehow involved. This led Essex County to call in their medical examiner, Dr. Harrison S. Martland, to investigate. He turned for answers to Dr. Sabin A. von Sochocky, founder and technical director of the company, as well as the inventor of the paint the workers used.

Martland and von Sochocky constructed a pseudo-Geiger counter and paid a visit to one of the dying women. When she breathed into the device, it registered deadly amounts of radiation. They then visited other former employees of the plant, both those who were showing symptoms and those who were not, and the device showed that all of their bodies contained radiation. Jokingly, von Sochocky breathed into the makeshift device and was shocked to see that his radiation levels were the highest of all.

Martland published his findings, for the first time establishing the true effects of radiation exposure on the human body. Five employees sued, and local newspapers began a crusade to support them. They were dubbed the Radium Girls by the press, and the papers began publishing articles about the workers' tales of debt, pain, and sickness—including stillbirths and the loss of limbs.

Public outrage eventually forced the company to capitulate, and in June 1928, it gave each of the five women $10,000 along with a $600 yearly pension. The company continued to fight subsequent lawsuits, though, and finally went out of business in the early '30s.

Over the years, employees continued to die horrible, painful deaths. Although most of them died within a few years of their exposure, the sins of the U.S. Radium Corporation would not be buried with the dead. In actuality, their crimes against the citizens of Essex County would be buried beneath the yards around, and laid squarely on the doorsteps of, hundreds of new suburban homes being built in the area.

Old Radium Never Dies

In 1980, Congress passed the Superfund law, which was aimed at cleaning up areas contaminated by radiation. An aerial survey of New Jersey showed that three neighboring towns—Glen Ridge, Montclair, and West Orange—had parcels of land saturated with gamma radiation. Like the luminous dials on the watch faces that were once manufactured nearby, these towns literally glowed in the dark when viewed with today's high-tech sensory equipment.

The problem was traced back to the tons of contaminated dirt from the Orange radium plant that had been used as landfill in low-lying neighborhoods built in the late 1920s and early 1930s. Homes, parks, and even schools were constructed on tainted ground.

The problems here were potentially more dangerous than radium itself. The discarded paint would eventually decay, releasing radon, a gaseous form of radium, which has been proved to cause lung cancer.

The EPA began initial cleanup efforts in 1983, but delays stretched the process into the next decade. Finally, in 1990, the EPA agreed to remove all the radium. Six years later, they had removed the contaminated soil from three hundred properties. Then began the removal of tainted soil from public areas—parks and streets.

The cleanup itself is ongoing. For more than twenty years, residents have dealt with the nuisance of men in radiation suits, huge trucks, and torn-up streets and property, not to mention the more troubling prospect of raising their children on a cancer hot spot. Needless to say, there has been much litigation filed by residents of these areas over the years. In 1991, after a seven-year fight, 237 residents collected $4.2 million from the remnants of the U.S. Radium Corporation. This worked out to $18,000 per household.

It has been nearly a century since the whole radium fiasco began. Only now, after dozens of deaths, numerous legal battles, and more than $150 million in cleanup efforts, does this dark, irresponsible chapter in our state's history finally appear to be drawing to a close.

***i**t is undeniable that some places* in New Jersey give off a distinctly strange and otherworldly vibe. For this reason, they have gained a reputation of being more supernatural than natural. Likewise, there have always been particular characters in the Garden State who are definitely not your garden-variety residents. We refer to such places and people as fabled. Sometimes the people are real and the stories are true, sometimes not. And sometimes we just don't know where to draw the line in that gray twilight zone that lies between the two.

Some of the characters and communities you will read about in this chapter are unquestionably real, like the enigmatic fire-and-brimstone specter of the White Pilgrim and the mysterious body of water known as Round Valley Reservoir. Others, well, you're just going to have to make up your own mind as to what you choose to believe. For example, did people from other planets really converge on (of all places) the rural farmlands of Hunterdon County to impart their intergalactic wisdom to us mere earthlings? How is it that not one but two places in the state have earned such an evil reputation that they were BOTH given the moniker of the Devil's Half Acre? And just what might lie at the very outer limits of our fair state, on the fringes of the known, miles down that last lonely road that seemingly leads nowhere at all? Let's find out—together.

Fabled Places and People

Weirdness in the Watchung Mountains

Rituals of the Forest

Back in 1986 when I was in high school, three friends and I were hanging out at the Friendly's in Mountainside. It was a Saturday night, and we were bored out of our minds. So when my friend Chris said, "Hey lets go to the Watchung Reservation," we said okay.

All but one of us had heard the rumors about Devil worshippers hanging out in the reservation but none of us really believed it. Anyway we got up there and parked next to the Magic Forest. Beyond the Magic Forest was what was called the Witches' Forest. I have no idea how these sections of the woods were given these titles. We got out of the car, and walked towards the Magic Forest. We had walked a few feet into the woods, which were pitch black, when we noticed lights flickering deeper in the woods, in the Witches' Forest.

At first we thought it was a bunch of kids partying, until we heard what sounded like the most unearthly moan or wail from a woman. We were so scared that we all grabbed hands and ran out of the woods to our cars. I will never forget how scared I was. I could literally feel the hairs on the back of my neck stand up.

Another story I heard came from a classmate, who happened to be an Eagle Scout. He and some other scouts were hiking up in the reservation one day, when they came across a stone altar-like structure, which had what he believed to be bloodstains. *–T2ee*

The Leaper

In the Watchung Reservation there are a series of trails which all lead in one way or another to Surprise Lake, which lies within the mountains. My sister, her dog, a good friend and I decided to take a stroll in an area known as the Magic Forest. It was early spring and everything was really muddy and slippery. As we were walking along, the dog's ears perked up and he started barking like mad. The three of us saw nothing and continued to walk on.

The trail leads down to the lake where you have two steep inclines on either side of you. They are not good walking grounds. Out of nowhere we saw this man running down one of the inclines at an incredible speed. Then he leaped across the path to the other side of the mountain. This was totally weird. The dog was still barking and we had all stopped in our tracks because the distance this man jumped was impossible and the fact of the matter was, he never stopped running. He kept on going, leaping along the way.

We continued with our walk and couldn't get the dog to calm down or the image of the strange man leaping across the mountain out of our minds. Somehow we got to a trail which none of us had ever been down before. We decided to take it, because it is pretty difficult to get lost up there, since you usually end up back at Surprise Lake and from there you can get your bearings.

As we walked on, the dog, who had calmed down again, went completely berserk. Ahead of us was an old red barn-like building, which had scorch marks around its window frames. As we got closer, we realized that squatters might be living in it because there was garbage and clothes everywhere. The weirdest part were the animal pens, which were on both sides of the building. There were no animals, but there were what looked like blood trails all over the dried up grass. There were also burnt candles placed in a circular pattern in the animal pens. We decided to high tail it out of there.

Over the years, many stories have filtered down about satanic rituals that occurred up in the mountains. We'd ignore those stories and still cruise around there at night to spook ourselves out. On one occasion about 8 years ago, I was driving around the mountains with my sister and a good friend. As we were rounding a curve, we saw flames in the distance. The cops and fire department were streaming in, and as we rolled by, we noticed that this wasn't any ordinary fire. It was a perfectly designed circle with a Pagan star in the middle. It was the creepiest thing.–*Melanie Quintanilla*

How the Suicide Tower Got Its Name

Our state has a legendary example of teen angst expressing itself in what has to be one of the most gruesome cases of murder in New Jersey history. It was 1975, and Mountainside was a quiet suburban community nestled right next to the Watchung Reservation. Gregg Sanders was fifteen years old and lived with his parents: Thomas, a banker, and Janice, a teacher at a church nursery school. He attended the prestigious Pingry School in Hillside, where he was an honor roll student. Gregg was a kid with a lot of potential. His freshman year he played football, and his sophomore year he managed the team. He was a solid student, particularly well regarded for his writing ability. In college, he planned to study either law or medicine. He had always pushed himself . . . and had been pushed by his parents.

Gregg had always felt a lot of pressure to do as well as his sister had done throughout her scholastic career. Kids from his neighborhood remember how Gregg was not satisfied with being a B student. They would tease him about it and often called him a momma's boy.

The combination of parental and peer pressures eventually took their toll on the young man, and with deadly consequences.

On January 15, Gregg left school at four forty-five p.m. Everyone who had seen him on his

way out said he seemed fine—but he was not. Gregg went home and wrote a suicide note. As his sister later told *The New York Times,* "For reasons which will never be known to me or to anyone, my brother could not cope with the pressures of his life anymore. . . . He decided, probably on the spur of the moment, that he could not stand it anymore. He wrote he was sorry for any trouble or distress that he caused for anyone by what he was about to do. What he was about to do was to end his own life. After deciding this, Gregg realized the pain he would cause our parents with his death. The only way he could die in peace, knowing he would spare our parents from any pain and sorrow, was to end it for them too."

That's right—in his twisted mind, Gregg decided he would spare his parents the pain of dealing with his suicide by killing them.

So Gregg took an axe and attacked his father in the dining room of their home. As his father staggered away, Gregg hit him in the back of the head five more times, caving in his dad's skull. He left him lying dead on the kitchen floor. His mother, who had heard the commotion from upstairs, came rushing into the kitchen, only to be axed

Teen uses ax to slay parents, leaps to death

By RICHARD CONNIFF

A quiet Mountainside youth methodically and without apparent motive murdered his mother and father with an ax, then leaped to his death from a nearby water tower late Tuesday night, police said.

Gregg Sanders, 15, a bright but shy sophomore at the Pingry School in Hillside, reportedly sat down about 9 p.m. in his bedroom at 1090 Sunny Slope Dr. and wrote—in a note addressed "To whom it may concern"—that he was sorry for what he was about to do.

He then went downstairs, got an ax and attacked his first at the . . .

48, had fallen dead on the kitchen floor, police said, the youth attacked his mother. Janice L. Sanders, 44, when she came downstairs. He left her dead on the dining room floor, with a single ax blow.

Police said Sanders then shut out the first-floor lights of the house and left by the kitchen door. Despite the freezing temperature, he walked without a jacket or coat the 10-minute route up to the 150-foot water tower in the Watchung Reservation.

The teenager climbed the winding staircase to the top of the tower . . .

Thomas Sanders Jr.
Respected bank exec

to live and work in Revere, Mass., outside Boston.

Neighbors and friends of Sanders, who had . . .

Gregg Sanders
A nice boy.

"Otherwise, . . . let us . . .

to death herself in a single blow.

Having already written his suicide note, which graphically described what he was planning on doing, Gregg took off into the freezing January night wearing only a T-shirt and a pair of khaki pants. He went to a popular make-out spot at the time, a hundred-and-fifty-foot-tall water tower in the Watchung Reservation that had a staircase circling up the outside of the tank. Gregg climbed to the top, then slit his left wrist, and leaped to his death. At around eleven fifteen p.m., four kids who were exploring the reservation came upon Gregg's body.

In the weeks that followed, people tried to figure out why Gregg did what he did. Rumors spread that he had been full of cocaine, but toxicology tests proved this to be untrue. It remained a baffling mystery. As one neighbor said, "He was the most normal kid on the block. He didn't break windows or anything like that. He was the last kid that you would expect to do this."

These days, Gregg's story is one of the most recounted tales of the area in which it occurred, a sad story of a confused kid who went to an awful extreme.

The EnCHANTed Forest

The Enchanted Forest was a constant theme of conversation when I was growing up. It was widely rumored that a coven of witches would meet there when the moon was full and they would do whatever it is that witches do. I was never really bothered by the story because from what I understand they are just religious people who give praise to the earth and then boil some roots and toads, not really bothersome unless you are Catholic and it runs contrary to your religious beliefs.

One Saturday afternoon a couple of friends and I decided to explore the woods of the Watchung Reservation. After walking about 1/4 mile down a path in the woods, we saw the spectacular sight of the Enchanted Forest.

It really is awe-inspiring. You walk through scrub bushes and old growth trees into a wide-open area where there are hundreds of trees planted in perfectly straight rows. They are all tall and straight, and there is very little foliage. The sun beats down in an eerie way so that it seems to glow off the floor of the forest.

We were roaming around the forest's numerous trails when one of my friends said there was someone behind us. We had just reached an area that had been cleared out and logs were placed in a circle around where a fire had recently been. There were a lot of tiny pieces of broken glass and the charred remains of logs.

We were sort of spooked and turned around to leave, only to find that there was no longer anyone behind us. There are a lot of places around the edge of the forest where people could hide, so we figured that was where this person was. Needless to say, we left pretty quickly.

A few months later, we decided to take another trip out there. This time we were going to go at night on a weekend with a full moon.

We got to the parking area after midnight and began to walk down the path towards the forest. As we got about two thirds of the way down we began to hear what sounded like singing, and not very good singing at that. It was very monotone and almost chant like, and it was definitely coming from the Enchanted Forest. Realizing that there was more than one person singing, we decided to leave, and fast.

It has been seventeen years since then and I have been back to the Enchanted Forest numerous times. But I only visit during the day. I will not go there at night. –*David Gaut*

History of the "Deserted Village"

Having grown up in Scotch Plains, I am familiar with a local spot known as the Deserted Village. It is located in the Watchung Reservation in Berkeley Heights and is owned by the Union County Parks System. Built in 1845, it consists of a number of cottages, a store-church, a pre–Revolutionary War cemetery, and the ruins of a mill.

My sister, who still lives in the area, tells me that the Park Service has fixed things up and the cottages are rented out now. But when I was going there in the 1970s and 80s, there were a lot of squatters in the cottages and, of course, teens went up there to party. There are tales of satanic cult rituals and witch covens practicing in the woods. I have also seen some strange rock placements and old campfires on hikes.

The Village was built by David Felt in 1845 to provide homes for the workers of his paper mill. Known as King David, he built dwellings, a combination church and general store, a barn, and a blacksmith shop. King David lived in a large manor house and was said to be a cold, reserved man who ruled with methodical strictness. All the people (the population of the village in 1850 was 174) had to buy from his village store. The villagers worked six days a week and had to go to church on Sunday. A bell at the manor house would ring at

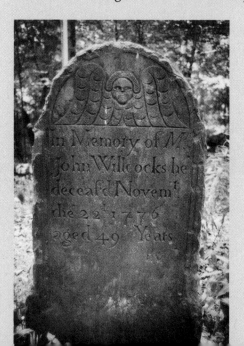

seven in the morning for work, at noon for lunch, at the end of the workday, and at nine at night when the people had to be in!

The village was kept in perfectly manicured condition by King David's decree and the village farms provided the food. Life went on like this until 1860 when David Felt retired to New York and sold the village. He was overheard to say on his departure, "Well, King David is dead, and the village will go to hell"—and it did, after several owners tried to make a go of it.

By 1882 it had fallen into ruin, and had become known as the Deserted Village. It was revived as a summer retreat for wealthy people at the turn of the century. In 1916 the Union County Parks Commission purchased the village and rented the homes to families that had lost their own due to the hard times. It is one of my best memories of NJ.—*Karen Sykas*

The White Pilgrim

For more than a century, residents who live along the border of Sussex and Warren counties have told stories of one of the state's most famous oddballs and one of its most apparent apparitions — the White Pilgrim.

Born Joseph Thomas in 1791, the White Pilgrim was an Ohio native who set out as a traveling preacher at a young age. Having visited hundreds of cities east of the Mississippi, Thomas attained a certain amount of national notoriety. While his legend has faded in most places, it will live on forever in New Jersey, since he not only preached here, but died here in 1835 — and some say, has haunted the area ever since.

Even today a person dressed all in white, right down to white boots, straddling a white horse, would turn heads. One can only imagine the reaction Thomas got when trotting through the quiet farm communities of northwestern New Jersey in the early 1800s. Some say that Thomas wore his outlandish garb to ward off evil spirits and diseases. Others say that he was a lackluster preacher and a fiend for attention, and that the outfit was his way of making sure he got noticed. Another way he gained his reputation was by doing drastic things in the name of religion, for example, renaming the town of Hainesburg "Sodom" due to its apparent lawlessness.

Part of why the White Pilgrim's legend grew so quickly was that he died shortly after delivering his first New Jersey sermon. A wave of smallpox was sweeping through the area, and the White Pilgrim succumbed to it in Johnsonburg. When he died, church officials, never too fond of Thomas's overzealous piety, decided that his contaminated corpse should not be interred alongside the upstanding, Christian, noncontaminated deceased citizens of the area. He was buried not in the town's official Christian Cemetery but in the far less respectable Dark of the Moon Cemetery, located near the Dark of the Moon Tavern.

According to local legend, this is the reason the White Pilgrim haunted the area. Enraged that he was denied his proper Christian burial, he would often be seen sitting on his white saddle on his white horse, frightening local residents. In 1846, eleven years after his death, the town elders decided to reinter his remains in the Christian Cemetery, and the townsfolk contributed $125 for the monument that stands there today. Interestingly, his memorial sits in the center of the graveyard, yet it is yards away from any other plot. Regardless of this apparent quarantine, locals say that since his reinterment, the White Pilgrim's ghost has been seen far less frequently.

NJ's Bermuda Triangle

I live about two minutes from the Round Valley Reservoir (RVR) and in my 10+ years living in the area, I have heard so many different accounts of strange happenings it makes me think that something weird is going on. I heard that when RVR opened in 1968, many people would drive up there and "park" with their sweethearts. Well, within the first week of its opening there were multiple eyewitness accounts of strange lights hovering above the reservoir. Recently, two young boys I know told me about a recent trip there one night when they spotted a strange green light hovering and bobbing above the water. At first they thought it was a boat light, but scratched that idea when it rose higher and drifted into the trees behind them.

RVR is 180 ft deep. It's the deepest body of water in NJ. The famous Jacques Cousteau supposedly paid a visit to the reservoir with his minisub and claimed that it was one of the weirdest places he'd ever seen. There was a small town that existed somewhere at the bottom of the reservoir and many of the buildings are still reputed to be there.

It's said that within the first year of RVR's opening, about 8 people drowned. Several rescue squad members (my sister and mother included) say that if one body comes up, then another one is going down soon. I can attest to this, as one summer, either 1993 or 94, my sister responded to a DOA call at the reservoir. A gentleman in a boat without a motor had his anchor stuck on a larger object. He requested a tow from a powerboat and up popped a missing drowned fisherman fully clothed; his 1990 fishing license was still attached to his vest and get this, his sunglasses were still on. Well, three days later two canoeists are paddling around when one decides to cool off and jumps in. He never came up! He's still missing to this day.

What's going on up there? Aliens in the reservoir? Is something pulling people under? Who knows, but any way you look at it it's weird. —*Brent Franklin*

Death in Drowned Valley

I worked at Round Valley recreation area from 1985 to 1994 in the maintenance crew for the State Park Service. Years before the reservoir was built, a town and several farms existed there.

Over the years, there have been numerous drownings and there are still unrecovered bodies in the water. Once in a while, one will surface, still clothed. When a person drowns in the reservoir, the body will get caught in the underwater trees, brush, and structures not leveled when the reservoir was built. Just before I left to a promotion at another park, a victim's body surfaced after approximately four years. He still had his pants, boots, shirt, ball cap and glasses on!

The water's temperature is cold down deep and this preserves the flesh to a certain extent. Round Valley (or Death Valley, as we called it) has its share of suicides also, two of which I'm aware of. One was by hanging and the other by self-inflicted gunshot.
—*Bob Parichuk*

The following is an excerpt from an Associated Press article by Wayne Parry dated March 9, 2006, which chronicles a small portion of the mysterious death toll of Round Valley and a search for some of the dozens of unrecovered bodies that remain in the lake to this day.

[Round Valley Reservoir is] a watery place where people disappear, never to be seen again. The description held true Wednesday after a 4 1/2-hour search of the sprawling Round Valley Reservoir failed to turn up any trace of six missing boaters and fishermen, some of whom were last seen in 1973. . . .

'It would be nice to bring some closure, not only to our open cases but to the families involved,' state police Detective Sgt. Jim Price said before the search began. All six men are presumed drowned

. . . A team of 30 state police, FBI and Bergen County Sheriff's officers fanned out on foot and in boats across the 180-foot-deep reservoir, looking for skeletal remains, clothing or other signs of the missing victims, all of whom are presumed drowned. . . .

'Since 1971, 25 people have drowned at the reservoir,' said Lt. Jim McCormick, supervisor of the state police's missing persons unit. The oldest unsolved case dates to May 4, 1973, when Thomas Trimblett, 27, of North Arlington, and Christopher Zajaczkowski of Jersey City, whose age was unknown, were fishing on the reservoir from a 12-foot aluminum boat that was later found capsized. . . .

On March 15, 1977, Craig Stier, 18, and Andrew Fasanella, 20, both of Trenton, launched a canoe from a reservoir boat ramp and were last seen paddling along the north shoreline. Four days later, their canoe was found washed ashore along with some camping gear.

On March 18, 1989, John Kubu, 37, of Rahway, and Albert Lawson, whose age and hometown were not available, failed to return from a fishing trip on the reservoir. Their 13-foot aluminum boat and various personal items were later found on the shoreline. Lawson's body was found that October; Kubu's body has not been found.

'. . . On two boats [during the search], specially trained cadaver-sniffing dogs were brought in to sniff for the telltale gases that decaying bodies emit. The next step will be to search sections of the reservoir with a special underwater robotic camera,' Price said. 'That search has not yet been scheduled.'

The death toll continues to mount.

The Devil's Half Acre

Deep in the southwestern part of Somerset County lie the Sourland Mountains. They run from the Delaware River to Hillsborough Township, then south towards the Princeton Hills. Though they are increasingly encroached upon by developers, much of the area is still wilderness and deep forest. Tales of bizarre places and strange creatures that roamed the area can be traced back over the centuries.

One such group of tales concerns a place called Devil's Half Acre. The name is incorrect because it is much larger than that. It is closer to a half-mile long and several hundred yards in width. Basically, it is a gorge filled to the top with boulders ranging in size from a basketball to an automobile. This is the result of centuries of erosion, exposing granite boulders left over from a glacial deposit. The boulders are piled one on top of another, creating what is known as talus caves. In some places, the openings create tunnels which run fairly deep, though most are too low to stand in and too narrow for an adult to fit in.

Early settlers avoided this place because it was said that the devil had a passage to the surface here. Looking

Early settlers avoided this place because it was said that the devil had a passage to the surface here.

at this remote location, it is easy to imagine some malevolent force or creature lurking here.

The only way to reach Devil's Half Acre without trespassing is to park at the Sourland Mountain Reserve on East Mountain Road in Hillsborough. The park is open every day from dawn until sunset. Walk up the northernmost trail, on the right-hand side of the parking lot. About 3/4 of the way to the top, leave the trail and head about a 1/2 mile to the north-northwest. The terrain is increasingly rocky and it is very easy to trip or get your foot stuck. You'll know you're getting close when you are only able to advance by jumping from one rock to another.

Wear good shoes and carry water, a watch and a compass. Remember, this place is very isolated. The trek is dangerous enough in daylight; at night it is downright treacherous.

This eerie and unique place is pristine. It is one of the last areas in our state like this.–*D. S. Gibson*

Devil's Half Acre of Middlesex County

There is another Devil's Half Acre, this one in Middlesex County. Lying along Half Acre Road in Monroe Township, this Devil's Half Acre was once part of a small village that was home to a notorious inn. The tavern was positioned at a point where two roads met, and a fence marked off the road, which ran behind the establishment. This fence was laid out as a border for an exact half acre of land. It was said that the area's most vicious men would meet at the site to participate in brutal brawls. The area was also a bastion of sexual deviancy. Since it was viewed as such an evil and immoral place, it was dubbed the Devil's Half Acre.

The Roaring Brook lies southwest of the Devil's Half Acre, in Hillsborough, Somerset County. It is said that the stones that lie along the bed of the brook possess strange qualities and ring when struck together.

Aliens Came in Peace

Fifty years ago, a man named Howard Menger and his wife Connie transformed the sleepy town of High Bridge into a mini-Roswell with their thrilling and enchanting stories of alien contact.

Menger, supported by a legion of other so-called "contactees" scattered throughout the country, claimed to be in regular contact with the resplendent "Venusians." Blond, blue-eyed, and sweet-tempered, the Venusians were our cosmic guardian angels, Menger claimed, here to act as a moral compass in the search for our repressed, spiritual selves.

The fact that the Venusians were also vegetarians left no doubt that they were truly advanced beings.

In 1956, Menger took his fantastic stories to the airwaves and became a frequent guest on the immensely popular "Long John Nebel" radio program, which then broadcast nightly from one to five-thirty a.m. on New York station WOR.

A brilliant New York attorney named Jules St. Germaine was also a guest of Long John's and frequently appeared on-air with Menger. Skeptical of his claims, he launched an intense investigation, traveling to New Jersey and conducting many interviews with witnesses. St. Germaine noted there were many inconsistencies—too many. In fact, the holes in Menger's story were large enough for an entire fleet of Venusian scout ships to have passed through them.

And Menger's Polaroid photos of what he claimed were spacecraft were obvious, crude fakes.

Menger, who now lives in Florida, has always denied there had been any chicanery. But during a conversation in March of 1995, Menger confessed (unexpectedly, and for the first time, I believe) that he had actually made sketches of what he saw and then photographed them. He maintained he did this because the original photos had been stolen.

Incredibly, Menger was incensed by the idea that anyone would consider a sketch of something a hoax! He stunned me further by maintaining that he had never said the photos were real and that the people who said he had "got it wrong."—*Peter A. Jordan*

AUTHENTIC MUSIC FROM ANOTHER PLANET

narrated and played by HOWARD MENGER

ACTUAL PHOTOGRAPHY OF INTERPLANETARY SPACECRAFT

Commander Valiant Thor

"Good evening, I am Valiant Thor and I am from Venus."
— *Val Thor, speech at Salmon Arm, British Columbia, Canada, July 22, 1994*

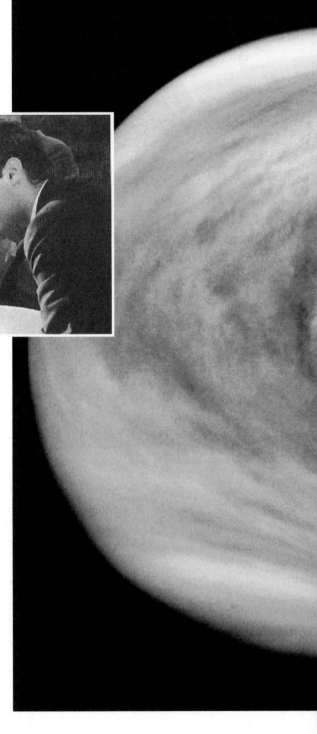

The legend of Valiant Thor started in the 1950s, an unprecedented time of UFO hysteria in America. Rumors spread of a mysterious man among us who claimed to be from Venus. Some said he could walk through walls; others claimed he had no fingerprints. Speculation on the location of his spaceship ran rampant. It was the beginning of a mystery that persists to this day.

Said to be Valiant Thor at far right, with his crew members, Jill and brother Donn

In the 1950s, the public's fascination with alien visitations was a relatively new phenomenon. One of the people integral to its widespread appeal was Howard Menger of High Bridge, who claimed to be regularly visited by Venusians (citizens of Venus) on his Hunterdon County farm. He went on talk shows speaking of these encounters, and hosted conventions on his property welcoming both fellow alien contactees and the public. These conventions were eventually visited by a handsome, charismatic mystery man claiming to be the commander of all the Venusians on Earth. He wowed people by being able to speak any language or dialect any member of the crowd could throw at him. The man's name was Valiant Thor.

According to Thor, he came from a race of beings who lived within Venus, not on its surface. This race was superior to us in most ways— they were smarter, better looking, and less violent. They were sent here to protect us from ourselves, and their number one mission was to make sure nuclear war never occurred.

When Val, as his friends called him, arrived, he immediately went to visit President Eisenhower to offer his assistance in solving all of

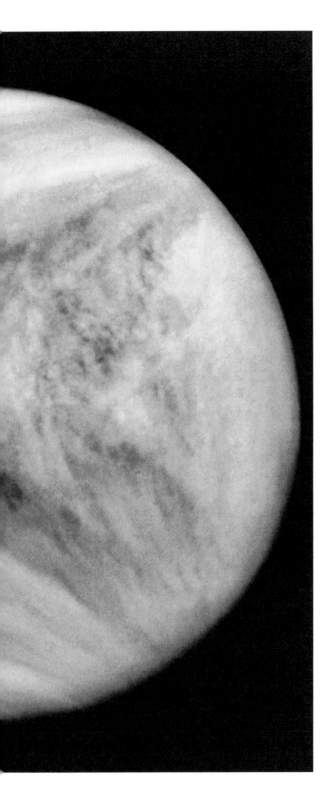

Earth's problems. He did not get to see the President, but claims he met briefly with the Secretary of Defense. After that, he was held by a government agency within the Pentagon, where he was questioned and studied.

The story of Valiant Thor has been disseminated by many, but most notably by one Dr. Frank Stranges. Stranges claims that agents of the Venusian escorted him into the Pentagon in 1959 to meet with Val. Since then, he has been periodically visited by Val, and he reports seeing Val's brother Donn walk through solid matter. He also claims that, during their first meeting, Val showed him a spacesuit that sealed itself without buttons or zippers but merely by a wave of Val's hand over it, and was made of a fabric that could not be destroyed. Stranges says Val told him that the government had been doing tests on him and had determined that his IQ was over 200.

Stranges, a preacher, believes Val and his shipmates are a race of people created by God before Adam, and never suffered the fall from God's grace that humankind did.

These days it is said that Valiant Thor's ship, *Victory One*, remains hidden near Lake Mead, just outside Las Vegas, Nevada. The ship is home not only to Val, but also to Donn, crewmates Thonn and Teel, and a medical officer known simply as Doc. Though he periodically returns to Venus, Val always winds up back here on Earth somehow.

Stranges says that while he still meets with Val to this day, the Venusian has chosen not to reveal himself to the masses yet because he is working on a very specific timeline to do so.

Is Val Thor really a superhuman responsible for maintaining peace on Earth? Is he just a strange guy looking for attention? Is he even real, or just a figment of Frank Stranges's imagination? No one is really sure.

Only one thing is certain—the journey that Val Thor began over forty years ago in High Bridge, NJ, where he first came to the attention of the public, seems to still be an ongoing mission. As Criswell said in Ed Wood Jr.'s *Plan 9 From Outer Space*, "Perhaps future events such as these will affect us in the future, where you and I will spend the rest of our lives. . . ."

In the words of Valiant Thor himself, "I leave you tonight and say alahoy."

Ong's Hat: Gateway to Another Dimension?

The New Jersey Pine Barrens have a plethora of deserted villages, most of them long abandoned. One of the most infamous is Ong's Hat in Burlington County. If you take the turnpike to exit four and follow Route 70 east, you'll come to Route 72 at Four Mile Circle. Taking a hard left leads to Ong's Hat and a trail that some say ends at a mysterious portal to another dimension.

The true reason as to why anyone would name a village Ong's Hat may be shrouded in mystery forever, but the folklore surrounding the town's name is well known.

Legend has it that at one time a resident of the area was a flashy young gentleman by the name of Ong (while his first name is unknown, his last is an old-time Pine Barrens name—one of the earliest Pines settlers was Jacob Ong). He was a fixture at local dances, where he wooed the ladies with his fancy dance moves and suave attire—most notably his silk hat.

Apparently, Ong was something of a "player," flirting and dancing with all the ladies he could. One of his love interests caught on to this practice at a dance and attacked Ong, taking his hat and stomping on it. Ong was upset that his chapeau had just been ruined. He ran outdoors and tossed the hat into the air out of frustration. It caught in the high branches of a pine tree and stayed there for years. It became a landmark by which people could find the small village, and the area was dubbed Ong's Hat.

As the Pine Barrens became less populated, Ong's Hat was all but forgotten. Today it is totally abandoned and would be nothing more than a footnote in history were it not for a very weird development—the opening of a gateway to another dimension.

The following history can be found in a book entitled *Ong's Hat: The Beginning*. The author, Joseph Matheny, is coy as to whether he intended the work as fact or fiction. Some claim that the book is pure fantasy and has set up a hoax that many have come to accept as real.

According to Matheny's history, a group of white jazz musicians and poets founded the Moorish Orthodox Church of America in the 1950s. The members of this small sect traveled the world, learning many different philosophies and spiritual practices. One of these travelers was known as Wali Fard.

When Fard returned from his travels in 1978, he spent all of his savings on two hundred acres in the New Jersey Pine Barrens. Along with a group of runaway boys from Paramus and two lesbian anarchists, he moved onto the property and formed an exclusive sect, the Moorish Science Ashram.

Fard published a series of newsletters proclaiming his beliefs. Readers on the fringe began flocking to his land, including two scientists, Frank and Althea Dobbs. The Dobbs twins were raised in Texas, among a UFO-worshipping cult founded by their father. Needless to say, they were used to life on the outskirts of the mainstream. When they arrived in the Pines they set up a laboratory inside a ramshackle trailer and began making discoveries that shook the small commune to its core.

The siblings had previously studied at Princeton, where they submitted as their Ph.D. theses a series of equations that led to what they called "cognitive chaos." They were dismissed from the university and found their way to the Pines. In the remote locale, they were free to work further on their ideas. Their theories promoted the

the dimension next door to ours. This was the opening of the Gate.

The members of the ICS had to leave their Pine Barrens compound due to a chemical spill from Fort Dix that was leaking nuclear material into the area. Instead of fleeing outward, they fled interdimensionally. They used the Gate to transport themselves and all of their possessions into an alternate dimension, where they still lived in Ong's Hat, but humankind did not exist.

Matheny first became involved in the Ong's Hat idea that people could tap into the unused portion of their brains and do things such as stop their aging and purge diseases from their systems. The ashram used their research to found the Institute of Chaos Studies (ICS).

Progress occurred more quickly than the scientists could have predicted. Within three years, they had stumbled upon an extraordinary apparatus that came to be known as the Gate. This was one of a series of devices the scientists referred to as the Egg. They hooked people up to computers and charted their brain waves. By experimenting with sex, drugs, and other mind wave manipulators, the scientists learned how to control the chaos they found within the mind.

The fourth version of the Egg was tested on one of the Paramus runaways. When it was activated, he and the device itself disappeared. Moments later both rematerialized. The boy claimed that he had traveled to saga when he posted a book catalogue he had found, known as the "Incunabula Catalog," on the Internet at the turn of the '90s.

Then he produced one of the essays reviewed in the catalogue, and from there, he claimed to have interviewed one of the physicists mentioned in these papers, as well as the original author of the book catalogue he had posted. These documents make up what are known as the "Incunabula Papers." It is somewhat unclear as to whether there ever was any documentation of these alleged events other than the ones that Matheny "found" and posted himself.

So was Ong's Hat ever the home of a mysterious cult of science nerds, or is this interdimensional gate merely one of the earliest known Internet hoaxes? Whatever the case may be, the story of Ong's Hat is bizarre and believed to be more fact than fiction by more than just a few sci-fi fanatics.

From Shell Pile to Sea Breeze

"Shell Pile is named for the great heaps of oyster shells stacked outside the packing sheds. This is a community of about 1,000 Negroes living in wooden barracks erected on stilts over the salt marshes. Negroes here live their own lives in their own way, and present a united and rather hostile front from the rest of the world. Strange whites are not welcomed in Shell Pile." —WPA guidebook to New Jersey, published in 1939

The Maurice River in Cumberland County was at one time the epicenter of the New Jersey oyster industry, processing much of the East Coast's mollusks for packing plants and the food industry. In the late 1800s and again in the 1920s, the town saw eighty train cars a day carrying out oysters from the Delaware Bay. In 1955, the industry was at its peak, but in 1957, a mysterious disease called MSX killed 90 percent of the oysters and clams that came out of the bay and adjoining rivers. This left many of the fishing villages belly up, beached, and left for dead. The population in the Port Norris area today (which includes Bivalve and Shell Pile) includes just nine year-round homes.

With billions of clams and oysters giving up their calcium crusts to the shucking line, what, we wondered, ever became of the shells? We were also curious as to whatever became of the "1,000 Negroes" living in barracks on stilts that the WPA report described. Were their descendants still as hostile toward strange whites as the guidebook claimed they were in 1939? With these questions burning in our minds, we set out for the most extreme outer reaches of the New Jersey mainland in a quest to see for ourselves where the shells line the shores.

The first thing one notices when nearing the town of Shell Pile is the pungent stench of fish in the air. Currently, most of the oysters processed there actually come from the Long Island Sound, but the local industry is witnessing something of a comeback of the native Delaware Bay oyster population. Today there are about twenty-five oyster boats working the bay, though many local fishermen have turned to crabbing as a means of support.

Berry & Sons mattress company, a firm that makes coffin liners with the slogan, "The last mattress you'll ever sleep on." We were almost too distracted by the open back door of the 18-wheeler parked there, coffin mattresses stacked to its roof, to notice what lay just ahead of us. There, at the very outer limits of the New Jersey subcontinent, stood the mother of all shell piles.

It was a gleaming white mountain, at least four stories in height and covering several acres. Way at the top, a lone tractor operator jockeyed his front-loader back and forth, reshaping the mound, immersed in a cloud of laughing gulls. This, we thought, must surely be the fabled shell pile of legend, though we were actually now west of that town, near Egg Island. The mounds are quite breathtaking, and a robust stench of rancid clams is pervasive, even in the dead of winter.

Not much of the scenery has changed since the WPA report, except for the lack of people (Negro or otherwise). In fact, not one resident was sighted during our entire expedition there. Heading out to the farthest point of Shell Pile, we spotted through our binoculars a huge white mountain along the shore to the northeast.

Leaving the main part of town (if you could say that there is a main part of town), we passed an apparently abandoned church. Upon closer inspection, we noticed a sign on the building that read SERVICES HELD OCCASIONALLY. Judging from the boards on the windows though, we surmised that even this modest promise was an overstatement. We also noted a multitude of MUSKRAT CROSSING signs along the side of the road on which we were traveling.

Following our noses, we turned down a small road that led us out through a seemingly infinite expanse of marsh grass. Finding ourselves in Port Norris, we passed the Miller

After pondering the awesome spectacle of the shell pile for a while, we decided to continue on our journey up the Delaware Bay shore, eager to find what might still lie ahead for us. Like Mohammed seeking his mountain, reaching the piles of shells along New Jersey's Delaware coast was for us an ardent, and almost mystical, adventure.

Coffins and Eelgrass

When we passed the Miller Berry coffin liner company earlier, we pondered why the firm was located in such a desolate spot . . . and then it came to us: eelgrass!

Eelgrass, kelp, and those blackish balls of seaweed can be found anywhere along the coast of New Jersey. At the turn of the century, eelgrass brought high prices in the Philadelphia and Boston markets; funeral directors and coffin makers used it to fill the liners of coffins because of its resistance to bugs and to fire.

Prisons and steamship companies also used eelgrass in making mattresses. Henry Ford even used it in the upholstery of his Model T. A blight in 1929 killed off most of the eelgrass growth, but you can still find it today mixed in among the discarded cigarette butts, beer cans, and beach whistles along the high tide line.

Caviar in Bayside

Located farther northwest up the coast, the town of Bayside has the distinction of once being the caviar capital of New Jersey. In fact, the original name of the town was Caviar. Around the turn of the last century, sturgeon were plentiful in the Delaware; their eggs, known as roe, is the stuff of which caviar is made. These giant prehistoric egg bearers were so plentiful in fact that caviar merchants from Russia, long hailed as the caviar capital of the world, would come to New Jersey to buy their roe and then ship it home to Mother Russia for processing.

Alas, though, like the oyster, the sturgeon population in the Delaware Bay declined sharply in the twentieth century, and the town of Caviar became known as Bayside.

See Ya in Sea Breeze!

After a brief sojourn to the all-too-normal-looking town of Fortescue, we set our sights on the most desolate spot in New Jersey, a little-known speck on the map called Sea Breeze. This town, we had heard, was a crusty, weatherworn village of stilt houses on the lonely wind-swept Delaware Bay shoreline. Like something out of an H. P. Lovecraft novel, this place supposedly had all the elements of a decrepit, dying shantytown. One would expect the inhabitants to have a swarthy froglike appearance, but to our surprise, we found a mysterious absence of residents (froglike or otherwise) to fill us in on the local history.

The road to Sea Breeze carries you through marshland, with the occasional sod or shrubbery farm to be seen here and there. A curious feature of the landscape is the innumerable little reed mounds that dot the marsh for as far as the eye can see. Something like beaver huts only smaller, we wondered what they were. It was then that we remembered the omnipresent MUSKRAT CROSSING signs that we kept seeing and surmised that this must be where the little critters hang out when they are not out crossing the road.

As we passed the bullet-ridden NO TRESPASSING and PRIVATE ROAD—KEEP OUT signs along our route, we began to feel like not so welcome strangers in this strange land. Although the landscape was beautiful in a most desolate sort of way, an underlying feeling of fear and loathing was pervasive.

Eventually, we reached the end of the line, where the road turns to sand on the little spit of shoreline known as Sea Breeze. Here once again, as in the other towns we had just visited, there were no local residents to be seen anywhere. A handful of ramshackle bungalows perched atop pilings lined the sand-swept street, with at least one dead or dying pickup truck outside each, which let us know that we were not alone.

We had come to snap a few photos, soak up some local air, and maybe even chat with residents about what it was like to live here, so far removed from the things that most of us in New Jersey take for granted—like indoor plumbing. These intentions went quickly out the window when we saw a ferocious looking mongrel dog bound out into the street a few yards ahead of our car. The brawny black beast just stood there barking insanely in the middle of our path. As we slowly attempted to ease our way around him, he actually charged headlong toward the grill of the Jeep, jumping and snapping furiously. When we did get past him, we realized that there was nowhere for us to go anyway, as the locals had piled sand across the

road to keep outsiders from getting any closer. Trapped, we had no choice but to turn back and take the dog for another run. We sped off toward the other side of town (actually just the only other road in the town), with Cujo running alongside us, barking and growling.

With our hellhound friend now a few hundred yards behind us, we felt brave enough to venture out of the Jeep, though not too far, and see what we could see. The Delaware Bay has a long history of shipwrecks due to the rough oceanlike currents, which can dredge up old wrecks after big storms. The beach (for lack of a better word) had the remains of an ancient barge that had washed ashore, its splintered boards strewn about like pick-up-sticks. Dead horseshoe crabs littered the shore.

A chill ran down my spine when to my left I saw another dog, wolflike in appearance, sneaking around the car. I slowly opened the door, jumped in, and yelled to Mark, who was taking photos along the beach, "You're on your own, pal. I ain't getting out." Totally defenseless out on the sand, Mark froze as the dog ran over to him at a half gallop. In my mind, I saw Mark turning into a big ham steak ready to be devoured, but fortunately, the canine just sniffed around, then relieved himself on a nearby tuft of marsh grass.

Satisfied that during our brief stay in Sea Breeze we had seen all that the town had to offer, or was willing to show, we set off on our long journey home. Our trip to the most desolate spot in New Jersey proved to be just what it promised. It seemed to us that the seldom seen inhabitants of Sea Breeze wanted to keep it that way.

Girl Sacrificed In Witch Rite?

SPRINGFIELD — Investigation into the death of 16-year-old Jeannette DePalma is focusing on elements of black witchcraft and Satan worship.

A review of death-scene photos, according to reports, is leading authorities to believe the girl's death. may have been in the nature of a sacrifice.

Pieces of wood, at first thought to be at the scene by chance, are now seen as symbols. Detectives thoughout Union County have been alerted to the possibility that a cult, or a cult member, played a part in the death.

A search party discovered her remains — she had been missing six weeks — on Sept. 19 in a wooded area of the Houdaille Quarry atop a 40-foot cliff about 400 yards from Shun Pike Road.

One searcher said two pieces of wood were crossed on the ground over her head. More wood framed the body "like a coffin."

Another person who was there said, "I guess if you were looking for signs, they were there."

The victim's own background, however, is thought to be remote from such cultism. Her parents, Mr. and Mrs. Salvatore DePalma of 4 Clearview Road, described her as "someone who tried to lead others to Jesus." She worked at an Evangel Church Assemblies of God community office on Eli

JEANNETTE DE PALMA
Police check possible Satan rite link in her death.

Police discover body of girl, 16

The body of Jeannette De Palma, 16, of 4 Clearview rd., Springfield, was found Tuesday by Springfield police in a secluded area of the township. Miss De Palma had been reported missing from her home on Aug. 7. 1973

The remains were discovered as the result of a search begun midday Tuesday when a hand and arm of a young female were reported found in the rear of a Springfield apartment complex. Town police were aided in the search by members of the Union County prosecutor's office and bloodhounds from the Ocean County sheriff's department.

Identification of the remains found not far from the apartments near Wilson avenue was made by means of dental examination. Doctors estimated she had been dead about six weeks. Police are continuing their investigation of the case.

Investigations into the Unknown

Everybody loves a good mystery, right? We read suspense novels and crime thrillers, piecing together the clues, hoping to figure out just who the REAL killer is before the intrepid sleuth in the story can. Of course, at the end of every great mystery, most folks like to have all the pieces of the wicked puzzle laid out on the table for them. They want the brilliant detective in the case to unravel the twisted scenario of the crime scheme and lay bare the evidence for all to see.

Well, friends, we're sorry, but this is no Agatha Christie novel you're reading. The mysteries that we like to investigate are true-life tales of curious events and inexplicable actions. We seldom manage to wrap everything up in a neat little bow. Quite the contrary—most cases end up raising more questions than they actually answer.

How does a hermit's ramshackle house full of hidden cash simply disappear? Where did the money come from in the first place, and where did it go?

Who would have risked their lives to place golden ceremonial daggers in a basin beneath the crashing waters of New Jersey's mightiest waterfall—and for what reason?

Why would some unknown artisan emblazon a primitive and enigmatic face on the center hallway wall of a rural eighteenth-century farmhouse?

Were satanists really responsible for the slaying of a suburban teenage girl whose body was found on a makeshift altar in the woods?

You'll find that few concrete conclusions are drawn in this chapter. Instead, we're pretty sure these stories will leave you wondering about the truly bizarre things that are going on all around us every day in this weird state we live in.

The Perplexing Case of the Brier Affair

On September 4, 1963, Bert Brier, a congenial but secretive man, died in a Piscataway hospital of a strangulated hernia. He was an older gentleman whom the townsfolk recalled as a bit eccentric and a loner. He was also thought of as a pauper, since he wore the same clothes every day, purchased near-rotten food at reduced prices, and did menial jobs around Dunellen to support himself in the one-room apartment he rented for $10 a week.

He lived there for many years, but no one seemed to know much about him. Brier never offered much information about himself or his past, and it was only in death that his bizarre life came to light.

In her 1969 book *The Brier Affair*, author Carol Beattie told Brier's strange story and how it intertwined with her own. Beattie's husband, an Episcopalian minister, was executor of Brier's estate, and soon after Brier died, Carol Beattie began keeping a diary on the weird events that unfolded.

Paper, Paper Everywhere

As executor, Carol's husband had to sort through Brier's belongings, looking, for one thing, for evidence of an heir. When the Beatties went to Brier's apartment they immediately realized that something was not right. Looking like a scene from a horror movie, every inch of the rented room was crammed with paper. Bundles of supermarket price tags, thousands of Christmas cards, old wrapping paper, bales of newspapers and magazines, stacks of milk bottle caps and raffle tickets (that went back to 1949)—paper was everywhere. Even the suits that were given to Brier by various charity organizations had every pocket filled with paper.

Then there was the money—lots of it. The first haul (in the form of bank deposits and dollars that were stuffed between papers) came to about $32,000. The bank deposits were in seven different accounts spread from Dunellen to New York City. Since Brier had been thought of as poor, the discovery of thousands of dollars was shocking.

As the Beatties had to read through every scrap of paper to find possible heirs, the life of Bert Brier became an

probably due to the newspapers stacked near kerosene heaters all around the house. After the fire, Brier took a room at a boarding house, but still returned to the farm to care for the few chickens and pets there. He slept in bedding that he had set up in the barn, chicken coops, and various other outbuildings on the property.

Hidden Wealth — and Food

When the Beatties visited the Middlesex County farm, the first site they came upon was the burned-out shell of a large house. Half the house still remained up to the third floor, but it was tangled in sumac, wild grape, and barberry vines. From the ground, they could see a spinning wheel in the attic. They walked to the back acres, where they found chicken coops stuffed with debris and junk: a senseless accumulation of toy plastic boats, Christmas ornaments, and more newspapers.

obsession for them. They soon discovered that he was the only son of Walter and Linda Brier. The family immigrated to New Jersey from England in the early part of the twentieth century. His father started a nursery in Nutley, but when that failed, he bought a farm in Piscataway. He died in 1939, leaving the farm to Bert and his mother.

The twenty-seven-acre farm had no electricity, heat, or plumbing, and Brier was known to pinch every penny he supposedly didn't have. Never one to welcome visitors to the farm, he kept a gun close by to ward off trespassers. It's not surprising that the neighbors knew little about the family, but they did tell Carol Beattie that in Mrs. Brier's last years, she was sick and half paralyzed, lying day and night on an old beat-up sofa in the parlor. The rest of the room was stacked with papers and magazines. She died in 1950.

The farmhouse partially burned down in 1958,

Sifting through piles of papers, they discovered uncashed checks, property receipts, $5 bills rolled together, and a map that gave evidence that the state of New Jersey had purchased a parcel of Brier's property for $25,000, for use as part of Route 287.

The strangest thing they saw on the farm was thousands of neckties hanging in trees. There were also countless holes dug into the ground that had food in them. Some of the holes were two feet deep. The rotting food created a feast for the vermin that roamed the estate.

With the money, bank certificates, and savings accounts found, Brier's wealth was soon reaching the $100,000 mark. It grew even more when the landlady who had been renting Brier his room asked the Beatties to take away his 1949 Plymouth that was in her driveway.

When they opened the door of the car, a shower of paper, empty envelopes, old razor blades, and soap coupons long expired came pouring out. Sorting through the mess, they found more money and uncashed checks. The mystery of where this money came from was baffling. Brier's menial job as a porter in a local printing company paid him no more than $40 a week.

Continuing to sift through the miasma of Brier's belongings, the Beatties finally found a letter from an L. Smith, postmarked Macclesfield, Cheshire, England. Finally, there was hope that an heir had been located. The Beatties wrote to the address and eventually received a letter from a Mrs. Lillian Smith, an elderly cousin of Bert Brier. Their responsibility to rightfully dole out the inheritance was coming to a close. For the next few months, correspondence between Lillian Smith and Carol Beattie became regular. Yes, Lillian knew of Bert's eccentricities, but hadn't seen him in many years. Lillian filled Carol in on the few details she knew about the Brier family and was excited that she might get a paltry sum from Bert's estate. (Lillian did not know Bert was wealthy. Legally the Beatties could not divulge that fact until everything involving the estate was settled.)

But It Was Right Here. Honest!

As things were coming to a close, the Beatties went back to the farm once again to see if they could find anything else that might be of help to their one-year odyssey of Being Bert Brier. What they found (or didn't find) is what makes this New Jersey saga a baffling and unexplainable mystery.

When they reached the farm, they saw that looters had broken into many of the outbuildings and stolen anything of value. The holes that were dug in the ground had obviously been searched, possibly in the hope that there was money buried around the estate. Even the thousands of neckties that were hanging in the trees were gone. As they stood on the property, the Beatties saw the wild grape vines, sumac, and other overgrown shrubbery that was surrounding the house. But to their bewilderment, the house itself was gone! It had completely vanished—not a splinter of wood was left, not a brick from the chimney. Absolutely nothing except a hole where the foundation once lay. Even the bricks that lined the foundation were missing.

They searched for tire tracks or any kind of machinery that could dismantle such a structure, but there was nothing. They stood there in amazement with no explanation as to what had happened. To this day, no one has come forward to reveal who the culprits were or offer a theory as to how a huge half-burned house could disappear into thin air.

Although Carol Beattie's book goes into many more details on the mysterious life of Bert Brier, there are some other questions that she still could not answer: Mainly, where did the money come from? A few months before his death, Brier took out a $4,000 loan from a bank. Why? He obviously didn't need the money. A year before his death, Brier bought two burial plots at his parents' grave site in the Bound Brook Cemetery. Being a loner all his life, he certainly didn't need two plots. And today a visit to the cemetery shows that the Brier family plot still has one vacancy. Is the spot truly empty? Or had Bert Brier, after fooling people for years into thinking he was a pauper, proved in death that you can take it with you after all?

Who Killed Jeannette DePalma?

Weird N.J. magazine published an article on the all-but-forgotten unsolved murder case from 1972 in which the body of a teenage girl was discovered atop a cliff, high above an abandoned quarry in the town of Springfield in Union County. The body belonged to Jeannette DePalma, a local teenager who had been missing for six weeks.

The details that had first drawn us to this sad story were the lingering rumors that Jeannette's murder had ritualistic overtones. The remote location where her body was discovered was said to have been strewn with cult-related symbols, and the body was reported by some to have been placed on a makeshift altar.

The various versions of the story that we had heard either blamed a coven of witches or a local group of satanists for her death. Strangely, we discovered that, even after thirty years, most people who remembered the crime were still too frightened to speak with us about it. Nobody wanted to go on record or have their name

published in our article—including the Springfield Police Department!

But the people we questioned all agreed on certain points: that it was in some way cult related, that there was a police cover-up in the case, and that Jeannette's killers were still most likely at large.

After the publication of that article in the spring of 2003, we received several new leads in the case. Some were vague or contradictory, some were cryptic, and others were downright creepy. Most came in the mail in plain white envelopes without any return address. Some of the letters were typed, others were handwritten—all were anonymous. They came from all over the state.

The information varied. Some would say the victim was a hitchhiker who was randomly picked up and killed. Several letters were similar to this one: "If I remember correctly, she was a very, very religious girl and many felt that she was a target for Satanists."

Shortly after the publication of letters like that one, we

---

8 THE STAR-LEDGER, Tuesday, October 3, 1972

'OCCULT' SYMBOLS REPORTEDLY SURROUNDED BODY

'Witchcraft' implicated in DePalma murder

By ARTHUR LENEHAN JR.

A Springfield teenager devoted to evangelism may have been murdered two months ago in a sacrificial rite of black magic, it was learned yesterday.

While Union County authorities declined comment on the mysterious death of 16-year-old Jeanette DePalma, informed sources confirmed there is evidence to indicate the involvement of teenage Satan-worshippers.

* * *

An Elizabeth minister said yesterday that Springfield police employed a "witch" to

a lofty bluff within the Houdaille quarry in Springfield after a dog roaming through the quarry uncovered part of a human arm.

According to one source who witnessed the discovered, wooden crosses were arranged around the body, within a trapezoidal perimeter of broken branches and logs.

"The logs and branches were supposedly arranged in a manner that would have indicated occult symbolism, and perhaps a human sacri-

fice," said the Rev. James L. Tate of Elizabeth yesterday.

Rev. Tate is pastor at the Assemblies of God Evangel Church, where Jeanette DePalma was a parishioner active in drug abuse work.

* * *

"I'm sure Jeanette herself was not involved in anything like that," Rev. Tate said, "but I know that many of the other young people in this area are involved.

"These kids tell us that

when they are on drugs, they are in the control of Satan. They do things they don't want to do, and say things they don't want to say, because of the power of evil."

It was revealed yesterday that both Jeanette DePalma and her older sister Gwendolyn had drug problems which were apparently solved a few years ago when Gwendolyn and then the entire DePalma family converted to the Church of God.

* * *

Rev. Tate said that before their conversion the girls may have socialized with teenagers interested in the witchcraft of drugs.

with witchcraft and the occult.

In the Elizabeth Public Library, the "Encyclopedia of Occultism" must be kept under lock and key, along with other works on the subject, because teenagers have stolen many such books.

Librarians in Elizabeth and Springfield said the popularity of books on the occult has increased dramatically within the last three years.

According to one librarian, the subject is often recommended by teachers as a paper topic, sometimes in connection with colonial history.

received a call from a detective at the Springfield Police Department. He said that he was looking for clues in the case and wanted to know if WE could help HIM! Apparently, someone had brought an issue of *Weird N.J.* to the attention of the police, and they wanted to know the names of the people who had written the letters to us so that they could question them. (This might explain why so many stories in our magazine are written anonymously or under a pseudonym!)

Of course we want to do all we can to help the local authorities, especially if it means helping capture a murderer, but I began to wonder, Were these the best tips that the cops had to go on? I asked the detective just how much he knew about the case and its original investigation.

"Not too much," he replied. "I was a rookie on the force at the time. This was around 1971 or '72."

"Don't you know exactly?" I asked in cross-examination. "Don't you keep records of a crime like this at the station?"

"No. All records prior to 1995 were destroyed due to flooding during hurricane Floyd."

This new bit of information seemed to put a real damper on the investigation of the Jeannette DePalma case, but the call from the police had reignited the spark in me to know more about this poor unfortunate girl.

Jeannette Disappears Without a Trace

It all started innocently enough. On August 7, 1972, Jeannette DePalma, a sixteen-year-old junior in high school, left her home at Four Clearview Drive in suburban Springfield at one twenty in the afternoon to catch a train to visit a girlfriend in Berkeley Heights. From there, she planned to go to her part-time job in Summit. She would never reach the train station or be seen alive by her family again. Jeannette's parents, Salvatore and Florence DePalma, reported her missing that evening, and a missing person's report was filed the following day.

A Gruesome Discovery

On Tuesday, September 19, six weeks after Jeannette disappeared, a gruesome discovery was made. A resident of the Wilson Drive apartments in Springfield reported to police that the family's dog had brought home the remains of a human arm after roaming the grounds of the nearby Houdaille Quarry.

At eleven forty a.m., Springfield police began a search using bloodhounds borrowed from the Ocean County sheriff's office. Six hours later a badly decomposed body was found at the top of a heavily wooded ridge that borders the quarry off Shunpike Road. The body, which was little more than a skeleton, was found lying facedown and fully clothed in dungarees, a sleeveless pullover shirt, and undergarments.

Dental records subsequently identified the body as that of Jeannette DePalma. Due to extensive decomposition, an autopsy failed to reveal the cause of death: There were no broken bones or skull fractures, no evidence of bullet holes or traumatic injury, though strangulation could not be ruled out. A tissue sample submitted for toxicological examination proved unsuitable for alcohol analysis, but determined that there was a lead content in the body of .694 mg.

Jeannette's death was termed suspicious by police and by the Union County prosecutor's office, which began an investigation.

Though there were no signs of a struggle near the body, there were some curious objects found arranged at the scene that would lead to much speculation as to just who might have killed the girl and why. The medical examiner's report contains a description of the site where the body was found and notes "a rock formation surrounding the body." According to the *Elizabeth Daily Journal*, "Around the body, police say, were pieces of wood crossed over her head, and other slats 'framed her body like a coffin.'"

From a *Star-Ledger* article dated October 3, 1972:

According to one source who witnessed the discovered, wooden crosses were arranged around the body, within a trapezoidal perimeter of broken branches and logs.

"The logs and branches were supposedly arranged in a manner that would have indicated occult symbolism, and perhaps a human sacrifice," said the Rev. James L. Tate of Elizabeth yesterday.

Rev. Tate is pastor at Assemblies of God Evangel Church, where Jeannette DePalma was a parishioner active in drug abuse work.

Was Jeannette Targeted by the Forces of Evil?

According to all accounts, Jeannette was a normal and attractive teenager. She was also a devout Christian, eager to help young people find their way off drugs and toward Jesus.

Jeannette planned to attend Trinity Bible Institute in

North Dakota after her graduation from high school. She worked at an Evangel Church Assemblies of God community office on Elizabeth Avenue, in Elizabeth, where youths with drug problems would go for help.

When asked if Jeannette had ever used drugs herself, her mother told the *Elizabeth Daily Journal*, "It was nothing serious, like heroin. She was on pills, maybe marijuana."

According to the article, it was Gwen, Jeannette's older sister of eighteen, who talked her family into discarding their Catholic faith for that of the Reverend James Tate. Gwen "received the spirit of Christ in her body" while at the Union County Youth Detention Center, according to the *Journal.*

"When Jeannette received Jesus she stopped using drugs," Mrs. DePalma said. A few days later Jeannette's parents would deny in the same paper that their daughter was a drug user. "Jeannette was not a drug user," her father was quoted as saying, "and by her witness of Jesus and with Jesus' help had turned children from drugs."

Florence DePalma told the *Star-Ledger* about Jeannette's work in the church's coffeehouse known as His Place. She said, "My daughter was a Christian more than anything else. I think the most important thing she loved to do was lead children to Jesus." (Curiously, the counselors' coordinator at His Place denied that Jeannette had ever worked there.)

Mrs. DePalma went on to tell the *Elizabeth Daily Journal:* "Jeannette may have met her death by persons possessed by the devil. She liked to help others, and prayed with and for those whose bodies were possessed by evil spirits . . . demons can possess a body and soul. When one prays with such a person, the devil's voice is heard. When that person allows Jesus to enter, the devil flees."

When Jeannette's mother was asked if she had ever witnessed witchcraft herself, Mrs. DePalma said she had not, but that Jeannette had. "She saw students praying to the devil" and came home "very upset." The next day, however, she returned to school to "preach the word of Jesus to the Satanists."

When asked about the allegations of Satan worship at the high school, an unidentified sophomore told the *Journal* that the son of a Springfield policeman had told him that some teenagers join in "seances" in an effort to get "in contact with spirits of the dead" afternoons and weekends in the Watchung Reservation.

The Reverend Mr. Tate expanded on this theme in a *New York Daily News* article on October 4, 1972, that carried the headline PRIEST'S THEORY: DEVIL'S DISCIPLES KILLED GIRL.

> The Pastor of the church that Jeannette DePalma attended said yesterday the 16-year-old may have been captured by Satanists and then killed when she tried to lecture the group on Jesus Christ.
>
> "It's just a theory of mine," said Rev. James Tate of the Assemblies of God Church in Elizabeth, "but, knowing Jeannette, it's possible. . . . She was extremely religious and a very devout parishioner. She may have been picked up by someone, or by a group. . . . She was so religious that she would often talk to friends and acquaintances about God."

Jeannette's siblings were quoted in a *Daily Journal* article echoing these sentiments. Darlene Bancey, Jeannette's sister, who was twenty-two at the time, said, "There are young people in the area who are forming worship groups that pray to the devil. They love and worship Satan and it's awful."

Her brother Salvatore, twenty-four at the time, called upon "the people of the world to open their eyes. Witchcraft and Satanism exists today," he said. "It is all over the world."

Retracing the Final Footsteps

Weird N.J. set out to find the exact place where Jeannette DePalma's body was discovered thirty-four years ago. We asked our friend Captain Lanidrac (pseudonym), a longtime *Weird N.J.* contributor, to tag along. The captain had worked as a police photographer for the town of

Springfield during the DePalma case in 1972. "Were you asked to take photos of the crime scene?" *Weird N.J.* asked as we drove up Shunpike Road.

"No," he replied. "To my knowledge, there were no pictures taken of the scene." Lanidrac did, however, remember the body being removed from the mountain and could guide us to the precise spot were Jeannette was found.

On our way up the mountain, Lanidrac pointed to the bumpy protrusions at the crest of the hill. "It all happened up there," he told us, "on the Devil's Teeth."

"The Devil's Teeth?" I asked. "What's that?"

"That's what we used to call it around here. You see those small ridges lined up across the top of the mountain? They look like the teeth of a skull that is buried upside down. They're actually mounds of debris that were removed from the quarry and placed on the edge of the cliff. Jeannette's body was found on them."

We drove as close as we could and then parked. The area is owned by the state, and trespassing is illegal. There was, however, a large breech in the chain-link fence conveniently located right where we intended to go.

We entered the woods on foot and began our ascent to the Devil's Teeth. As we huffed and puffed our way up, it was becoming clear that no one could have carried a dead or unconscious body up this grade.

Captain Lanidrac pointed out an old path where teenagers used to walk to get between this location and other popular "party spots" of the day, such as Suicide Tower and the Deserted Village in the Watchung Reservation. He told us that it was always his belief that Jeannette had come up to this remote location, perhaps with friends, and died, possibly as the result of drug use.

This scenario seemed unlikely. For one thing, people don't usually just keel over dead after smoking marijuana.

If there were harder drugs involved (and there is no evidence to support this theory), that would still not explain the location of the body. Even if she had been getting high when she died, it seems certain that she was not alone at the time. The arrangement of wood and stones placed around the body testifies to that fact.

And what of these strange "symbols" found around the body? Were they really evidence that some satanic or witchcraft ritual had been performed? Or is it possible that they were placed there as an act of remorse? Could whomever Jeannette was with at the time of her death, whether it was murder or accidental, have placed the

objects around her in sympathy? This too seems unlikely, as it is hard to imagine that a sympathetic person would have left the deceased lying facedown in the dirt.

All of these questions swirled around my head as we neared the summit. At the crest, a bitterly cold wind cut through the broken tree branches and rutty mounds of frozen earth. Captain Lanidrac pointed out the spot from which firefighters and police had removed the body using a truck with an extension ladder. It was a small flat patch of ground perched at the precipice of a cliff overlooking the abandoned quarry.

I climbed down to the plateau and inspected the area. I instantly noticed several large bleached white bones strewn around on top of the leaves and dirt. "They can't be human," I told myself under my frozen breath, and reasoned that they probably belonged to a deer or dog. There were also the remains of a blue jay, feathers and a skeleton, lying on the same spot. As the chill of the place cut through me, it became clear that this was a place of death. Living things had either come to this particular spot to die or their lives had been taken from them right here. After taking a few pictures, I was glad to leave it behind.

What did we learn from our foray to this enigmatic site? Far from answering any questions, new ones continued to pop into my head. For instance, if this area had been a popular party spot, how could her body lie around for six weeks and not be stumbled upon? Everything about the case seemed to beg more questions than it offered answers to.

Aside from her life, the only thing taken from Jeannette DePalma on that mountaintop was the gold cross she always wore around her neck. The necklace was never found.

Police Cover-up?

Weird N.J. recently spoke with one of Jeannette DePalma's nephews, who wants to be identified simply as John. He revealed that the family believes there was a police cover-up after the murder. He said that, although he couldn't prove it, there were rumors that a police chief's son might have been the perpetrator. Apparently, the son had liked Jeannette, but she had spurned him for another. He'd felt so guilty about killing her that he committed suicide. The family believes that somebody might have placed sticks around her body to make it look as though a ritual had been involved.

Most of all, the family wants a new detective assigned to the case, but so far the police haven't cooperated at all. The family finds that strange.

But Will We Ever Know the Truth?

At the time of Jeannette's disappearance, her bedroom was decorated with religious symbols and posters. One bore a picture of Jesus Christ and proclaimed YOU SHALL KNOW THE TRUTH AND THE TRUTH SHALL SET YOU FREE. Hopefully, one day Jeannette's family and friends will all know the truth and finally be set free of this horrible crime.

Keep Silent On Witchery

The Union County Prosecutor's office Monday continued to maintain silence on reports that witchcraft and Satanic worship might be involved in the death of Jeannette DePalma, 16, of 4 Clearview Drive, Springfield.

Asst. Prosecutor Michael Mitzner insisted that the investigation is proceeding along the same lines as any other involving a "suspicious" death.

Sources outside the prosecutor's office said cult symbols were found in the area where the teen-ager's badly decomposed body was found Sept. 19, in the Houdaille Quarry on Shunpike Road. She had been reported missing Aug. 7 by her parents, Mr. and Mrs. Salvatore DePalma.

The symbols were similar to those found at the List family house in Westfield, where five members of the List family were found shot to death last December. One of the victims, Patricia List, 16, reportedly owned a number of books on witchcraft.

There also are indications that

Kin Disclaims 'Drug User' Quote

The parents of Jeannette DePalma, whose body was found atop a cliff in the Houdaille Quarry, Springfield, Sept. 19 today denied they ever said their daughter was a drug user.

Mrs. Salvatore DePalma of 4 Clearview Drive, Springfield, said, "Jeannette was not a drug user and by her witness of Jesus and with Jesus' help had turned children from drugs."

Mrs. DePalma was quoted in Monday's Daily Journal as saying "When Jeannette received Jesus she stopped using drugs," and that "It was nothing serious like heroin. She was on pills, maybe marijuana."

Elizabeth coffee house aides doubt any link. Page 17.

young cultists may have used the vacant List home for various rituals before it was destroyed by fire in August.

Saturday, Mrs. DePlama said she had heard that police had taken a witch to the cliff top, where Jeannette's remains were found.

Springfield Police Chief George Parsell said, "I heard that some people from the department supposedly brought a witch out there, but I know nothing about it." When asked about the matter Monday, Springfield Detective Sgt. Sam Calabrese said, "no comment."

"The people from the county prosecutor's office were also supposed o know something about it (the witch). Why don't you call them?", Chief Parsell asked.

Elizabeth coffee house aides doubt any link. Page 17.

Not an Altar, but Logs Around Her Body

This is in regards to the story of Jeannette DePalma. When her body was found, it was not on an altar. There were logs around her body. She needs to be put at rest finally. I am sure something out there or someone must be able to give you some more information about the case. Maybe she did herself in, because at that time there was a lot of Satan stuff going on in the Reservation. Sorry I can't give you my name, for more reasons than one.–*Anonymous*

I Saw the Sacrifices

I, too, forgot about the death of Jeannette DePalma. But I can never forget all the weird stuff that happened in Summit, Mountainside, Springfield, and for me, the majority of it in the Watchung Reservation.

I lived next door to the observation tower in Mountainside. I walked the tower path and the bridle trails on a daily basis. At the time of Jeannette's disappearance I was 13 years old. I had just graduated grammar school.

I had come across a few sacrifices that spring and summer. I would find feathers strewn all around and see dead pigeons and a stone bowl that had their brains or hearts or some organ pulverized in it.

Now that I think back on it, it would make sense that Springfield would cover up the murder so as to not tarnish the reputation of the town. I know that the sacrifice that my friends saw was never reported or was in the newspaper. But I remember, and I sure as hell know they do too!–*Anonymous*

Descent into the Devil's Pathway

Life is a series of cycles of discovery, familiarity, forgetting, and rediscovery. The life of our state can be said to be something like this process as well. Sometimes, just when you start to think that there are no new frontiers to explore, you hear of one in the least likely place you would expect it to be. In some cases, our most intriguing adventures lie not in the uncharted terrain of some far-flung corner of the state, but rather in the oldest, most heavily developed urban areas.

We at *Weird N.J.* like to think of discovery as a stone tossed into a pool of still water: The waves of adventurous explorers will ripple out from the center of the splash to the farthest perimeters of the pond, then will reverberate back to their point of origin. In New Jersey, one such splash point is the pool beneath the crashing waters of the Great Passaic Falls in Paterson.

Paterson may be a rough and gritty town, but at its heart is the wild and primordial oasis of the Great Falls. Torrents of roiled water cascade down from the seventy-seven-foot-tall basalt cliffs, sending a swirling mist of spray up through the craggy chasm. Early Patersonians would eventually harness this power to run their mills, but they would never be able to tame its awesome force.

Down in the pools below the falls is another world. It is a world of light and shadow, mystery and danger. There'the city ceases to exist and you find yourself in a rugged and potentially hazardous place. The only way to get to this lost and forgotten world is through a narrow and treacherous cleft in the rock known as the Devil's Pathway.

One Paterson native who has explored the Devil's Pathway is artist and writer Nick Sunday. Nick called the *Weird N.J.* office in the early winter of 2002 and asked us to visit the pathway with him. He said that four old golden daggers in the shape of crucifixes had recently been found in the pool at its bottom. Were we interested?

I don't have to tell you what the answer was.

Before we visited, Nick told us that he discovered the pathway and the pool at its bottom by doing some research at the Charles Danforth Memorial Library:

"I read that the Lenapi sometimes referred to the waterfall as the 'Totowa Falls.' And that in their language, Totowa is defined as meaning 'It is between.' In one book, in parentheses after this phrase is written 'River and Mountain.' I realized that it was not the falls but the lake below the falls that the Lenapi named the Totowa.

"A relatively recent book describes various methods to enter upon the shoreless waters of the Totowa. The book is written by a man named Longwell, and he describes a crevasse that cuts through the rock to a basin.

"I traveled halfway down the crevasse that Longwell names the Devil's Pathway and saw that it led to a pool just above the lake. The Totowa's height is adjusted by a huge hydroelectric plant there, and I suspect that the pool above the lake has been revealed only because the power plant has kept the level of the Totowa quite low.

"The sound of water falling is the only sound that can be heard. The surface of the lake is remarkably still, just as Longwell described it."

Nick knew the operator of the hydroelectric plant, and that's how he was introduced to the four mysterious daggers. The employee had found them in the pool of water at the base of the Devil's Pathway. We asked Nick more about the find.

So what do you make of these daggers? What kind of metal are they made of?

It looks like a bronze or a brass. It wasn't gold. I believe that they were probably used by priests. They went down there, Catholic priests.

In what time frame are we talking about here?

Probably around the turn of the last century. The Devil's Pathway is sort of like a sacred place — it takes some doing to get down there. The priests could have been Greek Orthodox, and the Devil's Pathway could have been used for some sort of ritual, or exorcism — just because of that name. The falls is a mystical place. Your senses are suspended. You don't hear airplanes or cars. All you hear are the falls. It sort of changes you, and I guess it would be a good place for a ceremony.

Do you think that the daggers should be in a museum or a historical society?

They should be. But they belong to the guy who found them — they're his. I guess he doesn't want to give them up. I think he would hand them over if he were to be recognized. He's the only guy on the job over there at the power plant. He knows every inch of those falls and the Devil's Pathway.

It's extremely dangerous if you're alone. But if you're with someone, it's just a little mountain climbing. It's wide enough, and you can see your way through. It's not like you're gonna slip and fall. You've just got to be careful. It would help to have a little rope. If something happens—you know, if you slip—you want someone to be there. You don't want to take any unnecessary risks.

We set up a date to meet Nick a couple of days later at the top of the Great Falls. It was bitterly cold, and the Passaic River was at full volume as its foamy cascade plunged into the gaping maw of the crevasse, crashing angrily onto the monstrous boulders below. Nick appeared right on time. He looked to be in his mid-fifties. His bushy gray hair, brown tweed blazer, and black wool scarf made him look more like an Ivy League college professor than an urban explorer. As we shook hands, he apologized for the water that was trickling into the path we were to take through the falls. He had assured us that the Devil's Pathway would be dry.

We went over a fence of black iron spikes and down to the crest at the top of the falls. A white mist rose from the chasm and enshrouded us as we stood perched at the edge of the precipice. A treacherous glaze of ice and slime coated the dark, wet rocks on which we stood, poised before the abyss.

It was at that point that Nick, holding a few flimsy lengths of rope in one hand and a camera bag in the other, raised one arm and pointed to a cleft in the cliff's wall.

"There it is," he said at the top of his lungs so he could be heard over the din of rushing water, "the Devil's Pathway. It leads all the way down to the bottom. You ready to go in?" As he said this, he jumped into the

cleavage of stone and began to scurry farther down the crack.

We began to wonder whether Mr. Sunday might actually be insane. A steady stream of river water flowed into the narrow pathway from above, and the mist rising from the tumult below started to envelop him when he was only a few feet away. And just where did he think he was going anyway? If the pathway did in fact lead to the bottom of the plummeting falls, then that was the last place we should be headed!

"Nick," I yelled, "We'll wait until next spring!"

We decided that we might learn more by talking with Billy DiPillo, the man who discovered the mysterious

Do you have any theories about them?

Nope. The thing is, they must have been put down there. They couldn't have been thrown, because they would have all ended up in different places. And then, how did they stay there? We keep two hundred cubic feet of water per second going over that waterfall. That's a lot of pressure and a lot of movement. These just ended up in one spot. I've seen parts of cars, refrigerators, everything come down this river. And it all ends up being moved.

Were the daggers tarnished when you pulled them out?

They were greened up. I just cleaned them up a little bit.

Have you pulled anything else interesting out of the river?

Well, we pulled this doll out of the water. It was wrapped up in clear plastic and gagged. It had a ribbon across its mouth. The hands were tied behind its back, and the legs were also wrapped and tied. I asked some people about it. They say it's a voodoo doll. Ninety-nine percent of the people I've talked to say, "Get rid of it."

daggers, than we would from charging headlong into the jaws of a watery grave. So we left Nick to his exploring and walked over the chasm bridge to the power plant.

Billy has run the plant virtually single-handedly for more than a decade. He welcomed us into the impressive 1902 brick building, and we asked him some questions about his time spent on the river.

What can you tell us about these daggers you found?

That's actually Saint Michael on this one. He's the one that slew Satan.

What other strange and mysterious artifacts might still lie beneath the crashing waters of Paterson's Great Falls waiting to be discovered? That question can be answered only by those adventurous (or foolhardy) enough to brave an expedition into the Devil's Pathway.

Mysterious Evil Face on the Farmhouse Wall

"Outsider art" is created by individuals with little or no connection to the mainstream art world, or to any other world for that matter. Outsider artists are usually self-taught, self-styled, and rely heavily on their own personal experiences or visions for inspiration.

The term is a relatively new one, being first introduced in 1945 by French artist Jean Dubuffet, who coined the phrase *art brut*, which means "raw art." Dubuffet noticed that these artists seemed to live outside mainstream culture and society, and didn't necessarily even consider themselves artists.

Recently we learned about the work of a primitive craftsman who created a perplexing portrait that, like Mona Lisa and her smile, is enigmatic and beguiling at the same time. The bizarre work was in Boonton and was created nearly one hundred and seventy years ago. It may be the oldest example of outsider art to be found anywhere in New Jersey.

We contacted the Boonton Township Historical Society for more information, and they invited us to view the

piece—they referred to it as "spoon art"—which portrayed a devilish face and was found on a wall inside one of the township's oldest farmhouses. We were unfamiliar with spoon art, but the story of how the devilish face came to be on the wall intrigued us enough to accept the invitation.

We met with Jean Ricker and Carl Allieri at the Boonton Diner and asked just what the devil this devil face was all about.

"First, you tell me what you've heard," said Jean, "then I'll tell you what we know."

"We received a cryptic letter in the mail from a reader who asked us if we had ever seen *Mr. Kincaid's Nightmare* on his wall in Boonton," we said. "That was all she wrote, nothing more. After that, we had a few correspondences and managed to squeeze out a little more information. We heard that the owner of the house had contracted someone to paint the interior walls in spoon art, and that somehow the owner became dissatisfied with the job and refused to pay the artisan. In retaliation, the artist painted a hideous face on the wall of the foyer."

"That is almost the whole story," Jean said. "Mr. Decker, who owned the house, let the workman paint the walls, but the two men had an argument, which must have been a pretty good one, because when Mr. Decker left the house, the workman decided to paint this weird face over his spoon art. Nobody really knows whether the argument was about money or not, but when Mr. Decker returned later that day to find that face on his wall, he refused to pay anything!"

Painter Leaves His Mark

After leaving the diner, we hopped into our cars and followed Carl and Jean through the scenic rolling hills and farms of Boonton Township to the old Decker farmhouse. The house has been in the same family since it was built back in 1758. Its last owner, Oscar Kincaid, a descendant of the Deckers, was the former mayor of the township and a confirmed bachelor until he passed away in 2001.

Though the house is in exceptionally good condition for its age, it has few modern conveniences and even less decoration, except for the spoon art. The art itself is not pretty, and in our estimation, probably never was. The walls are dingy, and the darkened hallways give you the impression of walking through a house that has been damaged by a fire.

Here's what we've been able to gather concerning the technique of spooning: The craftsman would take a pewter spoon or ladle, heat it over a candle flame until the bottom blackened, then press it into wet plaster, swirling it around to create smoky one-inch curlicues. This process was repeated until every square inch of wall space was covered, floor to ceiling, with this bizarre pattern. This not only tinged the wet plaster, à la fresco, with an indelible tint, it also embedded a permanent texture in the surface of the walls. Someone spent a lot of time meticulously working on his creation. But why do it? we wondered. The house is very austere in its ornamentation and shows no other noticeable signs that any of its former owners had any predisposition toward aesthetic enhancements.

We asked Mr. Allieri if this was a popular form of decoration at the time, but he said he had no idea. He'd never seen anything like it before. He did say, however, that the Folk Art Museum in New York is excited about it and is coming to try and identify it. "Over here, there's a date of 1837, the time when this was made," Carl said, pointing to the large numbers stenciled onto the wall about six feet off the floor.

Though the whole issue of spoon art intrigued us, the real reason we were there was to see the devilish face that the disgruntled artisan had tagged on his benefactor's front hallway wall. It was indeed as hideous as we'd been led to believe, but to our eyes looked more like primitive cave art than a devil's mug. This grotesque visage, about a foot and a half in diameter and reaching about five and a

half feet above the floor, was baffling. It reminded us of a Native American or even African tribal mask. The facial features were rather well articulated and deliberate. Was the creator perhaps saying more with this image than the owners of the house, or we, can even grasp? Is it possible that the spoon artist was actually cursing the house with a portrait of some malevolent spirit from his own culture?

At this point, it is hard to say. No one knows who the artist was. It seems he just made his artistic statement, then moved on into obscurity.

"But why was this face never painted over?" we asked.

"That's the question that has never been answered," Jean said. "There was once a huge grandfather clock that hid it. We know that children growing up in the house used to be terrified of it. It's not a pretty face!"

It was the wish of the late Mr. Kincaid that after his death the farmhouse be preserved as a museum and community center. The historical society has taken measures to bring his wishes to fruition. It is currently restoring the house as a memorial in recognition of Kincaid's lifelong dedication to the community. In 2004, the society received a Cultural Trust Historic Preservation Grant of $12,000 to fund the replacement of the antiquated heating system of the house, ensuring that the delicate plaster wall will be maintained in a proper climate. That news should bring a smile to the strange and stoic face that has glowered down from its wall for the past one hundred and seventy years!

In Their Own Words

They walk among us—colorful characters with perplexing personas. They seem to go to great lengths to set themselves apart from the crowd—or perhaps they were just born that way. We see them in our daily travels, and we wonder just who the heck they are and what they are up to. To some they are just local curiosities, to others they are figures to snicker at. But deep down, who among us wouldn't secretly wish for the courage that these unique individuals must possess to go through life in a world of their own—no matter how weird that world might seem to the rest of society.

While we often marvel at them from afar, how often do we take the time to stop and talk to them to see just what kind of people they really are? Many people feel somewhat intimidated by such characters, while others just fear that they may be nuts or even dangerous.

So we decided to meet with some of the folks who have set themselves apart from the rest of us via some strange distinction. After all, their presence makes New Jersey a much more interesting place to live.

For this, we pay homage to their exploits, applaud their unique talents, and celebrate their eccentricities.

NO STEROIDS HERE

King of the Road

Most entertainers live to hear the sound of an adoring crowd's applause. For one of New Jersey's legendary performers, though, the best affirmation he can hope for is the sound of a car's horn being honked in appreciation. But then, Ed Geil is not your ordinary entertainer—he's an Elvis Presley impersonator like no other. Oh, sure, he's got the white, rhinestone-encrusted jumpsuit, jet-black pompadour, and pelvic gyrations. What he doesn't have is an audience—well, not a stationary one, anyway. You see, Ed performs his tribute show, "Memories of Elvis," for motorists passing along the back roads of Passaic County.

Most any day, weather permitting, you can find Ed, often accompanied by his lady friend Dolores, singing beside their station wagon—the car's cigarette lighter providing all the power needed for their sound equipment. Ed's voice bears such an uncanny resemblance to the real King's that many who have heard his show believe that Ed is really lip-synching—and those people might be onto something.

We first caught Ed's show on the shoulder of Fairfield Road near the Fairfield–Lincoln Park border by the muddy banks of the Passaic River. Ed performed there for a couple of years, until the gig was silenced by local authorities who did not appreciate the commotion he stirred up. Ed did what any cool rockin' Daddy would—he took his show on the road (to a different road, that is). Before long, the "Memories of Elvis" extravaganza reared its rock 'n' roll head once more, this time along the treelined parkways of the Garrett Mountain Reservation in Paterson.

Geil, who has been doing his one-man show since 1979, hails from "Stinking Paterson" (as he calls it) and performs Elvis Presley and Ricky Nelson tunes like you've never heard them before—or, more accurately, EXACTLY as you've heard them before. Dolores sits at Ed's side during the marathon six-hour daily concerts, often knitting booties and occasionally chiming in with a harmony.

We stopped by the Garrett Mountain parking lot on a hot summer day, and Ed was working up a steamy sweat. Between sets, he agreed to stop rocking long enough to share some of his thoughts with us about music, the King, and life on the road. As we spoke, perspiration rolled down his face, creating a dark stream of hair dye, which ran from beneath his bushy muttonchop sideburns and down his jowls and neck.

Ed, why don't you tell us a little bit about your history, why you're out here, how long you've been doing it?

Well, when I was eighteen years old, I started doing Ricky Nelson. Then I came across Elvis—I don't know, something happened when he was in *Love Me Tender*, the film. I said to myself, I'm gonna try to perform like him. At first, I tried to go along with everything that he did. And it's kinda hard, because he had done so much—religious, country, rock 'n' roll. I've done a lot of shows for children,

going to different hospitals, years ago back in the '80s. And they had told me, why don't you try to do an act, but I can't work with bands, I tried it.

So what brought you out to the road to perform?

What I'm in this business for is to help kids out, really. To help them stay off the street and not get into any trouble. If I had my way, I'd be in a hall or someplace where the kids could come by and watch. Being out here is like trying to tell people that the man is still here—it's like portraying Santa Claus. And people respond as if I was the man himself. I've seen other impersonators, and they don't get this like I do. I break my neck doing up to three hundred songs. . . . It's really hard work, but I try to bring the image back. When I'm doing a fast number, it's like he's right there.

When we first met you a couple months ago, you were in a different location.

Well, no matter where we try to go, they try to ban us.

You are out just about every day, right?

Yep, every day of the week. And a lot of people will stop by and throw money out the window, sometimes in envelopes. They're afraid to stop, because they tell me that I'm spooky in some ways.

What, they think you're a weirdo or something?

Nah, it's just that a lot of people look at me and say, "Wait, he can't be dead—there he is!" But there was only one Elvis, and there'll never be another. We've been to Florida and Georgia, all over the South trying to do this. I want to have a museum, really. Where I can show all Elvis's stuff to the kids. We have almost a million dollars worth of stuff in a storage room. I got more on him than I even have on my life! If I can only bring kids in to share the happiness over this, I'll be okay.

Move over, James Brown—Ed Geil just might be the hardest working man in show business today!

The King Is Dead? No, Long Live the King!

In May of 1997 I stopped with my father and sister to speak to the Elvis of Two Bridges Road in Wayne. Although the King could only briefly pause to take a picture, his ever-present mother [sic] was more than willing to tell his story. While her son rocked out lip-synched versions of "Heartbreak Hotel" and "Blue Suede Shoes," this woman would knit cup cozies and placemats that she hoped to sell to folk like me. We learned that Elvis had recently been the victim of a smear campaign orchestrated by his ex-wife. She had crippled his birthday and bachelor-party performance schedules by spreading word that he was dead. Until business picked up, Elvis planned to continue his free performances at Two Bridges Road, reminding all that he was not only still alive, but available for hire. I have not seen him in a few years, so I will assume he's again raking in the big bucks.—*Craig Jensen*

Elvis Stages a Comeback

A new phenomenon has recently appeared at the Garrett Mountain Reservation! Elvis performs LIVE!

An Elvis impersonator, recently (and officially) removed from his gig at the parking lots of Willowbrook Mall, is now appearing LIVE for your lunchtime entertainment at the lower parking lot by the pond at Garrett Mountain in West Paterson.

I couldn't believe my eyes when I first caught sight of him! My friend Tom Burns and I were driving out to the pond to have our lunch when I saw this tall lanky gentleman in his 50s, complete with mutton-chop sideburns and jet-black pompadour, crooning Elvis tunes into a microphone, speakers and karaoke machine set up on the roof of his car.

And as if this weren't a treat enough, Elvis brings his elderly MOTHER with him! Relaxing in a lawn chair, his faux "Gladys" sits adoringly in front of him while he croons the King's endless hit parade.

Tom and I sat on the lawn to enjoy the show with our lunch. The funny part was that everyone who entered the area simply ignored him—obviously I'm a bit behind with the local lore.

Elvis swung his arms and pelvis for a good hour and showed no sign of letting up. We didn't interrupt Elvis but were given an appreciative nod and wave from his mom.
—*Alan Rowe Kelly*

Birdman of the Pulaski Skyway

Offering good-natured salutations to frantic commuter traffic, the Birdman of the Pulaski Skyway, or Pops, as he prefers to be called, will often hold up a small sign for passing motorists that reads simply SMILE.

Perched high atop Route 1-9 in Jersey City, near the mouth of the Depressed Highway, Pops maintains a daily roadside vigil from a small island of sidewalk at the crest of an on-ramp to the westbound Skyway. But he's not all alone up there. Each day hundreds of pigeons drop in to keep Pops company, and to get a little day-old bread, courtesy of the Birdman.

"Are the pigeons waiting for you when you get up here each morning?" we asked Pops on a recent visit to his Skyway retreat.

"No, they watch from the rooftops." He pointed to the nearby houses. "And then," he said, flapping his arms like a giant pterodactyl, "they swoop down when they see me coming!"

And there they remain for the rest of the day, as Pops sits in his folding chair, greeting passersby who pause only long enough to assure themselves of a safe merge onto the perilous Skyway, then speed away. Pops places a hat at the curbside, just in case anyone is inclined to toss some spare change from their car window, but he is not a beggar. For the most part, he is content to just sit there, high above the traffic jams, feeding his birds, and offering a smile and a wave to harried highway travelers.

"Have you come to recognize a lot of these drivers?" we asked Pops.

"Oh, yeah," he said, "after all my years up here, day in and day out, you get to know people!" And pigeons too, we would imagine.

Stop, Smile, Drive Happy

There is a Waver near Hoboken, when you're merging onto the Pulaski Skyway from the Holland Tunnel. You can also see him if you're going up Routes 1 and 9 from Hoboken. He sits in a lawn chair with short dreads and sometimes an umbrella and always has a smile. Sometimes he has a little ringed book on a stick that has sayings like "Smile, Jesus loves you" or "Stay cool," and he smiles and nods at those who wave or honk. There was a while when he wasn't there, but he's back now—large and in charge.–*Megan Muckelmann*

Wailing with Woo-Woo

by Mark Moran

A couple of years back one of our readers sent us a letter telling us about the Woo-Woo Boy of Lyndhurst. The reader explained that Woo-Woo was a young man who has been riding his bicycle around town for the past few years chasing after fire engines and imitating the sound of their sirens. Not long after that we received a call from a woman named Anita at the Lyndhurst emergency squad. Anita informed me that the EMS squad worked out of the ambulance garage where Woo-Woo hung out— and that he was there with her at that very moment!

"Go ahead, Woo-Woo," I heard her say, "let 'em hear your siren." With that, Woo-Woo erupted with a wailing medley of his favorite siren sounds. I was shocked. Could this symphony of sirens actually be emanating from the throat of a human being? I told Anita that we had to meet him, and she invited *Weird N.J.* to come visit.

A few days later Mark Sceurman and I went to the EMS station, which is run by the town's police department and is located next door to the firehouse. It was a warm spring evening, and Anita and several other EMS workers were hanging out outside the garage as we approached. With them was a thin young man in a red Lyndhurst Fire Department T-shirt, hosing down and scrubbing an ambulance. Every once in a while he would spontaneously break out in a cacophony of siren imitations: EEE-OOO, EEE-OOO . . . oooOOOP, oooOOOP! This man, we presumed, was Woo-Woo.

Anita, who asked us to call her Princess, introduced us to Woo-Woo, who she said was sometimes called Siren Boy but whose real name is Brian Hughs. "He can do the siren of all the ambulances, the fire trucks—you name it, he can do it!" She then escorted us inside the cavernous garage so that we could get the full effect of Woo-Woo's unusual talent. There Woo-Woo launched into an ear-piercing barrage of assorted siren noises that bounced off the steel-and-concrete walls and echoed in my skull. I swear that if you closed your eyes, you would not be able to tell whether you were standing beside Woo-Woo or about to be run over by an ambulance. It didn't even seem possible that the noises were being made by a person. EEE-OOO, EEE-OO . . . aaaaAAAAAaaaa! He did police cars, ambulances, and fire engines. He even had some vintage sirens from the 1970s in his repertoire.

Anita, or Princess, told us that Brian had been making the sounds as long as she had known him, since he was twelve. He is thirty-two years old now. We asked Woo-Woo how he acquired his unique talent.

"Practice in the ambulance," he replied.

"So do you ride in the ambulance?" we asked.

"No, I wish. Sometimes they sneak me in."

Mark Sceurman asked, "Do you think if the siren on the truck was ever not working properly, they could just let you ride along and stick your head out the window to fill in for it?"

"It's been done!" Woo-Woo said.

Then Joe, another member of the squad, told us, "He pulled me over once! I had just moved into town, and I was riding my bike and I heard an ambulance, so I pulled over and thought, What the hell is goin' on? Then I turned around and saw Brian riding his bike in this 1970s *Emergency!* TV show coat."

"Do you have a license to do that?" we asked Woo-Woo.

"Don't need it," he said.

"He caused an accident one time," Anita added. "It was a pisser. He made an old lady pull over, and she whacked a parked car. He plays tricks on us too. He can imitate everyone on the squad and will get on the radio, and we'll think he's the chief or someone."

Brian showed us his ride, a fire-engine-red ten-speed

bike with a blue siren light mounted on the handlebars. "His bike has an official vehicle number—3258," Anita said. With that, Woo-Woo jumped onto his trusty steed and sped off as if racing to save the day, sirens a-blarin'! The boys next door at the firehouse gave a few sharp blasts of their engine's air horn in salute, and Woo-Woo answered in kind as he flew around the corner at lightning speed.

If you ever happen to be driving through Lyndhurst and hear the screaming wails of an emergency siren, pull over right away. That sound might just herald the approach of Woo-Woo, a duly appointed official local hero and one of Lyndhurst's finest.

Woo-Woo Is on the Job!

Ever since I was a kid I remember this "boy" riding around on his bike chasing the fire engines, mimicking the sound of the sirens. Over the years, his siren sound has gotten so good that people actually pull their cars over when he's behind them only to be furious after seeing a kid ride by on a bike.

Rumor has it that his garage is set up with police scanners and other equipment so he can monitor all the activities and then jump on his bike to meet up with the firemen.—*The Rollin-ettes*

Man Out of Time—The Ballad of Roy Downes

By Mark Moran

There he stood, behind the information counter at a bustling bookstore in a crowded shopping mall in Wayne, decked out from head to toe in a Revolutionary War–era costume befitting Paul Revere. He was bespectacled and bearded, long-haired, wearing a tricornered hat adorned with a rakish feather plume. His ensemble was a combination of the woolen garments of a Colonial American gentleman and the animal skins of a backwoods frontiersman like Daniel Boone or Davy Crockett.

As strange as it might sound, the first time I laid eyes on him, I didn't think him that odd at all. Since it was a Saturday, I presumed that he was dressed as he was because he'd be reading stories to children, perhaps James Fenimore Cooper's *Last of the Mohicans,* while dressed in the appropriate costume.

I was in the bookstore to deliver issues of *Weird N.J.* magazine, and I needed to get someone on the staff to sign for them, so I asked the man in the crimson leggings and brass-buttoned waistcoat if he would do the honors. After giving me a stern look, he obliged, without any pleasantries or other sign of cordiality. His no-nonsense attitude was not the sort of demeanor I would have expected of a performer hired to entertain children. As I turned to leave, I glanced down at the invoice on my clipboard. It was then that I realized there might be more of a story to this oddly attired individual than just his clothes. There on my bill was a signature that would have looked at home on the bottom of the Declaration of Independence. With all the ruffles and flourishes of the quill penmanship of John Hancock, it read Roy E. Downes.

We had been receiving letters for some time from readers describing a man they'd seen walking along the roadways of Montclair, Verona, Cedar Grove, and Little Falls dressed in outfits that were alternately described as Colonial dress, mountain man garb, or pirate wear. Nobody was really sure, but most seemed to think that his home was in Montclair. It dawned on me that the man that they witnessed was Roy en route to his job at the bookstore. This seemed almost impossible to believe, though, as the round-trip journey to his job and home each day would be a fifteen-mile hike.

I could hardly convince myself that he really did the commute, until one day while traveling along Route 23, I saw him for myself. Head bowed, walking with a moderate but determined gait, there was Roy Downes traipsing through the modern world in his full eighteenth-century finery — a man out of time.

Recently, on a warm sunny day, *Weird N.J.* stopped by the Upper Montclair house where Roy rents an apartment to chew the fat with this enigmatic roadside icon. We found him sitting on the front porch, whittling a walking staff out of a tree branch. We sat on the steps and soon found that there was more to Roy than just a weird wardrobe.

So, Roy, you've become something of a legend around here. People have written to us for years speculating about what you're up to.

Well, what are they saying?

Well, people say that you're a pirate, a mountain man, a Colonial war reenactor — even a ghost! Are you any of those things?

I hear the pirate thing mostly because I wear a cocked hat a lot of the time. And if you go back and do the research, that's just Hollywood and people not having, historically speaking, a clue as to what people would wear. 'Cause a cocked hat . . . not a real good piece of headgear for a seaman. Too easy to lose. Too expensive too.

How long have you been dressing in this sort of attire?
Um, maybe nine years, something like that.
And what started it?

I started looking for something. And I couldn't even have told you what it was. It wasn't even a conscious thing. It was just something really deep. I just started changing what I wore bit by bit. And I stumbled on a series of books called the *Book of Buckskinning*, which is about people who do black powder shooting. I just opened the books up and fell right into it. I was like, This is the way I'm supposed to go.

So where do you get clothes like that?

There are various places. I've never seen any place here in New Jersey that sells this stuff; more the pity, in a way. The shoes I actually found. It's funny, because prayer, in a sense, works. And the thing is you gotta be patient, 'cause they're not FedExed. I was walking, thinking very hard about needing a new pair of shoes. And I walked over down by the library, and on the side there are a couple of mailboxes. And there's something sitting underneath the mailbox. So I walked over there— pair of shoes! My size. These shoes.

You do a lot of walking. I remember when you were working over in Wayne . . . that's gotta be a fifteen-mile round-trip walk from here, isn't it?

I started walking to and from Willowbrook because getting on one of those buses at Christmastime is a lot of work. And I have a problem being in a closed space with a lot of people. I was standing there one night, and it had just snowed really lightly . . . and I looked at the bus, and everybody and his brother was getting on this damn bus. And I was like, You know what, I'm walking home. And that's exactly what I did. I can go through a pair of shoes in six months. Anyway, I've been known to walk from here to Parsippany and back, which is something like, I don't know, twenty-five, thirty miles. Of course I'm completely wrecked the next day. That's hard on the feet.

One of the reasons I walk is because it gives you time to work out in your brain what might really be going on. And it's a good way to get rid of stress, because if I walk to work in the moods that I wake up in some mornings, I'd kill some people!

Is it hard to find employment dressed as you are? Does that put people off at the interview?

Well, see the thing is, you don't want to scare people. And people around here, generally, are starved to death for anything different, but they're terrified of it. I mean, when I go walking, people look at me like I'm a piece of scenery. Like I'm a tree or a rock or a house, or whatever. And sometimes when I look back, they look away. They get scared, 'cause the trees and the rocks or the houses aren't supposed to look back at you.

Do you ascribe to other philosophies that go along with your type of dress? I mean, here in New Jersey we have a guy named Irwin Richardt who considers himself a Jeffersonian. He lives a sort of Colonial-era lifestyle, without electricity and things like that. Is that any part of your personality, or is it simply a wardrobe choice for you?

Well, the clothes are a lot more comfortable than most of the twentieth-century stuff that I've seen. But along with that, I think that a lot of the things that we're told we need, we don't. This country has always been built on a ridiculous amount of waste and folly. If your life is tied up with things, you get to a point where you simply cannot see anything but the things. They cloud your vision and maybe preclude you from having any vision at all.

Are you originally from Montclair?

No, I'm from Delaware. I came up here to go to college from about '78 to '80. I went to Princeton for a year and a half. That was a lot of fun. . . . I'm being sarcastic! And I came back up here again in '85.

Are you working now?

No, I'm getting ready to move out. My landlady said her husband wants the room back, so I've got a month to move out, after fifteen years.

Do you know where you're headed?

Well, I'm talking to some people in Upper Montclair about a room in an apartment. That's one of the nice things, in a way, about being this close to the ground—you don't have that far to fall. I mean, if I don't have a place to live by the time I have to be out of here, I'd just take a handful of things, and I'd just walk west, right out of this goddamn state. Wouldn't bother me one bit. Not at all.

Just keep on going?

I'd like to see some new country, and I need time to decompress from all that's happened to me, figure out who I am.

Have people ever been disrespectful toward you in any way?

I hate picture phones, because people think that they can just take pictures of me. I'm not scenery! Ask me first, because that's part of my privacy. When people ask, I have no problem. But when people just come up and put their phones in my face, I don't like it.

You're kind of a local celebrity. How do you feel about that?

I don't have any problem with that. You get different reactions when people drive by in their cars. People will honk, wave, nod, stare. I've only had one person stop and heckle me. And that was just like, dumb on their part. Because I'm going home from work and it's late and it's dark. And you're gonna stop your car and bother somebody who's dressed like me?! I am just somebody who wears funny clothes. I am not crazy—at least I don't think I am. I mean, I don't eat bugs or see things. I'm just trying to live simply and feel that people should respect one another, be kind to each other if they can.

After our conversation, Roy accompanied us on a trip to downtown Montclair, where he seemed to fit in about as well as a caveman in a spaceship. His attire soon attracted the attention of a woman standing at a corner waiting for the light to change. "Are you a pirate?" she asked Roy.

"No," he replied in a slow and even tone, without a hint of self-consciousness, "these are just my clothes."

Tracking the Montclair Mountain Man

Just where is it a man might find bear, beaver, and other critters worth cash money when skinned? The reply would be, "Ride due west and turn right at the Rocky Mountains!" However, if you are in pursuit of a genuine, real life, pioneer, there is no need to look any farther than the trails at the base of the Watchung Mountains right here in Essex County! While traipsing the footpaths and highways of this region, you may spy the Mountain Man of Montclair.

This gentleman treads the land decked out in regalia from the early 1800s. Besides donning buckskins and lace-up moccasins, he often wears Indian blankets, big wooly period pants of the day, and oversized leather belts with brass buckles. He carries a large buffalo skin trail bag, which must be filled with provisions for the long day on the march. His wardrobe includes at least three different kinds of hats. In wintertime, you will see him sporting a gray animal skin hat of some kind adorned with the face of a dead marsupial. In harvest season he will be wearing a sort of trappers cap topped off with a black turkey buzzard's feather. In the spring and summer months he'll have on my personal favorite, a black Continental three pointer, decorated with a white plume. He must be a man of peace, being he does not carry a Bowie knife, tomahawk, or Hawken rifle.

Some say that he is quite the "ornery fella if ya git to talkin' to 'im." I wouldn't know. I have never had the pleasure of conversing with him.

As legend has it, he has no use for the 21st century. He has no other means to travel other than by foot, although in extreme cold or rainy weather you will see him compromising these ideals as he steps off the bus coming back from his job. No one really knows where his cabin is but it is said to be in Montclair somewhere. If he has himself a mountain woman, she must be as dedicated as he is. I don't know; you would expect him to be shacked up with a female panther or something.–*Hatchet Jack*

He'll Be Comin' 'Round the Mountain When He Comes

Every morning at around 7:15, I drive down Pompton Avenue in Cedar Grove on my way to work. Every day I see a man walking toward me headed north. He is dressed from head to toe in full Colonial costume. He is large, with a full beard and mustache and long straight brown hair. I would love to ask him where he is headed dressed this way, but this is NJ, where people do not like to be approached by nosy strangers.

My best guess is that he does not drive and that he works at Jockey Hollow in Morristown doing Civil War reenactments. Either that or he's just very weird.–*Tami Anderson*

Revolutionary War Hero Spotted in Cedar Grove

I recently started a job in Wayne. Every day I notice a man walking north on Rte. 23/Pompton Avenue in Cedar Grove/Little Falls around 8:15 a.m., which wouldn't be so strange if it weren't for what he wears. He is completely decked out in Revolutionary War clothes.

The first time I saw him was on a Saturday, when I dismissed him as a guy meeting up with some friends to go to some sort of Revolutionary War battle re-creation (it was a Saturday after all). Then I was in Montclair Public Library a few months later and I saw the same guy, dressed in the same tri-corner hat with a feather in it, shirt with the frills, John Lennon glasses, socks pulled up to the knees, big buckle shoes, long coat with tails and gold buttons down the length. Plus, he had a really long Santa Claus-type beard.

Maybe he works at some historic site. Maybe he is some reincarnated war hero. Who knows? –*Dave Hunt*

Aaarrrgh! Pirate Sighting!

Could there be buried treasure hidden in Montclair? Well, a real live wandering pirate, who I saw with my own two eyes, might think so. Why else would he be wandering the streets of Montclair in broad daylight, dressed in authentic pirate garb? He's big, brazen, and stocky. He must know something I don't. Like the possibility of buried treasure hidden at the bottom of Edgemont Pond, where I spotted him walking bowlegged.

Maybe he's a homeless pirate on a mission. Or maybe he's trying to get back to the sea. Twice I glanced, but only for a second—I did not want to disturb his concentration. With fists clenched, chin down, he kept his eyes on the pavement. Next time you visit Montclair, keep your eyes open for buried treasure, and our pirate friend.–*Liz Enright*

Vive Miss Liberty! By Ryan Doan

A couple of years ago, I was pulling an all-nighter at the Brick Kinko's. Despite the steady injection of stale coffee, I could not wake up—that is, until the atmosphere changed around me.

Suddenly there was a thunderclap of presence, a burst of electricity in the air. Steamrolling into the place with her arms full of photos and documents, her flaxen hair fluttering behind her, was the smiling celebrity the Kinko's staff knew all too well. Some call her Miss Football, others Miss Liberty, Miss Millennium, former Miss Super Bowl, Miss World Series, Miss NFL, Miss Body Beautiful U.S.A., Miss Opening Day. But Sondra Fortunato is something beyond her many titles; she is bigger than life itself.

Chances are, if you live or spend any time in the Brick–Toms River area, you already know of Miss Liberty (my favorite of her titles). If you are a sports fan or frequenter of any local New Jersey parade, you are sure to have seen her.

Miss Liberty, a New Jersey socialite and onetime Playboy bunny, is not your typical debutante. A mascot of sorts for almost everyone's teams, she spends her time frequenting professional sporting events throughout New Jersey and even nationwide, holding up signs rooting for the players, hoping to get camera time, and making a general spectacle of herself. According to Miss Liberty, many professional teams have hired her to cheer for them and help fire up the crowd. And if you haven't seen her at a local arena, don't worry—she also drives a well-known car around NJ that touts her many titles on cardboard signs that have been carefully Scotch-taped to its exterior.

I recently met up with Miss Liberty, which was not an easy thing to arrange. She is very busy. I would've visited with her earlier, but as her voice message clearly stated, she "had that thing with De Niro."

When I arrived at her home, Miss Liberty opened the door of the Sondra Estate in full regalia—a green dress with a train and a Statue of Liberty crown. Several sashes were wrapped around her, and many more were strewn over the floor, along with hundreds of laminated signs. Here are some highlights from our conversation.

Sondra Fortunato: I've got to fix this dress. There is a malfunction. Well, you can airbrush it if you see anything you are not supposed to see. This is ridiculous. Vera Wang isn't used to big busts, and these are real too.

Good Lord, really?

I'm different. But that's a good thing.

You have many titles.

My titles are all legit. I was honored by the National Football League Players Association in 2003; I'm the first and only female in the world [to receive that honor], so I am very proud of that. I am also in *Who's Who of American Colleges.* I graduated from Trenton State College. I'm always a VIP guest at the NFL draft. It's fun. Fun life.

Do you live here alone?

Yeah, but I have a groundskeeper in the back upstairs. I have a girl that cleans who comes one or two days a week. My niece married the owner of Viacom. I have a brother who is a heart surgeon. Then I have two sisters who are much much older than me. I came after twenty-five years, and they thought I was a tumor, my mother was so elderly when she had me. I was born with a veil.

One out of a million babies are born with a veil. It means you are a little psychic, and I am.

You mentioned you know O. J. Simpson.

I've been friends with O. J. for over twenty years. I stood up after the press conference in New York with the five thousand cameras, and I said, "Hey, everyone, don't you think it's about time now to bury the hatchet?!" And he went, "Oh, my God! Bury the hatchet!" Everybody just stopped. I didn't mean it that way. Typical blonde, right?

You have been at this for such a long time. When did you first develop this persona?

Well, when I was about fourteen, I was on the beach and a former Mr. New Jersey came up to me and said that I should be on magazine covers. I said, "Oh, sure." And I started being on muscle magazine covers. And then I won Miss Body Beautiful U.S.A. and then this and that. It just kinda dominoed.

Let me show you all my baseballs. This was when I was Miss World Series. And I was featured on the World Series in 1983. And in Super Bowl '82, I was Miss Super Bowl City. It was so people would come to Detroit. Many years ago, at one game, all I did was walk in, and I literally stopped the game. Everybody stood up and clapped. That's how I got started—that and Giants Stadium. I don't know what it is that I have, but the people like me. My name means good luck in Italian. I'm not all Italian though; I am Swedish and Italian.

I was Miss Kentucky Derby a while ago, and the funny thing was [a horse named] Swell put his head on my chest, and this is terrible to say, but he died of a heart attack after that and I never heard the end of it.

He died from putting his head on your ample bosom?

Yeah, he died happy. What a shame. What a beautiful horse. I have done so many things. I've been in probably every publication throughout the country. The press printed my address once, and ninety thousand people

came. We had to call the police. My ex–mother-in-law said to me when we were guests of Bill Clinton that there is no sense telling people these things because they won't believe them.

Once when I saw Tug McGraw, I said, "Tug, what do you think, I'm an oldie but goodie?" He said, "I only see the goodies."

You are most noticed around central New Jersey because of your sign-covered car.

It's a little interesting that I do drive the car but, you know, to take all the pictures off and put them back on, with so many parades and appearances, it would take hours. I want to keep the car as an heirloom. Plus, I couldn't sell it with all the tape on it.

The police are very nice, and everybody honks, waves, or blows kisses. They leave love notes on the car. Of course there are one or two that maybe don't like it. But you can't please everyone, and I have a very good heart and I never get angry with anyone, because everyone is entitled to their opinion.

Tell me about the Sondra Estate.

A little history. My grandparents hail from Johnson & Johnson. I put a lot into this house, and it has been on the cover of many newspapers and featured in many magazines.

By the way, this dress is about three thousand dollars, and I have about thirty-two of them. I was born and raised in New Jersey. I have it in my blood, I guess.

Where would we be without people like you?

What a boring world this would be!

I truly enjoyed my afternoon with Miss Liberty. Her dynamic persona and countless stories make her a true original. She shares much in common with the two voluminous assets located just a foot or so below her radiant smile. Like them, she is right in your face in all of her glory, and like them, she is real and spectacular!

Red and the Tube Bar Callers

Long before Bart Simpson ever placed his first phony phone call to Moe's Tavern, there were a couple of young punks in Jersey City who never seemed to tire of pulling the chain of a local bartender named Red. Louis "Red" Deutsch was the owner of the Tube Bar, a blue-collar watering hole that was once across the street from Jersey City's PATH (Port Authority Trans-Hudson) terminal at Journal Square. This was back in the 1970s when the PATH system was more commonly referred to as the Tubes, hence the name, the Tube Bar.

The Tube Bar Tapes were recordings of prank phone calls that were made to Red by a pair of unidenti-fied callers. The tapes were so outrageous that they ended up being bootlegged and were passed around for decades at parties, in offices, and on college campuses, and through the burgeoning tape network that flourished in the pre-Internet underground of the 1980s. Red, the tapes, and the mysterious callers ascended to mythic status among the subculture of the time and eventually became an intrinsic part of New Jersey folklore.

As the years passed, excerpts of the tapes began popping up in mainstream media, and occasionally snippets could be heard on popular radio shows like Howard Stern's. When Bart Simpson began taunting a tavern keeper named Moe with dialogue lifted verbatim from the Tube Bar Tapes, well, it was apparent that the crank calls had truly entered the lexicon of popular culture. Of course, at the time, nobody seemed to know who made the calls in the first place, which did nothing to discourage a seemingly endless procession of copycats to take it upon themselves to make the world an unsafe place to pick up a phone. Anybody who has heard the Jerky Boys or seen the TV show *Crank Yankers* knows what we are talking about here.

The premise of the Tube Bar Tapes was simple: Two pranksters placed and recorded a series of phone calls to the bar. They would ask Red to inquire if a particular friend or relative of theirs was at his establishment. This required Red to yell the name out from behind the bar in his gruff and raspy voice. The hook was that the name was fake and a play on words. The call would go something like this:

Caller: "I'm looking for a friend of mine. Can you tell me if he's there? The name is Al, last name Coholic."

Red (at the top of his gravelly lungs): "Al Coholic! Is there an Al Coholic here? Al Coholic!"

Then back to the phone: "No, nobody by that name."

Caller (fighting back laughter): "Okay, thank you."

Red can be heard beckoning for phantom patrons with names like Ben DeBanana, Joe Momma, Sal Lami, Cole Kutz, Pepe Roni, Al Kaseltzer, Phil Mypockets, Phil DeGrave, and a long list of names that would be far too

anatomically explicit to list here. The results are nothing short of hilarious.

Red seems to have been the last person to catch on that there was a joke being played on him, as even some of the bar patrons can be heard on the tapes chuckling at the bogus names. But when Red finally does catch on, the fun really begins! The calls that are recorded thereafter contain a barrage of Red's profanity and threats to the tricksters that defy polite description. The language would make the saltiest Hudson County longshoreman blush.

After years of being ripped off by bootleggers, the original Tube Bar pranksters emerged to grant *Weird N.J.* their first ever interview, where they revealed their true identities to the world. John Elmo and Jim Davidson, who refer to themselves as the Bum Bar Bastards, now live in Florida but agreed to speak with us via telephone about their legendary exploits.

WNJ: First off, how do we know you're the real Tube Bar callers?

That's a good question. Well, we have all the tapes!

A lot of people have the tapes.

Well, I'm still trying to figure out how that happened. We used to work for Warner Brothers in Secaucus, and we used to bring the tapes in there. Every day we hear that the tapes show up somewhere.

What year were the Tube Bar tapes made?

We made the Tube Bar tapes in 1975. It wasn't until the early '80s that they started to surface all over. We started making prank calls around 1969, even before cassettes became popular. They were done on reel to reel.

How old were you when you made those tapes?

Twenty. Luckily we put them away and saved them.

What made you start taping the phone calls?

Boredom. There was no malice intended. We were just

Rocky Marciano, left, and Red

having fun. Let me tell you about the day we first called Red. I went to high school in Jersey City, and I used to take the bus to the Journal Square. I'd walk past the Tube Bar and always see people coming in and out. Inside you could see all types of characters. People in suits standing next to winos.

There were no chairs in the Tube Bar. Red was like the "Bar Nazi." If you weren't drinking fast enough, he'd push you out of the way and put someone else in there. It was always crowded. You'd always see people getting thrown out the door.

One day we were making random crank calls and we thought to call the Tube Bar. When Red answered the phone, I just started laughing and hung up. I told John, "Hey, you gotta hear this guy's voice." We called back and made lots of those calls in one day. The ones like Sal Lami, Cole Cutz, I couldn't believe he just kept calling out the names!

How long did the calls to the Tube Bar go on for?

From 1975 to about mid-1976. We made one more call in 1978. That was the last Red call, and nobody has ever heard that. We still got that one tucked away.

I've noticed that if you listen to Red yelling out, you can hear people in the bar laughing. Were there people planted in the bar?

No, they were just drinking. When Red yells out, "Al Coholic here?" you can hear someone say, "You're lookin' at 'em!" We went to a party and played the tape, and someone said, "Hey, that's Red Deutsch!" We started thinking, Oh no, these people know Red. Apparently, everybody liked him.

Did you go into the bar and come face-to-face with Red?

Yeah.

Did he know who you were?

No. We wouldn't be talking to you right now if he did—Red would have beaten us to death! A couple of times when we went there, we would have someone call up just to hear Red call out the name. One time I told someone to ask for Rufus Leakin. I just wanted to see the reaction from people at the bar. It was great.

What did Red look like?

He was an old guy. He actually didn't look like his voice. They used to call him the Tough Jew. He used to have a whole string of vegetable stands; then, when Prohibition ended, he opened the Tube Bar.

When did you realize somebody was selling bootlegs of the calls?

The first one we saw was in Hoboken in 1992.

How did you feel the first time you turned on The Simpsons *and saw Bart using your material?*

Well, you know, we should have copyrighted it!

How come your identity is still such a mystery?

We're trying to change that. When we finally got computers, we saw all this stuff about the Tube Bar on the Internet, and it's all wrong! We've got our Web site up now, and we're trying to set the record straight.

What year did you finally copyright the tapes?

1993. We had to cut Red's relatives in. We copyrighted all our stuff, but we couldn't copyright his voice, because he was dead by then. We put out a legitimate release on Detonator Records, but it only sold about five thousand copies. Meanwhile, everybody in the world has a copy of it!

How does it feel to be an infamous (if anonymous) local legend?

Well, I'm still broke! But people are starting to contact us now, and we're trying to figure out what to do. It seems like everybody wants to know about it.

Two years after John and Jim placed their final call to the Tube Bar, Red sold the tavern and retired to Palm Springs, Florida, where he died in 1983 at the age of ninety-five. The Tube Bar was sold to new owners, who moved the business across Kennedy Boulevard and changed the name to the Journal Square Pub. If you visit, be sure to raise a glass to Red's memory and to his arch nemeses, who made an art form out of rattling his cage.

John and Jim never did collect the $100 that Red offered them during one uproarious taped conversation if they'd show their faces at the Tube Bar.

To hear the tapes, visit the Bum Bar Bastards at www.bumbarbastards.com.

WARNING: This material contains extremely raunchy language that is definitely not suitable for impressionable minors or those adults who may be offended by a rapid-fire barrage of obscenities as exchanged by two snotty NJ youths and one tough old Jersey City barkeeper.

If you go down to the woods today, you'd better not go alone.
It's lovely down in the woods today, but safer to stay at home.
— "Teddy Bears' Picnic," by Jimmy Kennedy

When I was a kid, we lived near a wooded tract of land. Although I realize that the forested area probably covered only a couple dozen acres, at the time, those woods seemed deep, dark, and infinite. My friends and I would often make expeditions into that mysterious forest, wondering how far we could go before getting lost, what might be on the other side, and whom we might run into.

Perhaps it is a side effect of the *Grimm's Fairy Tales* that we read as children, full of witches, ogres, and trolls, that gave us the feeling that there was something evil in the woods. Or maybe the wary feeling is an archetypal characteristic of our unconscious, which teaches us to tread lightly in the primordial forest that was so dangerous for our prehistoric ancestors. Either way, the fear is what made our woodland wanderings so exciting — and so much fun!

One day my mother told me that we needed to be careful because "hoods" hung out in the woods we'd been exploring. I was fascinated by this bit of news, as I imagined processions of dark figures in hooded robes encircling a bonfire and chanting in strange guttural tongues. (That's what watching too many episodes of *Kolchak: The Night Stalker* will do to you.)

Weirdos in the Woods

Over the years, I have come to realize that, like my mother warned, weirdos often do gravitate toward the woods. This might be for any number of reasons: Perhaps the activities they engage in are best conducted out of sight, or maybe they are social outcasts who seek refuge on the outskirts of civilized society. Or these down-and-out souls might be finding sanctuary in a primitive environment. Hey, it beats paying rent and property taxes.

Whatever the reasons, one thing is for sure — weirdos love the woods! So heed your mother's warnings and beware, because you just never know who you might meet when you venture into the mysterious world of New Jersey's woodlands — but it is almost always someone that you will wish you hadn't. *–Mark Moran*

Indian Joe

On a summer day a few years ago, three friends and I hiked the New Jersey side of the Delaware Water Gap. We climbed to the top of Mt. Tammany, had lunch, then hiked back down the mountain. We still had the better part of the day ahead of us, so we decided to hike to Sunfish Pond.

Halfway into the second leg of our journey, we made a shocking discovery. Off to our left, about 100 yards off the trail stood an orange tepee. Upon further investigation, we came to the startling realization that about 50 yards from the tepee was a man, bound hand and foot to a tree. He wore only blue sneakers, and blue shorts, which had the name Joe across the waistband. He wore no shirt. Painted in red on his chest were the words Scalped Indian Chief. His face was painted red. Around his head was a headband with a single feather in it. We quickly nicknamed him Indian Joe.

Our arrival startled him and his face contorted with fear. He was bound in such a way that it would have been impossible for him to have tied himself there or to have freed himself.

Although he would not tell us his name, he did tell us that he was from Canada. He said that he and seven of his friends were camping by the river and that they were playing cowboys and Indians. Indian Joe had been captured and was awaiting rescue. He assured us that he had only been tied there for half an hour, and that his friends would soon return to free him. He did not want to be untied, and he refused the food and water we offered him.

Back on the trail, we talked about what we had just seen. Besides the obvious, there were three things that we were concerned about: Indian Joe told us that he had been tied up since 9am, and had only been there for half an hour. However, we did not find him until after 12pm. Our

second concern was the thoroughness with which he had been tied. Whoever had put him there had no intention of allowing his escape. And finally, our most unnerving concern was that there might be seven people running around in the woods tying people to trees.

Further up the trail we crossed paths with a Ridge Runner (a National Park Ranger). We related our discovery to him. He seemed to doubt us, but did agree reluctantly to verify our story.

While at Sunfish Pond we decided that on the way back we would see if Indian Joe was still where we had found him. We agreed that we would not untie him, but would instead question him further about how he had gotten there.

It was about 4pm when we left the trail and found Indian Joe exactly where we had left him. He looked even more frightened than before. This time we noticed a small lock blade knife sticking out of a tree. Below it, leaning against the tree were three sticks tied together. Two of the sticks ran parallel to each other, while the third stick was tied across the other two. Indian Joe told us that his friends had used the sticks to hold his head to the tree while they tied him. The knife, which had been left just out of his reach, would have been his only means of escape.

When we informed him of the time, his face dropped as he came to the sobering realization that his friends were not coming to free him. The four of us stared at him as he begged to be untied. We felt that was out of the question, since we had no way of knowing if anything he had told us was true, or if he was dangerous.

Before we were able to question the man further, the Ridge Runner returned. Having found our story to be true, he had left Indian Joe in search of higher ground to radio the ranger station. He thanked us for reporting what we had found and assured us that he had the situation under control.

It's been ten years since our discovery, and to this day we still do not know what became of Indian Joe.

My attempts to locate a report to substantiate my story have been unsuccessful. However, one of the rangers that I spoke to knew a Ridge Runner who had remembered hearing the story a few years ago.

I leave you with this advice: If you ever decide to hike the New Jersey side of the Delaware Water Gap and you find yourself on a trail headed toward Sunfish Pond, it may be in your best interest to stay on the beaten path.–*Matthew Rush*

Evil Clown in the Woods

My town of Howell has had a pretty weird guest. About four years ago, kids were getting spooked by a guy dressed up as a clown. He would jump out from the woods if you ever went near his "territory." It got everyone kind of scared until it was realized that the man was just a homeless guy living in the woods.–*Paul A.*

Death of a Clown

The story about the evil clown in Howell is not true. I live in Howell and happen to know what really happened. The homeless guy part is true, and so is him dressing up as a clown. But he didn't jump out and scare people. He went to a few different neighborhoods in Howell around Halloween and was putting candy on the driveways. That's all. He was just a homeless guy trying to make kids happy. When the cops found him he was laying in the woods dead.–*Anonymous*

The Beastly Brothers of Buttonwoods by Chris Gethard

Weird N.J. has received letters over the years about a place known as Button Woods, also known as Buttonwood and Buttonwoods for good measure, located in the town of Lincoln Park. For example, here is one such letter, which we received from a reader named J. P.:

In Lincoln Park there is a stretch of woods known by locals as Button Woods. Even though the name itself is weird, what's in those woods is something you have to see to believe.

I was playing paintball with friends back there when I first discovered the area. You can see cars burnt to a crisp and cars that are buried upside down with just the tops of the wheels sticking out of the ground. My friend said that as long as he has been going back there, new cars have managed to continually find their way there. We discussed how we wouldn't be surprised if there were dead bodies in the buried ones. Now I'm crazy, but not crazy enough to dig up a buried car to see if there are bones in it.

Another reader, named Craig, told us of his weird experiences in Buttonwood:

My dad spoke of a time when he was sleeping with the windows open. He heard a car driving down Buttonwood, when he suddenly heard the brakes slam. He heard the car doors open, some screaming and arguing, then a couple of gunshots. After the shots, he said he could hear someone jump back into the car, peel off down the road and then crash into a tree.

And one day my sister was on the back of her boyfriend's motorcycle going down Buttonwood when she was shot at by some men who came out of one of the houses back there.

With descriptions like these, we knew this was one location we had to check out for ourselves. So Mark Moran and I set out one sunny day for that waterlogged nether region of New Jersey known as Buttonwoods.

We made our way to the town, which is right around where Morris, Passaic, and Essex counties all converge. We found the entrance to a small neighborhood, hidden by trees, near where the Passaic and Pequannock rivers merge.

I turned onto a potholed road with large puddles all along it. The area floods on a regular basis, so the streets are almost always wet with a residue of smelly river-bottom silt.

As we drove, we saw that the entire neighborhood was surrounded by fetid, muck-filled ditches and stagnant backwater pools. We saw random objects scattered everywhere: TV sets, mattresses, ruined boats, bathroom sinks, and overturned cars. The putrid stench of raw sewage emanating from a nearby treatment plant hung heavy in the air.

A few feet down on the left side of the road, set back from the street, was the first house we saw. It seemed to have additions haphazardly attached at random points, and the side and front yards were littered with junk. There was a truck on some sort of blocks, boats, old engines, piles of wiring, and various other ancient machinery.

Other houses came into view; some were inhabited, others were abandoned. It seemed that everything that could be salvaged (or stolen) from the empty ones had been stripped away—windows, gutters, even aluminum siding. We made a few more turns and realized that, while the neighborhood was within earshot of the rushing traffic on Routes 46, 23, and 80, the place was totally hidden. So whoever lived on this floodplain might just be

hiding out, and they were hiding from people just like us.

Suddenly, a monstrous old pickup truck turned the corner from some hidden dirt path onto the road we were on. Moving toward us, the driver steered his rusty hulk into our lane and stopped. In the bed of the exhaust-belching monster was all manner of scrap metal, junked appliances, and disassembled machinery. The truck just sat there in front of us in the middle of this lonely road, blocking our escape.

It was two o'clock in the afternoon, but he turned his high beams on. I quickly tried to drive around him, but no dice. He inched his giant truck toward me, like a bully, forcing my little 1986 Chevy Celebrity to give away its lunch money.

Mark's eyes narrowed slightly, and in a slow suspicious voice, he said, "Now what the hell is this guy up to?"

The man stuck his arm out of the window and signaled with one finger for me not to move. Needless to say, I obeyed. He then pulled up next to me. There were two men inside, but I could see only the driver clearly. He was enormous; his head was the size of a pumpkin. When he waved his hand at me, I noted the monstrous size of his fingers. They were like five Italian sausages mounted on a hand the size of a catcher's mitt.

He was also filthy, his whole body covered in an oily black grime. His face, fingers, and shirt were especially caked in the stuff. His hair was swept out from the back of his oddly shaped head as if he were sitting in a wind tunnel. There was a strange-looking mound of fat at the very base of his neck out of which jet black hair grew. Tangled black tufts of hair also crept out of his ears. His eyes were almond-shaped and a pale, sickly yellow color.

As I stared at him, I rolled my window down about one-half inch. He began speaking. I amend that last sentence: He began making noises—low, guttural, rage-filled noises. The only words I understood were "stealing" and "community patrol." At this point, my instincts kicked in. "We haven't stolen anything," I swore. "We haven't even gotten out of the car." His demeanor instantly lightened. All I had to do was say I hadn't stolen anything, and he turned happy. He was obviously off his rocker.

He then launched into a round of twenty questions unlike anything I had ever heard before. Here I present to you his speech. Since the dialogue from my car consisted largely of my agreeing with this man while Mark attempted to ask for directions, it will mostly focus on the man's words.

Him: Lots of kids steal stuff back here with Glocks, nine-millimeter Glocks. The Wayne police had six Glocks. Now they found three. Know what that means? Three Glocks. Kid with glasses like you steals stuff back here, drives a maroon car just like this, we patrol. Community patrol. You steal stuff? No? Okay. You lost? Okay. You like Jerry Springer? I like when they fight. When the audience tears up, the security, throws them down, you know? Then we have the Second Amendment. You know what it is?

Me (as I angle myself to be heard through the half-inch crack in the window): Isn't that the right to bear arms?

Monster: Yes (followed by unintelligible rapid-fire commentary on the Bill of Rights).

Mark (bravely, no — death defyingly — interrupting him): We were looking for Riveredge Road. Do you know how we can get there?

Monster: River View? I live in that house. (He pointed to the first house we had seen, with junk all around it.)

Other man: Ohhhhh, Wolfson's!

Monster: Ah, yo, sho, wee, Wolfson's! You go up there, that's that market. You know, Dothead?

Me: Oh . . . okay. Dothead?

Monster (addressing me): Hey, can I have sex with you?

Me (absolutely petrified): No, no, you can't. (And with

that I make my first smart move of the day and inch the car onto the swampy shoulder of the road to circumnavigate his junk wagon. Then, just as I manage to skirt around his rear fender I hear him call out. . . .)

Monster: I'll give you twenty dollars. . . .

Me: Sorry (picking up a little momentum), talk to you later. (I called back to him as I sped off.)

We got out alive. I don't mean that facetiously. This was one of the only times in my life that I honestly believed I wasn't going to make it. Mark and I were like two lucky little flies who had somehow extracted ourselves from a big, hairy spider's web, just before being devoured. As I pulled away, I considered stopping to ponder what had just happened, but then I saw the hulking truck with its reverse lights on and realized this was no time to wax philosophic on adventuring. Not when the threat of being violated in unspeakable ways is glaring at you in your rearview mirror.

The Monster Is No Monster at All

The giant of a man in Lincoln Park is no monster, and certainly would hurt no one—unless of course you crossed him the wrong way.

Let me give you a little insight into this man. First of all, the Fairfield police tried to arrest him one day for some offense, but he snapped his handcuffs and beat up four cops. This man is a good neighbor—a little weird maybe, but he does qualify as one of the world's largest men.

I was coming out of the swamp from hunting one day and stopped to talk to him. He showed me pictures of himself and Senator Frank Lautenberg at the Pulaski Day Parade. He made Lautenberg's bodyguard look like a midget.
–*Anonymous*

The Beast Is Dead

On August 11, 2003, *Weird N.J.* received a phone call from a police officer from a station near the beast's stomping ground, telling us that the monster had died the day before. He said that the beast was not such a bad guy after all! The officer agreed to answer a few questions. We will refer to the deceased simply as John.

Weird N.J.: Describe John a little to us if you would.

Officer: He was about six feet three or six feet four, gray hair, somewhere around four hundred pounds. With hands like hams. He was a big man. Always very polite. But he had his good days and his bad days. His house was kind of like a junkyard. He once cut up an SUV with a hacksaw! His brother is kind of sick. And then the brother moved out. John was living alone for a while.

No serious crimes or anything like that?

Nothing all that serious with us. Sometimes, it was just something comical, like the time he put bread out in his yard to attract wild turkeys. He found one, beat it to death, plucked the feathers, and fried it in a pan, then got violently ill. He never gutted it or prepared it, he actually ate a few of the features too, as unbelievable as that may seem.

How do you think he'll be remembered?

In his own way, he was a Lincoln Park icon. Everybody who went back there in the woods pretty much knew of him. It would be impossible to go back there and not at least have him get your attention.

No Dumping in Channels or Ditches. The House You Flood May be Your Own. Report Dumping to Borough Police (694-5533)

Peculiar Parishioners

For some people, the everyday church or temple just doesn't seem to possess the ambience necessary for practicing their chosen faith. For such folks, it seems there is no better place than a deep dark forest in the dead of night to perform their weird ways of worship.

Satanists of the Sandwash

The normal evenness of the South Jersey landscape gives way to undulations, hills, gullies, and cliffs that make no geological sense. The pitch pines, gnarled and twisted, seem like the talons of monstrous carrion eaters, clawing at the sky. There are acres of blasted sand, where not even the most vile weed will grow. A labyrinth of waterways threatens to engulf the unwary traveler. And sometimes you will find evidence of ancient heathen feasts, held, perhaps, as part of the worship of some loathsome, pagan demigod.

Welcome to the Menantico Sandwash, a wilderness haven that is definitely off the beaten path in rural Cumberland County. This tremendous expanse of water, woods and sand was, oddly enough, a playground for me in my youth. During my high school years, my friends and I spent summers exploring, fishing, and swimming there. It seemed like Neverland to us. But like that fabled place, evil infused the shadows, an evil that oozed out of those shadows at night.

During the summer of 1970, my group of stalwarts and I decided to go camping overnight at Menantico for the first time. My brother Brad, my good friends Joe and Floyd, and I had all heard of the wild parties rumored to take place in these woods. We'd even heard about Satanic cult activities—but we didn't really believe them; or maybe we just didn't want to believe them. Even so, we selected our campsite with care; it was remote, accessible primarily by water, and far from any areas where we had discovered evidence of partying.

Late on a hot, humid afternoon, we loaded a pickup truck with our canoe and gear, and Joe's Dad dropped us off at the little dock on Menantico's main pond. Old Lou Nathan, a crotchety but likeable fixture at Menantico for years, was visible at the cabin he'd built on one of the many tiny islands that dotted the pond. We began the slow process of ferrying our gear over to our campsite on the largest island in the Sandwash, which we had ingeniously christened Big Island.

Transferring our gear took a couple of canoe trips because the Big Island was separated from the mainland by a very narrow passage, and the shallow sandbar between the two prevented a heavily loaded canoe from transiting it. Even with two guys and a moderate load of cargo, the bottom of the canoe scraped heavily on the sand and pebbles of the bar. But if we wanted to avoid a trek through the deep woods, we had to travel to the campsite by water; and that meant crossing over the sandbar.

Once everything was at the site, we set up camp on a small bluff overlooking a crystal-like body of water that branched off the main pond. We swam, sat around the fire, and talked. At dusk we settled down, wanting to get an early start fishing the next day.

As we lay quietly in our sleeping bags, we slowly became aware of an eerie sound drifting on the breeze. In a singsong chant, a deep, coarse voice bellowed an arcane phrase that was repeated by a number of others. A drum beat incessantly, with a rhythmic pounding that sounded like someone was using 55 gallon oil barrels.

Due to the wildly improbable acoustics of the Menantico area, it was impossible to tell how far the vile chorus was from our camp—it could have been miles away, or on the other side of the hill. We were all painfully aware of that fact, and the realization was chilling because we knew we were listening to some sort of cult ritual.

Then motorcycles roared and the chanting seemed to grow louder. Those drums kept hammering like the throbbing of the slave driver in the oarsmen's galley in *Ben Hur.* Our hearts pounded in our throats. I wondered how long it would be before wild-eyed, drug-crazed cultists on motorcycles stumbled upon our camp. "Well, lookit whut we got heer!" they would say with a sickly grin. My imagination was at full stoke, and when Floyd spoke up and said, "I'm seriously thinking of leaving," we all rose as one, jumped into the canoe, and shot out into the water. But to get to the safety of the main pond, we would have to pass through the bottleneck at the sandbar.

Now there were four of us in the canoe. We paddled at top speed and as we flew into the sandbar, the screech of rock and sand on aluminum was deafening. Surely the cultists would hear that! Panic driving us, we somehow flailed our way across the bar and into the main pond.

Luckily, Lou Nathan was there on his island, night-fishing. His lantern looked like salvation to us. Had he heard the weird chanting, the drums, the motorcycles? No. But he was concerned. I was relieved when he agreed to take one of us to get Joe's Dad and the pickup truck.

We all got home safely that night, with only our pride injured.

Today, 400 acres of the Menantico Sandwash are set aside as a State Wildlife Management Area and much of the surrounding land is owned by the Nature Conservancy. I still go there. It's really peaceful and beautiful. I like it out there. . . . I really do. I just never go at night.—*Stephen W. Jublou*

Shadows in the Woods

After one too many trespassing fines, I finally had a legal excuse to be at the Charlottsburg reservoir off Route 23 in the West Milford area. In my senior year of college, I did a term paper on New Jersey tree growth. Since a tornado had recently knocked down some 100–400 year old trees, I got permission to study the trees for one month. Every weekend my friends and I would go there to be "naturalists."

During the last weekend in August of 1996 we decided to stay the night at an obscure campsite about two miles from the reservoir. At about 11 p.m., we were getting ready for bed when we heard a low moan coming from the trail that led to our camp. We chalked it up to people partying.

At about 2 a.m. we were awakened by loud chanting coming from everywhere! I looked down the trail and could see shadows passing through the trees. About one mile ahead of the shadows there was a torch being carried through the woods. Someone was crying and the others were chanting over and over. The words were too low to be understandable. After a few seconds, one of my friends yelled, "Hey!"

The torch was gone, the chanting stopped. The crying continued for about two minutes then faded away. It was very strange.—*Kelly Norris*

Sometimes we don't actually get to see the weirdos lurking in the woods, but instead, we find the strange things they have left there—causing us to wonder, Just who were these weird woodlanders and what the heck were they up to?

Evil Tree

I live in West Milford, and several years ago my mother told me about a really cool old statue in the woods. I made her bring me there. We parked just off the main road and walked for a minute or two before I saw it. It's a statue of a tree about 12 to 15 feet tall, made from cast iron. It's anchored to the ground with concrete reinforcing rods and rods are used to form the branches. What makes it really creepy is that the end of each branch is shaped like a hand, four fingers and a thumb on each

branch, and they stretch up and out. The artist also added actual tree limbs around each branch.

There's more. Keep walking and the path bears right at the tree, crosses a small field, and slopes down to meet a stream. Here, alongside a beautiful waterfall is a stone fireplace, and stonework around the stream forms a small pool at the base of the waterfall. There are remains of an old stone house hidden farther in the woods.

My mom said that supposedly there was a group of artists living on the property about 20–30 years ago. They built the tree and did the stonework, and I assume they built the old stone house too, but that might pre-date them. It turns out that there was a fire and their house was destroyed.

My friends and I call the statue the Evil Tree. It's located just off Greenwood Lake Turnpike in Hewitt. The site is very tranquil yet unsettling at the same time, and you'll feel like you're miles from anywhere. *–Dennis Daly*

Sinister Singing Statue

Deep in the woods in Howell, off of Golden Way, there is a big statue of an old naked Asian woman on a stone pillar. Supposedly this statue is cursed by a woman who was brutally murdered in that area. They say if you spend the night at that spot you hear footsteps and a woman singing. And if you hear her stop singing, GET OUT OF THERE, because she then comes after you.

I don't really know if that is true or not because my friends and I are afraid to spend the night there. But every time we go by the statue we get the feeling we are being watched. It's a really spooky spot. *–Rob Vicari*

Habitats for Hermits: Wildmen Among Us

There are certain individuals who for one reason or another just can't conform to the rules and mores of modern society—rules, for example, that say we should all live in houses or apartments and bathe on a somewhat regular basis. These folks often end up going "back to nature" in one way or another. Turning one's back on our technologically advanced culture and getting back to the land is certainly a sane, wholesome, and admirable enough pursuit. But these are not the sort of nature enthusiasts we will be introducing to you in these next few stories. These weird woodsmen have found a small patch of forested land somewhere in our suburban backyards, where they can regress to a primitive state in their own hermit habitat, and have staked their claim to it. There, on the fringes of our neighborhoods, these not-so-noble savages roam wild and free.

Stalking the Woods at Crystal Lake by Mark Moran

When I first moved to the West Orange area, I set out to explore my new surroundings. One of the first places I investigated was an abandoned amusement park at the top of the Orange Mountain along the Eagle Rock Ridge. The park had flourished during the first half of the twentieth century. Locals would take a trolley car up the mountain to ride on the Ferris wheel, enjoy drinking and boxing matches in the beer garden, and paddle around the lake in small boats. The park had closed down decades before I arrived, but when I first discovered the site, there were still plenty of reminders of the place from its heyday. There were tennis and handball courts, a large pavilion, gaily painted walls, an enormous concrete swimming pool, and a cavernous shower house. All of this had been almost completely reclaimed by nature. Vines of poison ivy crept over everything, and the pool had developed its own pondlike ecosystem with fish, frogs, turtles, and water plants.

On one side of the lake was a bowling alley. Next to that was a small office building. The farther you went around the lake, the more natural the environment became, until it was a complete wilderness on the far side. Back then, there was a vast expanse of undeveloped land at the top of the mountain with fields, swamps, and a deep forest. I always felt a little uneasy being alone there—as if somebody might be watching me.

One afternoon in the dead of winter, just as the sun was beginning to set over the Orange Mountain, I went up to the lake to ice-skate. I was alone—I seldom ran into anyone other than people going into or out of the bowling alley. Their only interest in the lake seemed to be to see how far they could toss their empty beer bottles and old bowling balls out onto the ice.

I was skating around, being careful to avoid the obstacle course of half-submerged Brunswicks, when

Crystal Lake. Top of Orange Mountain.

LYMAN DALLY © 2002

Beer Can Billy and the Caveman of Crystal Lake

As a kid growing up in West Orange I used to make treks with my friends to the lake behind Eagle Rock Lanes. We'd grab our fishing poles and head up. If you fished on the bowling alley side everything seemed normal, but if you headed through the woods to the back of the lake, things got weird.

A guy we called Beer Can Billy lived in a shack and fished the lake for food using a beer can with line around it as a pole, hence his name. He was a nice guy and I've even seen him in the local bars down the hill. I heard his shack was burned down by a few punks.

The other person we ran into up there was scary! I call him the Crystal Lake Looney. We've only seen him once. We went deeper into the woods than usual one day. My friends and I noticed scattered deer bones everywhere, and that was enough to get us out of there until we heard a loud moan, or a scream. We looked in its direction and about 20 yards from us was this caveman looking guy. He was filthy, with a scraggly beard, wearing nothing but a loincloth. And he had a spear in his hand!

We bolted as fast as we could and he chased us for a bit. We never looked back, and never returned either.—*David R. Larsen*

something caught my eye on the far side of the lake. There was a bright red patch on the ice. I skated closer to investigate. When I reached it, I could hardly believe what I saw: Crimson blood was soaked into the half inch of pure white snow that blanketed the ice. The small tufts of tawny brown fur scattered about led me to believe that some small critter, perhaps a rabbit or raccoon, had met a violent end right there on the ice. The strange thing was that there was a single set of human footprints that led from the scarlet spot to the lake's shore.

Of course, I couldn't be sure exactly what had taken place out on that frozen lake, but I'd have to guess that someone had chased a small animal onto the ice and killed it, perhaps with their bare hands. But how could there be only one set of footprints? I began to peer more intently into the stillness of surrounding forest just a few yards away, once again getting that feeling of being watched. As I stood there quietly shivering beneath the darkening sky, I decided it might be wise to skate a little closer to the civilized side of the lake, where all I had to fear was being struck down by the well-thrown ball of a drunken bowler.

It seems that the Crystal Lake area has a long history of hosting reclusive nature dwellers. One older resident of the town told us he remembered a man living in the woods there as far back as the 1950s. This character was not your typical down-on-his-luck hobo, though. He was actually a well-to-do local merchant who spent his summers in grand style in a tent outfitted with Oriental rugs on the sands of Island Beach State Park. When summer ended, he would return to Crystal Lake, where he lived a solitary existence—up in a tree!

New pricey condominium and office complexes have recently sprung up on most of the land where the wildmen of Crystal Lake once made their homes. It's hard to say whether they still roam what remains of these woodlands or if they've migrated to greener pastures—in this case right across the street in the wooded tracts of the Eagle Rock Reservation. There they could easily live out their lives unseen and undisturbed without any worries of civilization's encroachment.

Mental Ed's Sanctuary

There is a bird sanctuary that borders Clifton, Montclair, and Bloomfield, where as a youngster I spent much of my time. It has everything from a swimming hole, a brook with tons of crawfish, and areas of very thick brush you could easily become lost in. We usually had the place to ourselves.

One hot summer day (I was about 10 years old) me and a couple of friends were playing G.I. Joe and running around with toy guns. I was walking up a path and out of nowhere this huge guy in full camouflage (face paint and all) ran across the path and disappeared. I flipped out and found the others to tell them what I had seen. We decided it was time to go and went home and locked our doors. No one could believe that this wacko was on the loose in what we thought was a sane suburban neighborhood.

The next day an older friend of mine named Ray told me that I had seen Mental Ed. He was a war veteran who lost his marbles and lived in the sanctuary. Ray said he had a small house deep in the woods and also dug out trenches to spy on people. Ray said he could find the house again.

Maybe since Ray was older, I felt safe enough for him to take me to Ed's dwelling. He led me into an area I didn't even know existed and the farther we walked the darker and more tree shrouded the sky became. The paths got narrower and thorn bushes ripped at my skin. "There's one," Ray said as he pointed down at a huge trench in the ground. I became beyond scared at the site of the hole that Ed had dug with his own hands. What was I thinking?

Then Ray said, "We're almost there," and pulled my arm. A few more feet and almost totally enclosed by bushes and trees was a wooden structure. We climbed through the bush to the house. It was very small and open on one side. It had a bed, a heater, a loaf of bread, a bottle of liquor and drug paraphernalia. Ray said, "Let's go, he could come back at any minute," and we jetted off.

I didn't set foot in the sanctuary again for several years. It seemed that the neighborhood I'd grown up in was no longer a safe place. I had a new outlook on life that would last to the present day—a darker one.

About four years later I told some friends the story of Ed and they wanted to look for his place. I was older and figured the house would no longer still be there, so I agreed to try to find it. After a long search I found it—but it was a new house, much bigger than the old one. It was covered with plastic, closed on all sides, and had a curtain door. I turned to my friends to see the look of astonishment on their faces. By the time I turned my head back I heard a noise, and a hairy arm flung itself out of the curtain along with a deep voice that moaned from within. I plowed through my friends in a fit of insanity, as they raced after me. Through the bushes, into trees I blazed my own path and didn't stop running until I was home. That night as I tried to sleep I felt that Ed was going to come knocking on my window.

Maybe every town has its own Mental Ed, and maybe not knowing is better, because I know all too well. And to this day on certain summer nights as I return to my house, I sometimes feel as though Mental Ed is watching me through the bushes.—*Ralph Sinisi*

The Hermit of Federal Hill

by Mark Moran

Most of the woodland weirdos that we have run-ins with are encountered when we are out looking for some completely unrelated weird site. Such was the case when *Weird N.J.* staffer Chris Gethard and I decided to explore the remains of an old German Bund camp that had been located on Federal Hill in Bloomingdale. The camp had been a rallying place for Hitler sympathizers in the years leading up to World War II. After war was declared, Camp Bergwald and the German-American Bund were disbanded, and the mountaintop sanctuary eventually reverted back to a wilderness.

Weird N.J. reader Jean Helm wrote us of her remembrances of growing up at the foot of Federal Hill: "When they [the Bund] were up the hill they walled in a lake, which is now referred to as German Lake, though the last time I saw it, it was a big mud puddle. Broken down cement buildings and foundations could be found all over the hill. The day after Pearl Harbor, the FBI raided the Bund camp and everything was left as it was."

Armed with only a hand-drawn map provided to us by a *Weird N.J.* reader, Chris and I ascended the southern slope of Federal Hill in search of Nazi memorabilia. After about two hours of hiking up, down, and around the hill in the sweltering June sun, we hadn't found anything. But we continued to search, and before long we began seeing stone fire rings. Some were obviously recently built, while others appeared to be quite old.

Chris wandered off into a shadowy ravine to explore further, while I walked over the ridge to see what lay on the other side. It was there that I spied a large brown tarp strung between two trees to make a tent. The shelter was hung up against the side of a rocky bluff with an open crag in it that formed a small cavelike enclosure. With trash and debris lying about, this looked like someone's

home. I decided to find Chris and move on before we came face to face with the mountain man.

Finding Chris was not as easy as I had hoped, though. I really didn't want to call to him for fear of alerting the hermit, but I had no choice. I hollered his name once, then listened for my companion's reply. It did not come. I tried again, my voice echoing back to me off the steep dark walls of the ravine, but there was still no answer.

I began to get a little freaked out. I was sure that Chris was either lost or had already fallen prey to the mad mountain man, who was no doubt watching me from his little hidey-hole, waiting to pounce. Just as my imagination was running away with me, I heard a faint voice off in the distance. It was Chris, who as it turns out, was not dead after all. I informed him about the nearby tent dweller, and we decided it was high time to leave his domain.

As we started our descent, we were surprised to actually find a walled-in pond of stagnant water. Could this be German Lake? The stone dam that contained it definitely seemed to be of about the right vintage. We walked carefully across it, and when we got to the other side and looked back across, we noticed some movement on the side where we had just been.

"There he is!" Chris said, and we both froze. On the other side of the dam was a man partially obscured by trees. After a few long moments, the figure stepped out into a clearing and we got a good look at him. He was bearded and disheveled, carrying a plastic shopping bag, and wearing the tightest pair of short shorts I have ever seen on a grown man. "That man," Chris whispered, "is clearly insane." With that, the stranger moved on down the trail, waving his finger and apparently conversing with thin air. Knowing no other way to get back down the hill, we reluctantly retraced our steps across the dam and continued down the trail, being careful not to overtake the weird woodsman. Before long, I spied him up ahead of us. He was emphatically trying to impress his point of view to a leafy green shrub. We decided to backtrack and take an alternate course through the forest.

We did eventually find what we had been looking for: the remains of Camp Bergwald, which consisted of a number of crumbling stone foundations, fireplaces with chimneys, and stone steps with walkways laid around them. There was also a variety of old debris from the camp, like

steel cots, enamel cookware, metal pots and pans, and antique-looking beer bottles. While the remains of the camp were fascinating, it was our unexpected sighting of the man of the mountain that really made the expedition memorable and weird.

Not long after our trip, we were back in the Butler area interviewing a local man about a completely unrelated story. I related the experience I had with the mountain man, and to my surprise he told me that years ago he had gone to high school with him! He said the man was named Andy and he had been living up on Federal Hill for years, perhaps decades. "He's not a bad guy," he told us, "just a little odd. And he just likes to live the way he does, up there in his cave on the mountain, in the woods, alone."

"Nothing weird about that," I said. "One man's cave is another man's castle, I suppose." As far as we know, Andy is still up there somewhere.

Home Is Where the Hut Is

Buried in the woods of South Toms River, on the fringes of the Pine Barrens and of society in general, stand some primitive structures that serve as the meeting grounds for an unusual group of folks who call themselves the Gatherers. Located on eighty-eight acres of land loaned to them by the town, the Gatherers have spent more than a year hunkered down on this property sandwiched between the Garden State Parkway and Route 9.

A nonprofit organization supported through grants from charitable foundations, the Gatherers state their mission as "to take human beings, born in captivity, re-educate them, and re-release them into the wild. In this way, we strive to teach people to become caretakers of the planet. Our efforts will allow the Great North American forest to be restored to 60% of its original size within the next 100 years." The group fulfills its mission statement by "working with Primitive Survival experts, outdoor enthusiasts, boards of education, Native American organizations, schools, communities and corrections departments [to] design and deliver primitive alternatives to conventional suburban development and community-building."

The Gatherers are a pretty idealistic bunch. Part spiritual sect, part naturalist commune, part survivalist training camp, the Gatherers hold regular

gatherings at their campsite and invite people to join in their community storytelling and sing-alongs. You might want to bone up on your Gathererese before attending one of these festivities, though. In the Gatherers' language, called mne94, traditional letters and numbers are changed around into Gathererspeak. The group's Web site (Gatherer.org) offers a crash course in their native tongue.

Weird N.J. decided to pay the Gatherers a visit and see just what was going on in the wilds south of Toms River. To find the encampment, we followed a sandy path into the woods off Surf Avenue in the town of Beechwood. It was a sweltering hot July day as we wound our way deeper into the forest. Suddenly, we saw it: a huge cone-shaped lodge

The Gatherers are a pretty idealistic bunch. Part spiritual sect, part naturalist commune, part survivalist training camp, the Gatherers hold regular gatherings at their campsite and invite people to join in their community storytelling and sing-alongs.

built with what looked like pine fence posts laid over a teepeelike framework.

As we approached, a young man emerged to greet us. He was in his early twenties, tan and thin, with bare feet and a large hunting knife strapped to his hip. We were happy to hear him speak English, as we had not yet perfected our Gathererese. We introduced ourselves, and he invited us into the lodge, instructing us to kick a stick suspended from a piece of rope as we entered.

"This releases your aggressions and leaves your anger at the door," he told us. The inside of the hut was surprisingly spacious, perhaps forty feet across. Despite the heat, there was a fire burning in a sand pit in the center of the room. The young man, who was smudged with soot and smelled like a smoky campfire, told us that he had come all the way from Israel to join the Gatherers in their work. He said that he and one of the other members actually lived in the hut year-round. Then he offered to take us to meet the "leader," who was off in the woods somewhere building huts with the kids.

"The kids?" we asked. "What kids?"

"We have a kind of day camp here," he replied, "where kids learn how to live off the land."

Before long we saw another young man, shirtless and shoeless, standing over a pit in the sand. Down in the shallow hole was a group of young children, perhaps six or seven years old, who were clawing at the earth with sharpened sticks.

I suddenly got the feeling I was in a scene from *Lord of the Flies*.

"What are they doing?" I asked our guide.

"Learning to build ground shelters," he replied.

Before long, we found the leader of the group. His name was Frank, though the youngsters, perhaps ten in all, called him Mr. Frank. Mr. Frank was also barefoot, and maybe in his mid-thirties. He was wearing black jeans, a bright red polo shirt, and a floppy suede hat. He was friendly and easygoing right from the start, and gave us a tour around the encampment. Barefoot children, all girls except one, tagged along and repeatedly offered Mark and me wild blueberries to eat. They all seemed happy and well behaved and seemed to like Mr. Frank and the other Gatherers. But there was no way we were going to touch any of their wild berries!

Frank filled us in on the group's plans to knock suburbia down to make room for more wilderness habitat. He said the land that they were currently occupying belonged to the town, and he wanted to show the town that it would be in its best interests to destroy the surrounding neighborhoods (which were admittedly looking a bit run-down) and revert them back to an environment where people would live in harmony with nature. He said that he envisioned a colony there in the future where people lived in primitive dwellings, and got up and went to work each day like they always had. The huts would be supplied with electricity produced through clean energy sources, such as solar power, and would even have wireless Internet access.

Frank then went into the logistics of his plan, telling us things about tax bases and rate tables, which I didn't really follow, but we listened and nodded politely. Now if he can just convince the local neighbors to leave their cozy homes to live in the woods with him—that would be the trick!

As we said good-bye, Frank and the children were standing around a heap of dried leaves and grass that they had recently built on the sandy ground. It looked something like a compost pile.

"It's a human nest," Frank said with pride. It reminded me of a prop from the movie *Planet of the Apes*, but I guess that when you're a Gatherer, home is what you make it.

A couple of years after our visit, we returned to see how far they had progressed with their plan to reclaim paradise. To our dismay we found that the makeshift shelters had all been disassembled, their timbers in heaps. The Gatherers were nowhere to be found, leaving us to wonder, Had they migrated to another woodland home deeper in the Pines? Or had they, like so many failed Utopian societies before them, been cast out of their own private Eden?

Jimmy and the Red Desert

I live in Point Pleasant, a small beach town, and I can still recall some weird events from when I first moved here. One is a story about Crazy Jimmy and the Red Desert.

Jimmy and his folks lived on the western border of the Red Desert (a spooky square-mile of pine trees and sand), and although not a vast wilderness, it seemed like a different world. Inside the square, the suburban noise and sounds mysteriously fade away.

One day Jimmy did something so psychotic that he ended up in Marlboro Psychiatric Hospital. Two weeks into his stay, Jimmy escaped to his own home and silently lived in his locked-up bedroom for a week before being discovered by his parents.

Not wanting to return to Marlboro, he headed for the Red Desert, and brought clothes, matches, and his BB gun. He began stalking the desert at night looking for kids having bonfire parties, and he shot at the motocross kids on their motorcycles. This was his home and he wanted no one to penetrate it. Kids began fearing going there until finally, after a month, Jimmy was caught by the authorities.

Up until four years ago, anyone could have viewed the spot where Jimmy camped. The tent, fire pit and an upside down metal shopping cart he used for a grill were still there.—*Sco-Jo*

Swamp Man Walks on Water

There is believed to be a man in Deptford who lives in the swamps behind a strip mall. He has been pursued by the police many times but never caught. Swamp Man has been coming up to the dumpsters of the mall and eating whatever he can find. People who have seen him have said he wears animal pelts on his body and head, and bones around his neck. In the swamps, he has laid down pallets over the mud for pathways. This created an illusion that he was running on water, according to a Deptford police officer. Also in the woods is a hut constructed of paper, pallets, plastic, and anything else he could find.—*Allen*

Personalized Properties

Personal space: The term means different things to different people. Most folks seem content just having a little home that they can call their own, where they can live their lives without drawing much attention to themselves. On the other hand, there are certain people who use their personal living space to make a statement to the rest of the world. Sometimes that statement is an aesthetic one, a visual representation of the homeowner's creative soul. Other times the message is a political one, railing against the powers that be. Either way, these folks live in a world of their own and of their own design.

Throughout our state, homeowners have transformed their dwellings, vehicles, and even personal possessions into something more than mere material objects. They have made them into unique environments that speak to us of their owner's individuality of spirit. Because of this, the term "private property" really needs to be redefined in many cases. For although all of the places you will read about in this chapter are privately owned, many of them have been created expressly for the purpose of grabbing the attention of the public.

It should be remembered, however, that these places are more than just odd sites to behold, they are actually people's homes. So have a gander the next time you pass one of them on your way down the street, but please respect the owner's right to privacy.

New Jerseyans, be grateful. In creating an awesome personal living space for themselves, these fine folks have enriched our state's landscape for all of us—granted in some very weird ways.

Luna Parc: Psychedelic Wonderland in the Woods

As we wound our way through the forests and farmlands of the Sussex County countryside, Mark and I wondered why Ricky Boscarino, owner of Luna Parc, decided that this remote locale would be the perfect place to create his own unique environment. We had known about this site for some time and were looking forward to finally seeing it for ourselves.

Upon entering the gates to Luna Parc, we were awestruck by the immensity of the project that Boscarino had been building for the past dozen or so years. The front yard was awash in brilliantly colored sculptures, walls, and spires. Everything was encrusted with swirling mosaics of tile, glass, concrete, and painted metal. The house itself looked like a multicolored gingerbread chalet in a psychedelic fantasyland.

Ricky greeted us in his front yard. He was friendly and easygoing and gave us a tour of his one-of-a-kind estate.

We asked him how he first found the property.

"I grew up in Piscataway, and I used to go to summer camp at Stokes, so I knew the area a little. I started a

The five-acre property is covered with an array of eclectic art: a chicken coop with fake chickens, a mosaic tiled wall of varying shapes and curls, and trees with things hanging from them.

Inside the house, the art gets a little more intricate. The place has a feeling of controlled chaos. The wall on the back of the stove is comprised of hundreds of cork tops. The doors are covered with bottle caps. The bathroom is tiled from floor to ceiling in a swirl of patterns and textures, with a stream of running water trickling down through pastel-colored gravy boats. Some rooms resemble a thrift store, others a museum, with collections of antique stringed instruments, taxidermied animals, and strange religious artifacts.

Back outside we find more works-in-progress behind the house. Walking amid the trees and sculptures, old movie set props, and odd junkyard finds, we come to a chapel that Ricky has built as homage to his grandfather, who, Ricky told us, once witnessed a miracle in Sicily.

"That's where the crutches come in," said Ricky, pointing to a dozen crutches leaning against a tree. "Kind of like 'Catholic kitsch.'"

"What do the neighbors think?" we asked.

"They're really cool. Bad neighbors can really make your life hell."

Next we came across hundreds of empty Mrs. Butterworth glass bottles set into concrete blocks. Ricky explained, "This is going to be a nine-foot replica of Mrs.

jewelry business in 1986, and I was looking for a place of my own. I really just stumbled upon this place. It was an old hunting lodge, and the family that owned it hadn't even been here for about ten years. As soon as I walked up the driveway, I knew I would be here the rest of my life."

The house is surrounded by art projects, some completed, some in the midst of construction. On the corner of the property is a foundation made entirely of blue glass bottles and concrete.

"Some are Skyy Vodka bottles and others are AriZona iced tea," said Ricky, scrounging through the pile. "Whenever I have an event here, I always get donations of various stuff I ask for. This project will be made entirely of blue glass bottles, which are the hardest to come by. I originally estimated I'd need fifteen hundred bottles to complete it, but now it looks like I'll need about three thousand. And I didn't drink even one of them!"

Butterworth built out of blocks which will be illuminated from the inside."

In the middle of all this madness is Ricky's studio, where he creates jewelry and pottery. He sells his creations at art shows throughout the year.

"I get a lot of visitors, but the place is not open to the public. I have an open house once in a while to sell the jewelry, and people respond well to it. Then they get to walk through the property. This woman left a message on my machine today saying, 'I've got to come for my soul.' What do you say to that?"

Standing among all the half-finished projects and piles of miscellaneous (but organized) clutter, we asked, "Where do you get all this stuff?"

"I'm constantly scouring the area. They have a good dump here in the area, and I put the word out if I need stuff. Like the wall in the kitchen covered with corks. I just asked if anyone had any corks!"

We asked how he balances his work for hire and his work on the house.

"The house takes priority. I'm very fortunate that my business is successful and takes care of everything. It gives me the freedom to do all this. I am working on a foundation so that there will always be money for the perpetuity of Luna Parc, but I don't know who will be the custodians of the place

yet. Maybe it will get deeded to the state or a university."

Don't deed it to the state, we urged, or you'll see a big McDonald's sign on top of it!

"Well, I plan to live to be a hundred and it's my intention to see that it's secure and safe. I also plan to haunt the place after I die. I'm planning on building my mausoleum in the back."

Luna Parc is a private home not open to the public other than by invitation. If you'd like to take the cyber tour of the property, you can visit www.lunaparc.com.

This Place Is for the Birds—Literally!

The Birdsville Church of South Toms River was built by Albert P. Greim with his own two hands and no set plans as to what it would look like when completed.

A builder of birdhouses, Greim established a woodworking shop in Cedar Brook, near Camden, but in 1914 moved to Toms River, where he could find the better quality cedar needed for his birdhouses. He moved into a wooden cabin and, with the money he made from his craftwork, began construction of what the local population would dub Greim's Dream.

Greim began the Moorish-looking structure by making molds and pouring concrete to form his first room, the "cathedral." Using hand-painted religious tiles, he began to build his church as a sanctuary for humans, but it was mainly for birds, for whom he had great affection. Greim also constructed many birdhouses and birdbaths on his property for his feathered friends, and cultivated rows of flowers for them.

As time went on, Greim added more rooms, domes, and vaulted archways to his strange temple. Oriental rugs were hung, and large concrete candelabras were placed alongside the altar. Greim, who was Episcopalian, put crucifixes, figures of the Madonna, and wooden figures of Christ all around his shrine. Above the doorway to the chapel, in tile, is the name Oratory Bethlehem. He even had a pipe organ installed and two pews built. The church was sanctioned in the 1920s, and seven couples took their marriage vows before the altar.

Although Greim constructed his building as a sanctuary, he also lived in it. There was a kitchen and bedroom off the main chapel. He was not an engineer, and he discovered his one great mistake: A concrete home could not be properly heated. The roofs (also poured concrete) had to be taken down and insulated.

Greim had big plans for his church, including adding another fourteen rooms and making the structure three stories high. But he died on April 27, 1930, before his dream could be completed. He had never married, and the property and his entire holdings were given to a local resident, Stanley Grover, who often assisted Greim with work around the church.

Over the years, the church had many incarnations. At one time, it was a sewing machine shop, and then an electrical repair store. Today it is all but in ruins, a mere shell of what was once a quiet, but odd retreat for a religious bird lover.

Whirligigs in Weehawken

Rudy Bram, of 63 Highwood Terrace in Weehawken, is a retired postal worker and Madison Square Garden usher who has created what he calls "eccentric architecture." Encrusted with an armor of found objects and bric-a-brac of all kinds, the gleaming, whirling façade of Rudy's house has attracted much attention over the years. It has been featured in *The Star-Ledger* and the Sunday *New York Times,* and on TV's *Good Day New York.* Old bicycle parts, toys, hubcaps, and dolls might look like plain old junk to some of Mr. Bram's neighbors, but to Rudy it's high art.

A Guided Tour with Rudy Bram

Rudy Bram creates art out of everyday objects. He displays them throughout his house, both inside and out. When I first found his place, he was just leaving, but he offered to give me a tour.

As he led me through the garage and the house, Mr. Bram told me that he got the components for his work from a variety of places. "People give me things. When things come into my possession, I use them, and it works."

The house is really one flowing piece of art. Individual pieces blend into designs made on the walls and ceilings, and you really can't tell where one piece of art ends and another begins. The art is created from common items like brooms, toys, Formica tiles, jars, and miscellaneous doodads, and Mr. Bram says that many pieces are meant as dedication to family and friends who have passed away.

So many people have commented on Mr. Bram's house and his art that he should have a show at an art gallery. "But unfortunately I'm an artist, not a business man, which means I'm not an artist either."
—William Angus

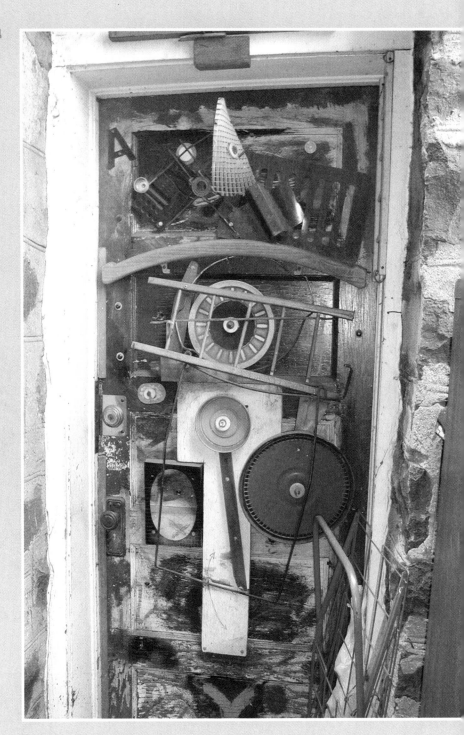

A Tale of Two Pink Ladies
The Pink Lady in West Orange

"How do you do, gentlemen?" asked Madame Mildred Johnson as we approached her while she was doing a little front-yard gardening at her house in West Orange one mild summer day.

"We love the colors of your house," we said.

She smiled and said, "Pink is my favorite color, as you can see."

And see we did. All decked out in pink-and-white accents, Mildred's house reminded us of a Good n' Plenty candy box. Not only is her home an homage to her favorite color, but her mailbox and clothing also sport the same rosy blush. And don't think for a minute that Mildred's luxury ride is a Mary Kay car.

"I paid every penny for this car with my own money!" she told us proudly of her customized 1985 Cadillac Biarritz.

Mildred, whom most locals refer to simply as the Pink Lady, works out of her Gregory Avenue home as a spiritual consultant and counsels as many as fifteen clients a day. But don't call her a psychic, because, as she tells us with authority, she sees far beyond what your run-of-the-mill seer sees. Madame Mildred first realized her amazing gift as a mere child of six in her native Virginia—and that was eighty years ago! Since then, she practiced her trade in Newark and Irvington before settling in West Orange about twenty years ago. And don't expect her to stop any time soon.

"My grandmother lived to be one hundred and eight," Mildred told us. So she should be feeling in the pink for a long time to come.

Her calming demeanor affects you the instant she speaks. And you really get the feeling that you are in the presence of a uniquely intuitive person.

"You fellows should come for a reading sometime," she told us with a knowing smile. "I can tell you're up to something!"

Indeed, Madame Mildred sees all.

Pretty in Pink in Metuchen

Just like Madame Mildred, a pink sensation graces another New Jersey town. Gracie Knox, the Pink Lady of Metuchen, has been enjoying her pink paradise for over seventy years.

Weird N.J. visited Ms. Knox just as she was preparing her outfit and her convertible Cadillac El Dorado (one of her two luxury pink-and-white rides) for the town's annual Memorial Day parade.

Gracie invited us into her century-old home, where we sat ensconced in pink pile carpet and pink, plastic-covered furniture. She told us that someone in town had shown her the copy of *Weird N.J.* magazine that Madame Mildred had originally appeared in. To that she remarked simply, "That other Pink Lady in West Orange must be copying me."

Nyukking It Up in Colonia

Susan Hunter wants three things out of life: an Amish carriage to put behind her fiberglass horse in her yard; a low rider automobile, complete with a monster sound system; and to be in the pages of *Weird N.J.*

Why *Weird N.J.*? Well, one look at Susan's property and you just might figure it out. Right on the front lawn, we found—in addition to flamingos, a hubcap tree, and a fiberglass horse—the Three Stooges imprisoned in an oversized birdcage.

Passersby have more than once stopped in front of her house on Chain of Hills Road in Colonia, thinking that there were children locked up on the lawn. Susan dresses the Stooges to fit the season. In winter, they wear jackets, and on Halloween, they have costumes. This summer we found them sporting Mets baseball caps, making this site full of woo-woo-woo weirdness!

"I purchased the Stooges at a hardware store," said Susan. "I had to have them."

Susan is also a pink flamingo junkie, with hundreds of flamingo-related objects placed all over the property, and some even adorn her skin in tattoo form.

As she peeled off her cowgirl boots, she showed us some of the thirteen tattoos she'd gotten over the years, with themes from Native Americans to cowboys and her favorite pink bird.

"My grandfather was a full-blooded Blackfoot, and my grandmother was Cherokee." Showing us her calf, she revealed a cowgirl surrounded by a lasso. "My father had the same tattoo. I had it copied."

The Hub Cap Tree in the rear of the property has over two-dozen caps Susan found on the roads throughout New Jersey. And the fiberglass horse? It's Sonny, the former mascot of the JFK Memorial High School of Iselin. Susan said the mustang horse used to be in all the school's parades. "And it's anatomically correct, if you want to know," she said.

As for future displays, Susan said she'd have to be careful, because her husband, Chip, didn't approve of all the lawn adornments. "Once Chip gets the lawnmower out, you never know what will happen. Sometimes he turns the Stooges around!"

Though Susan was battling cancer at the time of our visit, she was one of the most cheerful and optimistic people we have ever had the pleasure to interview. As we bade her farewell and made our way back to our car, she called out, "I hope you think I'm weird enough for your magazine—everyone else thinks I am!"

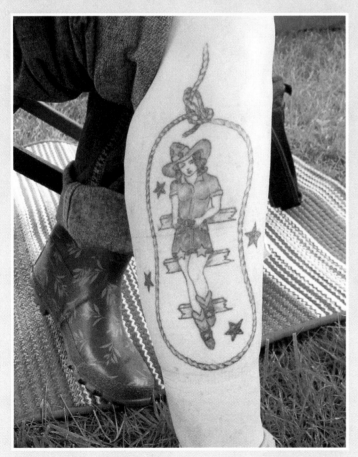

Good-bye to Colonia's Weirdest Resident

Dear *Weird N.J.:*

I just wanted to let you know that my mother, Susan Hunter, passed away last month. One of her greatest enjoyments was your magazine and she was so proud to have been in it. On behalf of her family, I just want to thank you for making one of her dreams come true.—*Gabrielle*

From Susan's obituary:

Susan will be remembered by family and friends for her unique personality and for her love of the strange and unusual. She enjoyed reading, fishing, gardening, Harley Davidson motorcycles, tattoos and collecting all things flamingo. One of her proudest achievements, aside from her family, was being featured in the magazine *Weird N.J.* for her extraordinarily decorated home in Colonia.

Paint Bucket House of Salem

This photo is from a house near Salem. The front has rows of what appear to be tin cans painted black with assorted colors dabbed on them. The side of the house has cans and milk cartons painted black. They are about 5 to 6 feet high and create a fence along the property.—*B. Kafer*

Pumpkin House

Located on the western shore of Culvers Lake in Sussex County is this gourd-crowned cottage, which the locals have dubbed the Pumpkin House (though the sign over the door says HICKORY CORNER). It's painted orange and gives passersby that Halloween feeling all year round.

A Study in Weirdness

Very little is known about the origins of this bizarre desk other than what is handwritten on a small scrap of paper found beneath a secret little door on the front. It reads, "G. P. Ailers, Sussex, New Jersey, 1878." The ornate piece of rustic hand-made furniture features highly detailed carving of flora and fauna, tree branch knots, and a built-in calendar. It stands 78 inches tall, is 38 inches wide and 45 inches deep. Both whimsical and functional, this curious cabinet was designed either as a utilitarian piece or as a work of sculpture. Either way, it's considered folk art now and is part of the collection of Gael and Michael Mendelsohn of Westchester County, NY.

Chipmunk Run, Home of Boss Sutter

Riding along the quiet upscale suburban neighborhoods of Upper Saddle River, you don't see too many sights that would strike you as being weird or even out of the ordinary. There are just too many pristine houses and manicured lawns to catch a weird wave in this Bergen County community. But then you approach the corner of Lake Road and Upper Saddle River Road. There at the crossroads is a stately looking abode with the surrounding property adorned with a plethora of junque—thousands of neatly arranged figurines, lawn ornaments, wheelbarrows, signs, and frying pans. A huge wrecking ball sits on the side of the road, and next to it a sign that proclaims CHIPMUNK RUN—HOME OF THE SUTTER FAMILY AND SOME OF THE HAPPIEST CHIPMUNKS IN TOWN.

We soon were chatting with Ann Sutter, who was giving the dogs their daily constitutional. We asked if the place was an antiques store. She said no, this was her home, and the grounds were the work of her husband.

From reading the signs on the property, we surmised that her husband is Ted "Boss" Sutter. And we learned from other placards that Ted is a "soldier, statesman and lover." According to one inscription, he's also the greatest parking lot painter and sealer in the universe.

When we pulled away, a sign bade us farewell by saying HE WHO THROWS BEER CANS IN MY GARDEN . . . MAY LEAVE WITH A FREE KICKINAZZ—Boss Sutter.

Touring the Collected Works of Ted Sutter

When you hear the words "lawn art" you might think of pink flamingos, concrete rabbit planters, and road signs. Although what Ted Sutter has done with his home could be called lawn art—that would be an injustice to what he does. Whatever you want to call it, it's definitely hilarious. Like other people who have decorated their homes with all sorts of things, Ted Sutter marches to the beat of a different drummer, and he's been doing it for 25 years.

Perhaps the best stuff on his property are the humorous collectibles, from the stove used by the NASA astronauts on the moon, to a propeller from Air Force One. He also has a commemorative marker for the spot where he gunned down a T-Rex, as well as a giant safe where he keeps his family jewels.

Ted freely allows people to wander his property, but being a polite person, I rang the doorbell. His daughter answered, and she gave me a tour and told me a little about Mr. Sutter. Apparently he has always decorated like this, going back to the days when he lived in Edgewater. He gets his materials from garage sales, off the street, but most often from friends and relatives who say, "Here's something weird I found, thought you could use it." There are several sections to the property, each showing off a different collection, such as the 169 cast iron frying pans on his barn, and the cake pans on a fence.

Ted's still decorating. He recently covered his van with over 2000 different objects, bolted on for safety. He turned to the van as a mobile form of art because he was "done with the house," or so said his wife.— *William Angus*

The VHS Walkway of Fort Lee

My Aunt Mamie and Uncle Tony have lived in Fort Lee for over 50 years. Uncle Tony has collected VHS tapes and recorded every show and movie you could ever think of. Now he uses all those videos to make patios and walkways at his home. Please keep in mind that Uncle Tony is 90 years old!—*Donna Kampner*

How the Other Half Lives

We guess for the families that lived in the "other half" of these structures, you can't go home again. These half houses are a curious site along the streets of Trenton.

Gargoyles of Somerset

In the county of Somerset, there is a large, almost gothic looking house. During the day, anyone who looks at the sides of the house near the roof will see gargoyle statues overhanging the house. While this may seem cool enough, each gargoyle has lights in it so at night the eyes shine red!–*Erik Dresner*

Burlington Lawncraft

I came upon this roadside weirdness on somebody's front lawn in Burlington Township.

Seems like a frustrated Italian-American pilot lives in this house. Note the red, white, and green colors on the tail wing and also on the pole holding up the helicopter. I call it aeronautical weirdness.–*Stephen Conte*

I recently moved and noticed something new in my neighboring town of Burlington. It was a house with a rather colorful display of sculptures of helicopters and airplanes! As I took these pictures I noticed random aircraft parts in the backyard. There does not appear to be anything other than a decorative purpose for this weird lawn art.–*Monica St. Clair*

North Plainfield's Totem Pole

Some people move to Florida after they retire. Others travel and see the world. And some carve totem poles out of trees in their suburban backyards.

That's what John J. Dwyer of North Plainfield did. He had all the branches removed from a forty-foot-tall oak tree that stood in the middle of his yard and started planning his totem pole. John, a retired U.S. Air Force major, had served in Alaska during World War II and had become fascinated by the totem poles he'd seen there. Eventually, he researched totems and began to plan his own pole.

Dwyer mapped out a series of six-foot-tall figures and began his project. First he carved a bear out of the tree's base. Then he used a chain saw to add a raven, a medicine man, a wolf, a beaver, a thunderbird, watchmen, and an eagle to the tree. He even hung wings on the thunderbird—each wing weighing close to two hundred pounds.

Residents of North Plainfield have embraced the totem pole as part of the fabric of their community. John has passed on, but the totem he created still stands, serving as both a landmark and a testament to one man's personal obsession.

Takin' It to the Streets with Hoop, "King of Art"

The death of pop art icon Andy Warhol in 1987 left a cultural void in American society. We had lost the only living artist most people could name—or so believed Steven "Hoop" Hooper of Clifton. Fortunately for the art community and the residents of New Jersey, Hoop was prepared to fill that void and ascend to the art world's highest throne as the self-proclaimed King of Art.

Hoop's chosen medium was, and still is, his ever changing livery of automobiles. He had begun modifying his cars into works of art as early as 1985. These were not just your ordinary custom jobs, though. Hoop's creations are high-concept masterpieces—on wheels! There's the Fiat 850 festooned with hundreds of aluminum cans and christened the Can-Vertible, and the black van encrusted with wall clocks, alarm clocks, and watches, dubbed the Time Machine. There's a 1930s Packard hearse decked out in black-and-white faux fur. Actually, fur is one of Hoop's favorite mediums to work in, and several of his eccentric vehicles sport furry coats.

Another favored canvas for Hoop is his stable of Italian Isettas, small three-wheeled contraptions with two wheels up front and one in back, with a glass bubble for a driver's cockpit. Hoop has crafted several of them into works of art including the Heli-Hoop and one that is even a self-portrait of the artist. Hoop uses Day-Glo spray paint to make sure they keep their "just off the assembly line" newness.

All the cars are in a constant state of flux. A vehicle that is a Time Machine today might be transformed into the Hi-Tek Hoop mobile tomorrow or perhaps into a van with a front end at either side so that you don't know if Hoop is coming or going. That one had the police in Clifton and Montclair scratching their heads for a while!

Hoop does all the maintenance work on the vehicles himself. And when it's time to unveil his latest creation, Hoop dons one of his regal outfits befitting his royal Hoopness: King of Art. These getups usually consist of a white jumpsuit spray-painted with the same neon colors emblazoned on his cars and a high crown, feathery and bejeweled.

When Hoop isn't brightening up the roadways of the state, he can usually be found outside his home on Charles Street, hard at work on his next motorized masterpiece. You never know what might roll out of this guy's garage next—but you can be sure it'll be pretty weird!

The Backyard Bowling Ball Pyramid

Possibly taking a cue from ancient Egyptian bowlers, Roland George built his own bowling ball pyramid in the backyard of his Mendham home using discarded balls from various bowling alleys throughout Morris County. The structure consisted of two hundred balls and was held together with nothing but gravity.

When news of the bowling ball pyramid hit the media, George's home become a depot for unwanted bowling balls from all over the state. Bowling alleys, neighbors, and even nuns were dropping off balls on a daily basis. *Weird N.J.* had the opportunity to speak to Roland in 2002.

"I have people from all over delivering bowling balls. Forty-one just arrived from a New Brunswick German American club, and he even polished the balls!"

We asked how the bowling ball pyramid came about.

"My daughter suggested I build a pyramid. I found a spot and just started arranging them nine across," said Roland, who, by the way, has no interest in bowling whatsoever.

Eventually, Roland amassed over three hundred bowling balls for his pyramid creation when he called it quits. He and his wife, Anne, decided to retire to Tennessee. Roland wasn't sure if the new owners of their house would keep up the ball collecting, so he placed an ad in local newspapers to see if anyone would like his collection.

Roland George

Fred Kanter, owner of Kanter Auto Products in Boonton, thought that the bowling balls were right up his alley. Kanter, sixty-one, said he was inspired by George's creativity and wanted to honor him by re-creating the pyramid on his own lawn.

Fred is no stranger to eye-catching roadside architecture. For years, his office roof has sported a yellow 1937 Packard. In 2004, he had put a seventeen-and-one-half-foot-long Glastron Runabout up a hubcap-festooned oak on his property in Mountain Lakes. The boat was cut in half and wrapped around the trunk. He gave the sculpture a name, *Democrasee,* which means "see what you can do in a democracy."

Fred Kanter

Mosque in the Meadows

Nestled among the high reeds of the Meadowlands and within wafting distance of the horse manure of the racetrack stables is a plot of land belonging to a self-described gypsy named Jamil. A devout Muslim, Jamil uses the land, which he says his family purchased during World War II, as a sort of religious retreat for himself. Locals call the site Squatterville.

"No one lives here," Jamil insisted when we made our pilgrimage to the site; then he inquired if we were with the town. "My family uses the property for getaways from the city."

Jamil told us he is a social worker in New York City and explained that the peacefulness of the Meadowlands is the perfect summer vacation spot.

"I have six kayaks that we use to travel through the waterways. There is some good crabbing, but I was told you shouldn't eat more than one a week because of the pollution."

The Meadowlands property was recently zoned as commercial, and Jamil was told he couldn't build a home there. The original house that once stood on the property was condemned and razed to make room for a jug handle off Paterson Plank Road. Jamil's property was not even given an entrance through the newly built curb. Undaunted, he somehow managed to maneuver several cars and various other vehicles onto the overgrown property. Most look as though they have found their final parking place.

"At one time there were houses all along here, but they were all knocked down. I pay residential taxes though, because of a grandfather clause. It would be a lot higher if I were to pay for commercial."

The most prominent structure on the property resembles a mosque. The other structures are "under construction," and Jamil says he hopes to complete them soon. "No one bothers us here. We're very religious, and we have family gatherings and picnics. My family wants to sell the land, but I don't think we ever will."

Unfortunately, neighbors complained and the display was found in violation of local zoning laws. Kanter is appealing that decision.

After moving to Tennessee, Roland George, the creator of the bowling ball pyramid, lost his battle with cancer and passed away in May of 2004. But the pyramid he designed continues to attract attention from all who pass by Kanter's home. It even enjoyed a brief stint as a legitimate piece of outsider art in 2005 when it was dismantled and reconstructed at the Here Art Gallery in SoHo, Manhattan, as part of *Weird N.J.: The Exhibition.* We think Roland would have been proud.

Now safely back at its home in Mountain Lakes, the pyramid continues to thrive.

Gods and Monsters in the Yard

A statue that had been on the side of U.S. 13 in Delaware since 1984 has moved to join the weirdness that is New Jersey. The statue is eleven feet tall, weighs three thousand pounds, and is alternatively described as looking like either Buddha or a demon. It has weathered a bit—its eyes are no longer illuminated by sinister red bulbs, and the writhing serpent it once held has been beheaded.

Originally a movie prop featured in two Tarzan films and in *The Prodigal* (1955), it was purchased at an MGM prop auction. After its long stint in Delaware, it was bought by a Lumberton man named Denney Van Istendal for $6,000. He's intending to restore it and use it as a mascot for his landscaping business. There's a good view of Van Istendal's backyard from Main Street, part of County Route 541, so don't be surprised if one night you happen to drive past a black-and-gold demon that stares at you with newly restored fiery red eyes.

But not everyone is happy with the Main Street statue. Lumberton's Land Development Board wants Van Istendal to move the statue to a spot where it can't be seen from the street. Attendees at a board meeting called it "despicable," "demonic," and an "eyesore."

Mr. Van Istendal has some simple advice for those who do not care for his horny lawn ornament: "If it offends you, don't look at it."

Bearded Bull God?

A strange statue appeared in the backyard of someone's house right after Halloween. They have it set up facing the road about a mile north of the Rt. 70 intersection. The creature looks like some type of Bearded Assyrian Bull God holding a human-headed snake in his hand. Remember, of course, that you're only seeing the part exposed over a six-foot stockade fence.–*Greg and Maureen Sapnar*

ATLANTIS, THE LOST CONTINENT

What better way is there to get your message across to the world than to simply spell it out in big bold letters on a sign on your front lawn? Here are a few stories of NJ residents who had something to say and wanted their neighbors to hear them loud and clear—so they did just that.

Stickin' It to the Man

Sometimes you just want to stick it to the system. Marc Snyder is one person who literally is sticking his frustration to his May's Landing home in hopes to get Congress to notice the high cost of prescription drugs.

Snyder has plastered his house with prescriptions he could not afford to fill. His neighbors are supportive of Snyder's idea. They don't feel it's an eyesore, but rather a good way to get people to notice the problem.

So far Snyder has amassed over one hundred and sixty prescriptions that would have cost $100 or more if he could have afforded to fill them. The way Snyder figures it, that's about $16,000 worth of paper he has glued to his house.

Snyder needs five different types of medication to help the sciatic pain in his leg. He feels he's found a good way to send a message to the government, which recently approved a prescription drug benefit for elderly people.

"If it helps the seniors, fantastic," Snyder said recently in an Associated Press article. But Snyder, who is fifty-one, wants to know what will happen to everyone else.

Sending a Message in Mine Hill

At a shack on Randolph Avenue in Mine Hill, near East Randolph Avenue, there are huge signs on someone's lawn denouncing lawyers and local media. All the signs carry messages with themes like alimony being unfair, a lost custody fight, the court system. All are crudely written with glaring anger.—*John*

Diss All the Lawyers

My parents live down the street from a sign guy in Mine Hill. Apparently from what the sign says, he went through a very messy divorce where he was made to pay alimony and lost custody of his children, and ever since he has been pissed off at the legal system in Morris County and New Jersey in general. Everyone looks to see what battle he is fighting when they come to see my parents.—*Karen Ullmann*

Clean Up Elmwood Road

Here are some signs in a yard in Mt. Laurel. It seems North Elmwood Road has some environmental issues!
—*Lisa and Jon Kaufman*

TO: P.S.E.& G. RIP-OFFERS & LIARS

NOW YOU CAN SEE HOW THIS BLACK MAN WAS RIPPED-OFF BY RICHARD MURRAY, THE REPRESENTATIVE OF P.S.E.&G. THIS WILL SHOW YOU THAT HE IS A DAMN LIAR! AND THE OTHER LIAR WHO SAID I WAS STEALING GAS IS MR. PETERSON FROM THE MAIN OFFICE IN ORANGE. 1ST LOOK AT #6 DATE OF PURCHASE. 2ND LOOK AT 22 TO 28 ONE YEAR LATER. I WAS FORCED TO PAY $10,000 OR ELSE BOTH BUILDINGS WOULD BE CUT-OFF. AS YOU CAN SEE, THESE ARE THE ESTIMATED BILLS, THEY SAID THEY HAD PROOF, BUT HAVE NEVER PROVEN TO ME. DAMN LIARS!. LOOK HOW THE 1ST $10,000 WAS PAID. NOW LOOK AT #45, THIS IS THE ADD'L AMT. NOW #30 THE LAST PAYMENT TO THE LAWYER. BEFORE THEY GAVE ME A METER IN 85', I HAD A COAL BURNING STOVE, KEROSENE HEATERS, OUTSIDE GRILL, ELECTRIC FRY PAN & TOASTER OVEN. THIS IS THE TRUTH & HERE IS ALL MY PROOF. THE PHOTO'S ARE HOW THE BUILDING LOOKS INSIDE.

If you think discrimination doesn't exist! Listen to this!!!

This is my 2nd sign & my 2nd warning! About PSE&G ripping-off people w/ reps like Richard Murray. Everything I am saying is the truth & as long as Im telling it, Nobody can do a damn thing to me. From 1984 to present, I have been ripped-off for $22,000.00 by PSE&G & Richard Murray, Atty. I will fight until the end. They cant & they wont keep my money that I worked hard for. Phil Fenituck, who was my attorney told me that Richard Murray had a judge deny my a hearing. Now I am asking the community, the church, the people of the county, the state to please help me before someone gets hurt. We need to boycott PSE&G. We should have choices in our demand for services that are rendered to us. Please get on the phone & call your friends, family, etc. Do not let PSE&G put in your furnaces & hot water tanks.

Below is my information from beginning to end with my fight with PSE&G Please take time to review & help me win this fight!!!

Please help me by calling Sen. Lautenberg at 1-609-757-5353 and Sen. Bill Bradley at 1-609-983-4143

Ripped-Off House

Question: What can one man do when the system is trying to bring him down?

Answer: He can plaster his utility bills on the front of his house in an attempt to obtain justice!

Located at the corner of Haywood and North Park streets in Orange, directly across from the PSE&G office, is a building that the owner claims has been targeted by the mega-conglomerate to the tune of more than $22,000 since 1984.

Adorned by signs that tell the whole underhanded story (from one side at least), the three-story building has its landlord's past decade of PSE&G bills and photos of the meager appliances inside, all posted on its façade.

The owner of the property has vowed to fight the giant monopoly to the bitter end. To keep the public abreast of

TO PSE&G & RICHARD A MURRAY,

GUESS WHAT RICHARD MURRAY. I TOOK ALL THE PROOF OF THE ESTIMATE BILLS TO THE FBI, WITH 2 REPS FROM THE COMMUNITY WHO IS HIGHER THAN YOU, YOUR JUDGE FRIEND & PHIL FEINTUCK. EVEN THEY KNOW YOU RIPPED ME OFF. THATS THE KIND OF SON-OF-A-BITCH YOU ARE. AND TO THE BLACK COMMUNITY THIS IS THE KIND OF GUYS THAT PSE&G HAVE REPRESENTING THEM. THERE MUST BE TWO SIDES OF JUSTICE 1 SIDE FOR WHITE, 1 SIDE FOR BLACKS. THIS IS HOW THIS JUSTICE SYSTEM TREATS BLACKS & POOR PEOPLE, LIARS LIKE YOU, CROOKS LIKE YOU. EVEN THE COMMUNITY KNOWS I LIVED HERE FOR YEARS NOT USING YOUR GAS. ALSO YOUR WORKERS ACROSS THE STREET KNOW DAMN WELL THAT THIS BUILDING WAS BOARDED-UP WITH NO METERS BEFORE I PURCHASED IT. SO THEREFORE YOU KNOW DAMN WELL I DID NOT BURN NO $22,000 OF PSE&G GAS. WHY DIDN'T YOU APPEAR IN COURT ON MAY 5th, 1995 INSTEAD OF SENDING YOUR FUNKY? HMMMM...

the case's developments, the signs are updated with every court appearance or new litigious frustration.

This is one angry homeowner.

Bumblebee Man of Paterson

I was traveling in Paterson the other day and saw a very crazy-looking house on Preakness Street. Everything around the house is painted black and yellow, including the garage and the guy's car! On the roof of the house is a huge satellite dish.

On the second story of the house is a very large sign. It's yellow and black and has a man's face on it with one of his eyes covered with an eye patch. The sign has the man's name and below that, it says ONE EYE ON PATTERSON. What the heck does that mean?

He also has an interesting way of watering his lawn. He has one of those oscillating sprinklers, not on the ground, but sticking out from his gutter above the first floor!

There is also a sign on the side of the house, yellow and black also. I walked up to read it. I got a quick glimpse and read something about bees just as someone pulled up in a car and started walking towards me. So I left quickly. I was worried I'd become part of an experiment or something.
—*Christal Liebenthal*

Bumble Bee Man Has One Eye on Weird N.J.!

Hello,

I am the Bumble Bee Man of Paterson.

Actually, I am not a bumblebee man. My hobby is the honeybee and I am president of the New Jersey beekeepers. I sting people, make lectures, bake Paterson Pecan honey pie and brew wine from honey with no grapes at all. The wine tastes smooth but has a little sting (none for sale).

Honeybees, you know, are responsible for the production of most of our food, including orange juice and applesauce. I sometimes find schoolteachers who don't know that. My lawn sprinklers are overhead out of the way, and the hoses are not underfoot. Only water goes on the lawn and it works so well it deserves a patent.

The message One Eye on Paterson has two meanings. First, I have a handicap in one eye and can laugh about it when I keep watch on city government. Second, when I was a candidate for city council, I designed a Safe City program called One Eye On Paterson—Yours and Mine. The people lost more than I lost. My services were available to improve my city, but some voters were so ignorant that all citizens must suffer the loss of my talent to improve our city.

Sincerely,

Tom Fuscaldo, Antenna Specialist, Honeybee Expert

The Ark Woman of Newark

If you were traveling through Newark's Central Ward back in the mid- to late 1980s, you might have thought that the time of the next big flood was close at hand and that one church might have the inside scoop on God's impending wrath. For back then, in a vacant lot adjacent to the Humanity Baptist Church on Bergen Street, stood a massive wooden ark reminiscent of Noah's own. The three-story-tall vessel was eighty-six feet long, about twenty feet wide, and had a main mast that towered above its twenty-eight-foot-high deck. But how did this ship of biblical proportions come to rest here, far from the nearest navigable waterway? Was this vessel, like Noah's ark high atop Mount Ararat, stranded here by the ebbing waters of some prophetic deluge?

The answer is no, this ark had never sailed, nor would it ever even float. It was known as Kea's Ark, and its hand-hewn keel and ribs were made from timbers salvaged from abandoned buildings in the Central Ward. Its builder, a gruff-looking middle-aged woman named Kea Tawana, spent twenty years combing derelict buildings in the area looking for timbers, boards, bolts, and whatever else she could find in the way of materials. Other on-board amenities included stained glass windows, ornate oak fixtures, two-hundred-year-old brass locks, and paving stones to fill the ship's bilges as ballast. Ms. Tawana even found a forty-eight-star American flag in the locker of an abandoned school to unfurl from atop the ship's mast.

Tawana, or the Ark Lady, as she was often called, was a self-taught structural engineer. She shaped the ark's timbers by hand and drilled and chiseled them to fit together. She began working on the project around 1983, and by 1987, the city of Newark began to take notice. It was originally erected in a vacant lot adjacent to the Baptist church where Ms. Tawana worked as a caretaker. However, when the city condemned the ark, it was moved twenty-five feet onto church property. Newark also served eviction papers on the old bus and shed in which the Ark Lady lived, which sat atop a flatbed trailer, calling them "unfit for human habitation." Ms. Tawana said that the city's argument "just doesn't hold water," arguing that she had a generator for electricity, running water, and a stove to keep her warm.

According to Ms. Tawana, she was the daughter of an American civil engineer and a Japanese mother. She claimed that she was stranded in Japan when World War II broke out, and lost her mother and sister in Allied bombings. After the war ended, she and her father set sail for America aboard a converted cargo ship. After the ship nearly went down at sea during a typhoon, Tawana vowed that she would "become a ship's master, and never again be its cargo."

To many people the Ark Lady's ship was a beacon of hope. They saw it as a monument to the determination of one woman, who struggled to create a symbol for Newark's Central Ward, parts of which were still in ruins from the riots of ten years earlier. Visitors from the Smithsonian Institution, the Library of Congress, and the Folk Art Museum of New York reportedly called the vessel a work of art.

City officials called it a violation of the building code, a fire hazard, and an eyesore. Supporters of the Ark Lady collected thousands of signatures of residents in favor of saving the ark. Though the pastor of the church supported Tawana in her struggle, he could not afford the fines for code violations that the city threatened the church with.

In a 1987 interview, Tawana said that no matter what happened, she would not be swayed from her ultimate vision of turning the ark into a floating museum of Newark memorabilia. In March of that year, she asked the city of Newark for three more months in which to sheath the

ship's hull enough to keep it afloat. Desperately trying to save the ark from demolition, she sought riggers who could move the vessel down to the Passaic River, just one mile away. Meanwhile, under the watchful eye of city officials, Tawana dismantled the top two levels of her beloved ark so that it could fit under the telephone, electrical, and cable television wires on its hoped-for voyage down to the river.

"It will be little more than a scow," she said of what would be left of the ship by the time it reached the water, "but it will still be the ark. It will be all I have to show for five years."

"They are squeezing me like a grape," Ms. Tawana told *The New York Times* in an interview at the time. "I'm being pushed out by developers and politicians. Unless I get the extra time, the ark is doomed. I'll have to break it up and sell it for firewood."

Which is exactly what she ultimately did.

Subterranean Views

I'm originally from Merchantville, but for the past few years I've lived in Cherry Hill. Every now and then during my time in Merchantville, my family and I would make trips to Cooper River. One of the highlights of our trips would be a visit to an underground house that was located just off the road that runs along the north side of the river.

The underground structure lies at the end of a dead end road. It would be easy to miss if it weren't for the concrete entranceway with the name Malcolm B. Wells emblazoned on it.

Recently a friend and I decided to go back to see it. I say "back" because we'd been there before, but never inside. It was late at night, so we grabbed some flashlights and a camera and made our way over to the house.

It was about 11:00 p.m. by the time we got there, and the only lights came from our flashlights and the street light on the other side of the road. We passed through the concrete entranceway and down the stairs that led to the entrance of the house. As we stepped off the stairs, we were greeted with a strange quote that was painted on the wall. ALL WORK PASSES OUT OF THE HANDS OF THE ARCHITECT . . . and on the second half of

the wall . . . INTO THE HANDS OF NATURE. Puzzled, we moved on.

It was a surprisingly small place. As we explored more, we realized that the building was not abandoned. Not only were the plants that had been overgrown last time we visited cut down, but the entire place was much cleaner. As a result, we dared not enter the house itself. Instead, we walked around the small pavilion that was constructed around it. We could see inside the house since a majority of the walls were made of glass. Inside the building were many filing cabinets and a desk. After some thorough exploration, we decided to call it quits.

The architect, Malcolm B. Wells, is apparently well-known as a designer of "earth-sheltered" structures. He has declared May 14 to be Underground America Day. I'm pretty sure that he's the only one who celebrates this holiday.—*Jeff Baldwin*

Going Underground with Malcolm Wells

Malcolm Wells spent ten years as an architect, spreading asphalt and concrete to build his buildings. Then, in 1964, he had an epiphany. In his own words, "The earth's surface was made for living plants, not industrial plants." Mr. Wells began designing homes not just across America, but underneath it. Today Malcolm Wells is the world's most recognized pioneer in the field of underground housing.

There are roughly six thousand underground dwellings in North America. Wells takes great pride in this achievement and has even declared a day to celebrate underground architecture. May 14 is Underground America Day, according to Mr. Wells. "On May 14th each year hundreds of millions of people all across this great land will do absolutely nothing about the national holiday I declared in 1974, and that's just the way it should be."

Wells now resides in Massachusetts and still designs plans for those who wish to build or convert their homes into subterranean dwellings. For more info, visit www.MalcolmWells.com.

Vineland's Lunar Landscape

I was heading west on Landis Avenue, a very nice section of Vineland, when I saw something so amazing I had to pull over and take these pictures.

The owner of this property, one of the wealthier residents of Vineland, who used to own a chain of Shop-Rites, has turned his lawn into a strange lunar landscape. He dumped at least six inches of sand over his entire front yard and has huge rocks scattered around and piles of smaller rocks at the entrance.

I asked around and heard that this guy's wife kept bugging him for a beach house, so he decided to give her one. I also heard the neighbors are quite upset with him, probably because the sand blows everywhere. Sometimes I go by and see big tire tracks all over the sand (a lunar land vehicle from NASA, or maybe just a monster truck?). The other day I swear I saw a kid mowing along the edge where grass has managed to grow through the sand.–*Pam Fiocchi*

When *Weird N.J.* visited this almost Zen-like yard, we spied a local man getting into his car across the street. We quickly rushed over to ask him what he thought of his neighbor's austere choice of landscape design.

"It's his property," he told us with a shrug. "He can do what he wants with it."

We couldn't have said it better ourselves.

What Lies Beneath

Did you ever wonder what's going on beneath your feet? It might just surprise you! New Jersey is a veritable hive of caves, man-made tunnels, and abandoned mines that wriggle for miles just beneath the surface of the state. Legends abound of Revolutionary War Tories and Prohibition Era bootleggers using these subterranean passageways for their own nefarious purposes. Unfortunately for us though, the stories that these hidey-holes have inspired have proved much easier to come by than the holes themselves.

Our state also has many natural cave formations, though they're quite modest by geological standards. Experienced explorers of such places will tell you that none of our caverns extend for more than a few hundred yards and that short distance is often a wet and claustrophobic journey. Still, these unpleasant conditions have done little to discourage adventurous molelike people known as spelunkers. These cave explorers are a breed all their own. Undaunted by the dangers of climbing into dark and foreboding cracks in the earth's surface, these cavers have mapped almost every nook, cranny, and crevice in our state's crust. Some are so enthusiastic that they will even strip naked and grease themselves up to slip more easily through the tightest of cracks.

On the other hand, several people have told us tales of vast underground networks of tunnels that connect natural cave systems to a labyrinth of man-made structures. They have assured us that a person can walk upright for miles underground through this hidden maze.

Unfortunately, many of New Jersey's most interesting tunnels were sealed up years ago, allegedly due to concern for the public's safety. This has only added to their mystique, and most of the people we talk to about these caves seem to believe that there is a conspiracy afoot to keep them a secret from the general population. This feeling has inspired many a subterranean traveler to wonder what may still lie just below the surface of our state, waiting to be rediscovered.

Moody's Cave

Perhaps the most legendary of all of New Jersey's subterranean passageways is Moody's Cave. Named for the Tory renegade James Moody, this storied passage was said to connect Moody's Rock, on the southern edge of the Muckshaw Swamp in Fredon, to the Devil's Hole (a.k.a. the Devil's Den), located half a mile southwest of Newton in Sussex County. History tells us that during the American Revolution, Moody used the rock as a hideout from which he could conduct raids on local farms. Legend holds that Moody and his men could not be brought to justice because they could escape by traveling a mile underground between the rock and the Devil's Hole.

The Devil's Hole is the largest known cave in the state. It consists of several rooms, some as large as 105 feet long and 40 feet wide, with 10-foot-high ceilings. Moody's Rock, on the other hand, is just a large overhanging cliff of dolomite that forms a natural rock shelter. The many Indian artifacts recovered from the Moody's Rock site are evidence that it was once used by Native Americans as a rock house.

Though recent forays into these two caverns have produced no evidence of a passage connecting them, rumors still abound that it exists. We asked Matt Little, a Stanhope resident and local cave junkie, what he knew of this great lost passage.

"During the time of the American Revolution," Matt told us, "James Moody, a British Tory, made a jailhouse escape from Newton and rode to a place called the Devil's Hole. Supposedly, he was told of this tunnel by Indian chief Allamuchy's daughter Kittatinny. Moody used these tunnels to fight the Americans. After the war, he returned to England and was given Nova Scotia by King George. His family came back to New Jersey in the 1960s to look for these tunnels and were told they did not exist. The search for Moody's tunnels has been going on forever.

"Where I went in at Andover, which is called the Devil's Drop, there were stalagmites from floor to ceiling, and ancient campfires along the way. It's a maze of routes. You're walking upright all the way through."

Many legends of Moody's exploits have been handed down by word of mouth. Augustus Schooley, a native of Newton, wrote down eight legends of Moody's Rock in blank verse. One passage describes a visit to the cave by a friend of Moody's. These lines were published in the *Sussex Register* on July 8, 1885:

When the rock they had arrived at,
Moody gave a long shrill whistle;
then a small door slowly opened,
opened in the solid limestone,
and the twain a passage entered,
leading to the secret cavern. As the
door was closed behind them, this
dark passage was illuminated as
by magic it was lighted, and
revealed the Tory's armor—
weapons, civilized and savage—
hanging on the walls and ceiling.
Moody leading, through the
passage went the pair some little
distance, now to right, now left, they turning, till they
came to where it ended. Here they halted, Moody
whistling as before when forthwith opened, swung
upon its creaking hinges, a huge door of massive limestone—swung and opened in a chamber cut by nature in
the boulder; cut in form a quadrangle; cut as if by some
hand human. This they entered. It was lighted by a
chandelier suspended from the center of the ceiling, and
its brilliancy illuminated every nook and every corner of
this spacious limerock chamber. On the floor were
Turkish carpets; on its walls were Persian hangings; all
of oriental pattern; all of colors warm and gorgeous
paneled in between the hangings on all sides were
polished mirrors; rugs, fauteuils, divans and sofas
added luxury and splendor, while an English grand
piano graced the center of the chamber. . . . On one side
of this cave-chamber, where the walls bulged slightly
outward, was a dais, sort of a throne room, which in
regal style was fitted, and contained the bust and
picture of the wicked English monarch, George the
Third, whom Moody worshiped. . . .

Judging from the above account, Moody's quarters
compared favorably with the best in English castles.
One wonders what the chancellor of the exchequer said
when he saw Moody's itemized expense account.

Moody did not have long to enjoy his luxurious
cave though. He was captured by American troops and
imprisoned. He later escaped and made his way to
England.

But whatever became of the elegantly appointed
secret cave? Perhaps it still lies buried somewhere
beneath the hollowed ground of Sussex County, just
waiting for some curious caver to unearth it.

Devil's Drop

There are mine caves in Andover that are known as Devil's
Drop. The story goes that a man pushed his son over the
edge of the cliff there and then jumped himself. We used to
throw parties in one of the big caves during high school, and
one girl swore that she saw a little boy wearing a baseball
glove standing in a corner. She wept hysterically, and we all
left with a serious case of the spooks.—*Terry O'Sullivan*

Haunted Church Tunnel

When I was 6 or 7, my uncle would tell me his New Jersey legends. My favorite has always been the legend about the haunted tunnel in Belleville.

The story starts with a 300-year-old church, located on the Passaic River, at the Belleville end of a bridge on the Kearny/North Arlington border. Apparently, far beneath the church's foundation is a tunnel which extends far beyond the church, going under the Passaic River. Some say that the tunnel was used for artillery storage during the Revolutionary War. Others argue that it was used as part of the Underground Railroad at the time of the Civil War.

One night, according to the legend, a group of people were traveling in the tunnel. All of a sudden, there was an explosion. Most of the people died.

Well, even today, the tunnel remains. So do the ghosts of all the victims. Some say that on a quiet night, at about midnight, if you pass by the church, you can hear the ghosts of the dead souls trying to get out. –*Ms. Sara Callori*

Mining for the Tunnel

When I was in Kearny High School in the 1920s, we spent many Saturdays exploring the old Schuyler Copper Mine on the east side of the ridge," Merrill Harvey told us in a letter. "The mine was opened by Schuyler in the 1700s, the richest mine in the colonies, according to Ben Franklin."

To construct these tunnels was an amazing feat. The Dutch Reformed Church of Belleville, a historic landmark built in 1692, is said to have a tunnel that leads underneath the Passaic River into North Arlington. Legend has it that General Washington's troops would use the tunnel to conduct surprise raids on the British troops camped on the other side of the river.

"There was a folk tale regarding a tunnel from the mine to the church which no one believed," recalls Harvey. "But I do remember a tunnel in the mine that was always flooded and a flashlight showed it going down and under the water. A few years ago a young man organized a Schuyler Historic Foundation to research the mine. I talked to two members of the foundation who, in the 1930s had followed that tunnel down and under the river and came up to what was the church wall! They found no exit apparently and went back as they had come.

"I talked to a young man who told me that he saw the entrance in the basement of the church. 'I lifted the door in the floor and there it was!' he said. The church people were interested but afraid of publicity so there was no follow-up."

The Devil's Kitchen and Wheelwright Shop By Mark Moran

Weird N.J. is all over any place that has the word Devil in its title. And if that site happens to lead underground, it's all the better. So when we found the names Devil's Kitchen and Devil's Wheelwright Shop while perusing the pages of Henry Charlton Beck's book *Tales and Towns of Northern New Jersey,* we were ecstatic. Beck mentions the sites only in passing, but we were able to surmise that they are caves that just might be located in the area of Johnsonburg, in Warren County. Beck writes,

> . . . an elusive crossroads called Southtown was given the same typographical status as Johnsonburg itself. But only from the lips of the reticent, who remembered what their grandmothers and grandfathers had said, and in the text of a little-known pamphlet, was I to hear of caves under limestone ledges celebrated as "The Devil's Kitchen," and "The Devil's Wheelwright Shop" on a road called "The Dark of the Moon Road" which wound out of Johnsonburg. More surprisingly, for most of two centuries there was a narrow passage close by referred to by those who know it well as "The Pass of Thermopoly." My most impressive dictionary would indicate that "thermopoly" is a place of radiant heat, but whatever it is or was, I feel sure that with all the others it was well-known by one who was known far and wide as "The Old Pig Drover of Log Goal."

As everyone knows, the Battle of Thermopylae took place during the Greece-Persia war in roughly the fifth century B.C. To hold off an invading Persian advance from the sea, the Spartan king Leonidas led his army to the pass at Thermopylae, a narrow valley adjacent to the Persian landing point. There an outnumbered three hundred Spartan warriors fought savagely against thousands of Persians in a suicidal, yet successful, mission to delay the Persian advance until Greek troops could amass their naval forces.

What this battle had to do with a cave in Johnsonburg, NJ, I had no idea. And since Mr. Beck published this book in 1964 and died shortly thereafter, there was no way that he was telling.

So Mark Sceurman and I set out to find these mythic caves. Of course we all know what a kitchen is, though it might be unclear why the devil would need one. But just what the heck is a wheelwright shop? I wondered. My most impressive dictionary indicated that a wheelwright was "one whose trade is the building and repairing of wheels." Okay, but still a curious name for a cave. I wondered if the devil had his meals cooked for him in the kitchen and his wheels righted in the wheelwright shop, or if he himself was said to be toiling away doing his own cooking and wheelwrighting. Sort of menial work for the prince of darkness, in my opinion.

Johnsonburg is a tiny farming community comprised of only a handful of streets, a few old homes, and even fewer shops, surrounded by miles of open fields. Dark of the Moon Road (Route 519) runs right through the heart of the town, though no street signs can be found that bear that name. The town is just a stone's throw from Shades of Death Road, which should need no further introduction to readers of *Weird N.J.*

We stopped at the diner in Johnsonburg to ask a few questions of the locals. A couple of flannel shirt–clad patrons, nursing their coffee and cigarettes at the counter, seemed as if they could offer the information we sought. We eased into the conversation cautiously, knowing how some locals tend to clam up when out-of-towners start pumping them for information.

"So, this is a nice area around here," we began. "We're just passing through. Anything interesting to see while we're in the neighborhood?" This is an act Mark and I refer to as Routine B. I won't tell you what Routine A is, because we might want to use it on you someday. The question seemed to dumbfound the diners.

"Well," a grizzled-looking bearded fellow finally said, "that big white barn across the street used to be the town jail. There's a sign on it from 1800 and something that says Jail."

Okay, I thought, that's a start, but it ain't no Devil's Kitchen. "What about caves?" I blurted out. "Got any of those around here?" I quickly got the impression that I had tipped our hand prematurely. The counter folk, though not too forthcoming before, seemed to become visibly suspicious after this question was asked. "No," the man said, turning back to face the waitress, "no caves around here."

Since the cat was already out of the bag, we decided to pursue this line of questioning a little further. "What about a place we've heard about called the Devil's Kitchen, or maybe the Devil's Wheelwright?"

"Yeah, that's a cave," the man said. "Used to have a bunch of hippies livin' in it years ago. They painted up the inside with all this freaky stuff." He added, "The cave is in the woods on private property."

It didn't take much to see that this guy was done talking to us. We paid our bill and got out of Johnsonburg, knowing that the Devil's Kitchen did exist and that we'd never find it based on what we had learned there.

As luck would have it, before long we received a lead on a site from a reader. The letter said, "Walk several yards east along the Erie Lackawanna Rail Road from its underpass at Marksboro-Silver Lake Road. It can be found on a rocky point several hundred feet across a swampy area on the right. Marksboro (Frelinghuysen Twnsp.)" Checking our maps, we could see that this was not far at all from the crossroads of Dark of the Moon Road and

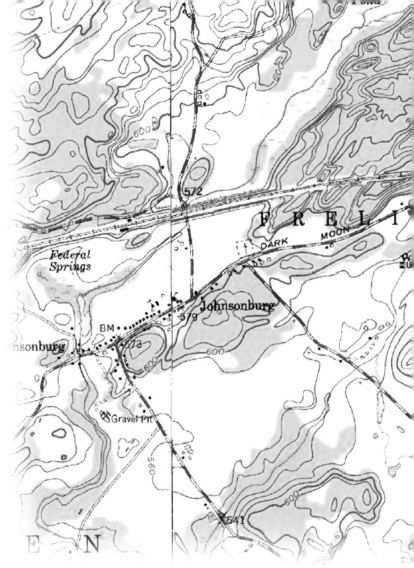

Southtown Road that Henry Charlton Beck had written of in his book.

Researching further, we came upon the 1976 NJ state geological survey conducted by the D.E.P., which confirmed the exact location of the Devil's Kitchen, but informed us that the cave we were looking for was actually one of two caves in the area with that demonic moniker. The other Devil's Kitchen, referred to as Devil's Kitchen #2, is located about a half mile north of the Johnsonburg station on the Erie Lackawanna Railroad.

So we decided to look for the cave we had the best

directions to—the Devil's Kitchen #1. To help us, we contacted Diantha Quick, who lives in the vicinity and whose family history in the area goes back for generations, and she agreed to accompany us on our journey.

We headed out to the overpass on Silver Lake Road that crosses the abandoned tracks of an old railway line. We walked down to the tracks and headed east. After several hundred yards of peering through the thick foliage on the side of the tracks, we began to think we were headed in the wrong direction.

It was then that we found ourselves overlooking a grassy hollow of land with a small pond in the middle of it. There was a car parked by the pond with two men standing beside it one hundred and fifty yards from where we stood. We debated whether we should venture down into the hollow to ask these guys if they knew where the devil's caves were. We didn't know if we were on private property, so I took just one step off the rail bed toward them. That's when the shots rang out, putting an end to our debate.

One of the men shouted up to us, "You lookin' for something?" I stepped back up onto the railroad tracks. It seemed ludicrous to yell back, "We're looking for the Pass of Thermopoly." Just then Diantha shouted out, "Earl, is that you down there?"

"Who's that?" the man with the rifle replied.

"It's Diantha," she said.

"Hey, Diantha, what are you doin' up there?" Earl's voice had warmed up considerably.

"We're looking for a cave," she said. "You know of any in this area?"

"Yeah, there's one down in the other direction," he yelled, then added that it was by so-and-so's property.

"Okay, thanks," she said. As we turned around to walk back down the tracks, Earl offered one last piece of advice. "Be careful, it's bear season, you know." This last bit of information, while undoubtedly sound and valuable, I could have done without.

It was December, and the temperature had just recently started to get very cold. We all know where bears go when the weather gets cold—caves.

As we backtracked, we once again began surveying the land for signs of a cave, although this time we were perhaps a little less eager to find one. Before long, the land on our right began to slope down to a low, swampy area, exactly as described on our lead sheet. Beyond that rose a dark outcropping of rock. I scanned the mound with my binoculars and saw, about halfway up the stone wall, a blackened hole that seemed to be a cave.

We traipsed across the wet and mucky expanse to the hill. When we got there, I had no doubt that this hole was at least one of the devil's hangouts that we had been searching for. Sceurman fired up his video camera and stood a safe distance from the cave's entrance to, as he put it, get a good shot of the bear mauling me, while still allowing himself enough head-start time to beat a hasty retreat. Diantha was also smart enough to stay a safe distance from the cave. I, on the other hand, am the guy who must take pictures to share with you, dear reader, so it was my job to venture forth.

It was December, and the temperature had just recently started to get very cold. We all know where bears go when the weather gets cold—caves.

The entrance was only about three feet high, so I had to squat down to enter. The first chamber was like a little stone foyer. There were no signs of anyone or anything living or having lived there, but there were no leaves or other debris either, leading me to think that maybe something had kept it tidy. Beyond the first chamber, the tunnel turned sharply to the left and another low rock arch led into a larger room. Since I was not carrying a flashlight

or tranquilizer darts or anything else one might find useful when venturing into a bear den, I stayed in the first small room of the cave. The only way for me to see what lay beyond in the larger room was to stick my camera in at arm's length and take a flash photo. But the flash illuminated the chamber for just so far, and what lay beyond its light remained a mystery.

The 1976 geological survey had described the inside of the cave like this:

. . . there are about 130 feet of branchwork type passages in the cave, although most of it is less than four feet high. It contains cave coral, flowstone on the wall, and a column. Cave life included one small brown bat, a good many spiders and crickets, and a few daddy-long-legs; the cave is intermittently used by larger animals. Silt, containing an abundance of bones, covers all of the floor of the first section.

Okay, I thought, that description is vivid enough for me. I decided that I was satisfied that we had found the cave that was referred to in days of yore as the Devil's Kitchen. There was no discernible "radiant heat" or any suicidal Trojan warriors present, so I'll have to assume that we had not found the Pass of Thermopoly. Not being a spelunker, I cannot say for sure what mysteries might have been found in the farthest recesses of this gloomy cavern—perhaps some good ol' home cooking from hell's own kitchen.

Faery Hole

Located in Jenny Jump State Park, near the shores of Ghost Lake on Shades of Death Road, is a small cave known as the Faery Hole (*faery* is an Old English spelling for fairy). Evidence of Indian occupation, including a few pieces of pottery and evidence of a fire pit near the opening, has been found there. From the parking lot, follow the rocky trail along the lake's edge about two hundred yards, then turn to the right and climb up a steep rocky slope to the cave.

The cave is about ten feet wide and fifteen feet deep, and the ceiling is high enough for a person to stand up. There is a natural chimney in the rear of the cave that sometimes contains blind cave crickets.

When the Faery Hole was excavated in 1936 by archaeologist Dr. Dorothy Cross of the New Jersey State Museum, more than ten thousand bone fragments from twenty-three different species of animals were recovered. Among them was the tooth of a giant extinct beaver that has been found nowhere else in the state.

Down in the Darkness

Under a seemingly uninteresting industrial park in Wood-Ridge lies a wartime artifact so massive that it used to hold 17,000 people a day. What is this gargantuan relic built into a hillside? It's an abandoned Curtiss-Wright Corporation defense plant, and at two million square feet, it's more like an underground fortress than a former factory.

In 1942, the Wright Aeronautical Corporation built the plant as an aircraft engine factory that would become essential to the U.S. war effort. It was here that thousands of plane engines were churned out, including one that eventually wound up in the *Enola Gay,* the notorious B-29 that flew over Hiroshima and dropped the atomic bomb.

In the plant's heyday, men and women worked feverishly to provide the juice to our frontline defense. The plant operated twenty-four hours a day, seven days a week. Inside, they ran engines at full speed in ten two-story "test cells," before packing them and shipping them off to meet their planes.

While most of the employees were machinists, riveters, and assembly line workers, some were waiters serving the management at the plant restaurant, nurses at the infirmary, or teachers at the training school. The windowless building was designed with one goal in mind: to produce aircraft engines and, oh, yeah, to make sure that it was impervious to enemy attack. The thirty-two-acre roof of the building, which is at street level, was reinforced with concrete, and during the war, armed men with machine guns stood watch over the plant from nearby towers.

When World War II ended, the factory began to make jet engines that would eventually be used in the Korean War. Later the plant manufactured gas turbine generators, until it finally closed its doors in the early 1980s. A few businesses remained aboveground.

In 2001, the plant site was purchased by developer Cammebys International, who installed its current sixteen business tenants—all aboveground—and anticipates its future as an enclave of shopping, housing units, and parks. Until then, the former factory remains a glorious specimen of abandoned underground New Jersey.

Lost in the Netherworld

From 1991 to 1993 I worked for a small plastic bottle manufacturing company located in the old Curtiss-Wright industrial complex. As a foreman I had lots of time to walk around the place. Out in a corner of our warehouse area there was an old staircase but it was boarded up at the bottom. I never really paid any attention to it until I had a conversation with Ben, one of the security guards. I knew that during World War II this had been a factory for making planes or engines for the military, but that was all I knew. Ben told me that there were numerous underground levels where the planes had been built and stored. I asked him if he had ever gone down there and he said yes, but only a couple of floors down. He told me it was "spooky" down there.

At the next opportunity I went down the short flight of stairs in the warehouse. I examined the boarded up doorway and discovered it was very makeshift. Within ten minutes I had removed enough of the planks to ease my body through the opening. I found myself standing on a small stairwell landing looking down another flight of stairs. I went back upstairs to the tool room and returned with a flashlight.

I went back through the doorway and made my way down a flight of about twenty creaky wooden steps. I found myself in a long corridor. The walls were concrete with lots of graffiti all over them. There were hundreds of broken beer and booze bottles everywhere. The corridor went on for a long distance and eventually terminated at another flight of stairs. These steps were made of concrete. I proceeded down and continued down another corridor almost identical to the one above except there was far less graffiti and only a few broken bottles.

At the end of the corridor I discovered yet another staircase leading down into yet another long corridor. Gone were the graffiti and the bottles. In their place were large dust webs from ceiling to floor. My clothing, head, and face were quickly covered in dust. Off this corridor were rooms that looked like they had once been offices and had desks, tables, file cabinets, and old typewriters. Everything was covered with a thick layer of dust. I made my way to the end of the hallway, and went down yet another stairwell.

These stairs, unlike the previous three flights, had small landings every twenty or so steps, which turned into another flight of twenty or so steps. At each landing was a door into another corridor area. I did not go into these corridors because I wanted to see what was at the bottom of the stairs. When the stairs finally ended I found myself in a huge open area. The beam of the flashlight was too weak to illuminate the high ceiling. Quite possibly this was one of the airplane hangars or rooms where the planes were assembled.

I carefully walked across the large floor, which had junk all over the place: big spools of cable, old wooden crates, piles of metal ducting pieces. I felt uneasy about the size of this room because the beam from my flashlight was insufficient to reach the walls on either side of me. I hoped I would not become disoriented. The eerie silence was broken by the scampering of little feet off in the distance, hopefully mice and not rats.

When I finally reached the opposite wall, I found an open doorway. I walked through and found a room with all sorts of machines. There was an old lathe and a couple of milling machines, racks of long pieces of metal tubing neatly stacked on one wall, and metal shelves with machine parts on them.

I left and continued down the hall. Just then my flashlight flickered, and I was seized with the terrifying thought that if these batteries went dead I would never be able to find my way out of there.

I started retracing my steps. I walked back out of the machine shop rooms and came into the large hangar area. I prayed my light would not go dead. I was sweating profusely and was starting to panic. I suddenly questioned whether I was walking in the right direction towards the stairs. The terrible answer came to me as I reached the wall and did not recognize anything! I panned my light along the wall and decided to simply walk along it until I reached the stairs. In a few minutes I finally reached the staircase I thought I had come down. I started up, one flight, and then another. However with each step I wondered if I was coming closer to getting out of there or was becoming more lost.

At the top of the stairs I found myself in a corridor I thought I recognized. I back tracked down this hall and to the next staircase and proceeded up. I eventually made it back to the boarded up doorway. I replaced the boards as best I could and ran up the stairs to the well-lit comfort of civilization.

Several days later I saw Ben and told him about my adventure. He told me I was crazy for going down there and that I could have easily gotten lost. I asked him how far down those levels go and he told me he had heard they go down for thirty or more floors! I was amazed.

Ben told me I was lucky I didn't find any bodies down there. I asked him what he meant. "Well," he said, "don't you think more than a few people have gotten lost down there over the years and had never been able to find their way out?" The thought sent chills up my spine. I never ventured back down there but I never forgot my experience.—*R. Kevin DiPeri*

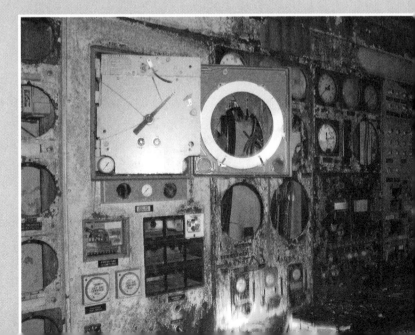

A Different Kind of Playboy Grotto

In the summer of 1983, my three friends and I had just graduated from high school, and were enjoying the summer. One friend lived somewhere near Marlton, although I am not sure which town. At the time there were still lots of woods and a creek by his house, so we went to check it out. We found a large (8' tall) drainage culvert and decided to explore it. We went back to the house and retrieved flashlights, and someone brought a roll of electrical tape, to mark the way we entered.

It was close to 7pm when we finally entered the culvert. We were all telling stories about the Jersey Devil, trying to scare each other. It was large and dank. We went past old shopping carts, dead rats, pieces of wood, etc. Pretty much anything that would wash down a drain in a rainstorm was there. Every once in a while we would find stairs that led up to the road. We made several turns and marked the direction we were going with small arrows of tape. We were underground for what seemed like hours when to our amazement, the culvert came to a large open area.

The room we entered was huge. It was the main hub for the runoff water to collect. But this is the weird part: This room had a house in it! Mind you, we were 20 feet or so below the ground. In front of the rundown house was a shopping cart FULL of the current issue of *Playboy!* We thought that was bizarre—literally hundreds of copies of the same issue!

We all started to laugh until we saw a light go on inside the dilapidated house! I can tell you that the four of us ran like hell to the place we had entered from, which seemed like miles away. We followed the arrows and ran at breakneck speed. When we looked back, we could see the illumination from a flashlight following us! We were four scared kids. We finally made it outside to the small containment pond where the water would collect. Whoever was holding the light never came out of the tunnel. It was a bizarre experience, and as I said, 100% true.—*Jim*

Doin' the Locomotion Underground

As many train enthusiasts will tell you, abandoned train tunnels can be just as exciting to explore as any cave you may wander (or fall) into. These man-made corridors, bored through mountains of solid rock, possess many of the same elements of wonder, history, and legend as their more ancient counterparts. There are abandoned train tunnels all over northern New Jersey, tucked away in small rural communities and urban areas alike. Here are a few of our favorite dark passages. But be forewarned: Sometimes that light at the end of the tunnel is not an exit. Some of these tunnels are still in use, and if that light you're looking at turns out to be a highballing locomotive, it just might mean it's the end of the line for you!

Dead Man's Tunnel

My sister took swim classes one summer at Dickinson High in Jersey City around 1970. It's a gigantic neoclassical structure, built for the federal government around the time of the War of 1812.

Behind the school is a playground, then train tracks where the Erie Lackawanna trains went into Dead Man's Tunnel. Going down the hill from there, the next thing you would come to was a medium size cemetery.

After one of their midsummer swims, my sister and some friends noticed that the door to the subbasements of Dickinson were open, and they went exploring. They were soon hopelessly lost in the dark, having no light with them. They wandered in the pitch dark for hours before stumbling out into the Newark Avenue graveyard! She said they thought that towards the end, they were in a train tunnel. They later went back and thoroughly explored Dead Man's Tunnel, but never found the place they emerged from. When we inquired at the public library, we were told that Dickinson High School was originally a U.S. Naval Academy and that its basement was riddled with secret tunnels traveling underneath Dickinson Hill to provide escape from a potential British invasion.–*Jeff B.*

The Dead Irishman of Dead Man's Tunnel

Growing up in Jersey City, my friends and I would go down into Dead Man's Tunnel in the day but we were always scared to go at night. We heard that many people died there. Many people say that a ghost would appear there at night. This was supposedly the ghost of an Irish immigrant who blew himself up with dynamite when the tunnel was being excavated.

Once when my friends and I walked through the tunnel, my friend freaked out because he felt someone tap his shoulder. It was a weird experience.–*Letter via e-mail*

Manunka Chunk Junction, What's Your Function?

Tucked away in the woods of a Warren County mountainside, just north of the town of Belvidere, are the remains of what was once a thriving rail line. In 1876, the tiny village of Manunka Chunk became a major rail center when two lines—the Delaware, Lackawanna & Western from Hoboken and the Pennsylvania from Philadelphia—decided to form a junction there. Soon trains arrived from major cities, carrying wealthy summer vacationers to the cool waters of the Delaware River. A grand hotel was built on an eighty-five-acre island in the middle of the river to accommodate the visitors in lavish style.

The hotel flourished until a flood in 1903 submerged the first two floors, forcing the owner to give up the enterprise. The building would be renovated and reopened under a new name, The Manunka Chunk House, but its misfortunes would continue. First, the train station at the junction was abandoned; then the Great Depression hastened the decline of vacationing customers. The hotel finally closed its doors in 1935 and burned to the ground in 1938.

Today the island is once again a lush wilderness. The train tracks have been removed, and the junction is no more. All that remains are two gaping black holes bored through the mountain that once ushered adventurous sojourners to these bucolic shores. But that seems to be all it takes to lure leisure-time travelers to this weird New Jersey destination.

A Dark, Dark Passage

Early one morning I set out for the town of Manunka Chunk to walk the two abandoned train tunnels that run through the mountains there. I parked in the general area where I knew the tunnels to be, at a crazy little roadside hot dog joint called King Cole's on Route 46. I darted across the highway and into the woods. After climbing a bit up the mountain, I located the old rail bed. The tracks had been pulled up, but I knew that this path would lead me to the tunnels.

After a short hike down the trail I found what I was looking for—two huge, gaping holes in the side of the mountain. A cold breeze emanated from within the caverns. The two entry arches are about 20 feet high, and framed with chiseled granite blocks. Other than good sense, there was absolutely nothing stopping me from going in—so in I went.

The tunnels start to curve just a few yards in, leaving any light outside a distant memory. After ten paces I was immersed in total darkness. I had my trusty Mini-Mag Lite, but that was not much of a match for the overwhelming darkness of this place. The tunnel floor was wet and muddy in spots, and here and there the walls had collapsed, leaving large mounds of rubble, which I had to climb over.

I walked for a long way, maybe a couple hundred yards, before I saw the proverbial light at the end of the tunnel. This sight was a relief, as I was actually starting to think seriously about turning back. Not knowing the actual length of the tube, I wanted to be sure that my batteries did not die while I was inside.

Fortunately I soon emerged into the lush green forest on the other side. After a few minutes, I plunged once more into the dark damp abyss of the second tunnel to begin my trip home. This time, knowing exactly how long it would be made traveling through the darkness a little more relaxed journey.

When I emerged on the other side I stood for a moment, soaking wet and full of mud, reflecting upon my trip. I've heard that due to accidents inside, officials have considered blasting the Manunka Chunk tunnel entrances shut forever so I highly recommend checking these dark passages out while you still have the opportunity.—*Myke L.*

The Edgewater–Fairview Train Tunnel

One of the great lost passageways of New Jersey, this tunnel stretches from its western entrance beneath the Fairview Cemetery in Fairview (Bergen County) to its eastern opening at the foot of the Palisades in Edgewater. Starting around 1892, this was the railway for the New York, Susquehanna, and Western Railroad Company, and was used to get coal from Pennsylvania to the Hudson River coal docks. The yards shut down in the late 1960s, and the tunnel has been unused ever since.

Ah, but what stories such a dark and forlorn passage can inspire! Here are just a few.

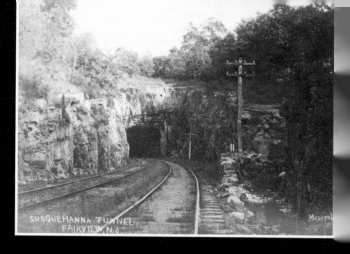

SUSQUEHANNA TUNNEL
FAIRVIEW, N.J.

Wild Tunnel Dogs

There is an old train tunnel that runs underground from the Hudson River to Fairview. It's about three miles long, and it's dark and really freaky. From time to time a pack of wild dogs roams through the tunnels, so be prepared!
–*Rev. Tom Moan*

Death on the Fairview–Edgewater Express

One weird area I explored is an abandoned rail line that goes right into one of the cemeteries of Fairview, then goes under it into a tunnel! This tunnel has been abandoned since about the 1960s, after a little girl was supposedly hit by a train blazing out of the tunnel. It is said that her body was not noticed by the engineer until he reached Pennsylvania.–*Dan Lopez*

The Hole Story

The Fairview portal was used as an atomic bomb shelter during the cold war. My friends and I once walked through the tunnel when we were about 12, with makeshift torches. As it was flooded, we had to walk along a four-foot wide metal pipe placed off to one side. I remember feeling scared, wondering if a train would enter while we were in there, or if the bats would get us! The way back was even scarier since our torches went out.

It's sad to see the chain link fences up at both ends now. I actually pondered driving through it, but I guess that wouldn't happen now.
–*Kenneth Accomando*

The Old Cedar St. Subway

Due to my job, I travel all over the state. On one trip, my co-workers and I ended up in a building in Newark. While in the basement of that building we came across a small hole in the wall. With flashlights in hand, we had to investigate.

The hole opened up into an abandoned subway tunnel. We squeezed through and found out that it was the old Cedar St. subway line. The Cedar St. subway was built in 1916 and ran trolley cars between Washington St. and Broad St., where it split at Broad. The split sent the tunnels up Broad St. and toward the train station. In 1938 Newark stopped running trolleys in the tunnel and started running diesel buses there until 1966.

As we descended, our flashlight lit up the past. We first walked across an old platform, which turned out to be the old Kresge's Store entrance from the subway. The displays held artifacts from when the place was alive. Old signs, wooden figures, and tables covered with sales posters were scattered across the platform. Across the two tracks was another platform that was the old McCrory's Store entrance. The tunnel ran about a mile before ending at a wall, which blocked it at both Washington and Broad streets.

I must admit that during the exploration of the tunnel we were a little spooked, because of how the old platforms were preserved. Entrance is prohibited, and because of this we do not see ourselves going back down there any time soon. –*Dave Crum*

A backyard bomb shelter in Clifton was completely stocked with food and water from 1961, with virtually nothing touched in the last forty years.

Gimme Shelter (Of the Backyard Cold War Kind) by Mark Sceurman

Many of us who were brought up during the cold war period, from 1958 to the early 1960s, remember the school drills for "duck and cover." If you were a student, you were ushered to the ground floor of the school and told to get on your knees and put your coat over your head. You would then wait, intensely listening for the sirens that would signal a nuclear attack was imminent. The NJ school system issued dog tags for every student, and the rumor was that the tags would withstand a nuclear blast, in case your body needed to be identified when the Big One was dropped.

Yellow-and-black fallout shelter signs were posted on larger buildings to let you know that if an attack did take place while you were out and about, you would have safe refuge, at least for the moment.

WHERE WILL YOU GO?

a safety zone shelter is the answer!

Backyard bomb shelters were also being built for the safety of the family, and some still exist throughout the state. *Weird N.J.* was invited to see a backyard bomb shelter in Clifton; it was completely stocked with food and water from 1961, with virtually nothing touched in the last forty years.

Patrick DeLage, whose parents had the bomb shelter built, tells us his story. "One day this salesman came to the door and told my father, 'If you really want to protect your family, you have to buy one of these bomb shelters.' After talking to my mom, they decided that, 'Well, we gotta save the kids!'"

Weird N.J.: **How was the bomb shelter made?**
They brought in a big steam shovel and dug the whole backyard up. They flatbedded in this giant metal tank. It also had a few other big pipes for the shaft, ladder, and the escape hatch.

Weird N.J.: **Do you know of any other bomb shelters in the area?**
None that I know of. But everybody in the neighborhood knows this one's here. When I was younger, I always got to be quarterback in the football games because if I wasn't, well then, the other kids couldn't go into the bomb shelter if we were attacked!

Weird N.J.: **What kind of supplies did your father keep down there?**
There are old boxes of cake mix, soup, sugar, baking powder, etc. But I don't really know how they planned on using or cooking the stuff. He did replenish the supplies once in a while. I think he had a box of cereal that he mixed with chloroform to keep it safe!

Patrick opened the weathered, cone-shaped hatch in the middle of the backyard, and we saw a three-foot-wide cylindrical tube with a metal ladder attached to it. Shining a flashlight into the hole, we saw that it went down at least twenty feet. It was full of cobwebs.

Weird N.J. correspondent Dean Cole was the first to enter. Next went Mark M. and myself, followed by Patrick, his sister Marie Gerhart, and their friend Janet Martin.

Reaching the bottom, we entered a small cement chamber that led into the shelter. The safe room was no more than twelve feet long and about seven feet wide. It was actually not much more than a round metal tank—

and with six people, it was getting more claustrophobic every minute. Since the walls were round, one got the feeling that the room was spinning. Either that or the air was getting thinner.

"Wow, your parents really stocked up on the sugar," Mark M. said, noting the forty to fifty pounds of vintage Sucrest stashed away beneath wooden benches.

"Well, that was for the coffee," Patrick said.

Dean pulled out a can of Tropical Treat fruit drink, a little weathered and rusted, but still sealed.

"Condensation has ruined most of the stock," Patrick said.

We started to pull out boxes of cake mix, peanut butter, and bottles of water and instant coffee purchased at Two Guys. We even found some aspirin.

"I think the aspirin is still good because, you know, there were no expiration dates back in the '60s!" joked Patrick.

The escape hatch was bolted and filled with sand, and there was a hand-cranked air vent that allowed fresh air to be brought in. Patrick explained the theory of the hatch: "In case you're locked in here, you could use the other hatch. The sand (as we all know) prevents radiation from permeating. The sand would fall, then you would pull the ladder down and get out—to what, I don't know!"

There were no comforts of home in this shelter. The commode was nothing more than a wooden box with

lime in it. There was no electricity, stove, refrigerator, or beds. Just the wooden seats to sit on while you waited for the end of the world.

"Can you imagine staying in here for two months? I would go nuts!" I said.

"Well, you'd get to know your family very well," said Dean.

We asked Patrick again what possessed his father to have a bomb shelter in his backyard.

"My father was pressured by my mother. He was scared, like most of us were. At that time, this place wasn't that funny. He just wanted us to feel safe. The shelter cost twenty-five hundred dollars to install. I still have the receipts."

As we exited, the climb back up into the light was a refreshing change, even though we were in the hole for only about twenty minutes. To come out of that shelter after a nuclear attack would be unimaginable.

The DeLage family home was recently sold to a new owner, bomb shelter and all. It may have turned out to be an added selling point in these uncertain times we are living in—again.

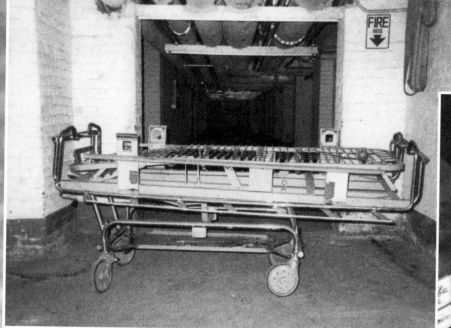

Remains to Be Seen

The eight or nine buildings that make up the Jersey City Medical Center were constructed during the 1930s. Only some of the buildings are in use now, the rest have been left to rot. However, there are tunnels underground, at least two different levels of them connecting all of the old buildings. I work there and over the years have explored several of them. They are very eerie.

One of the buildings had an enormous amphitheater in it (near the morgue). In the 40s and 50s, medical students would gather there to view experimental medical procedures. There is supposedly a room off of this amphitheater where there are still jars filled with formaldehyde that contain bizarre fetal remains such as those having two heads, three eyes, etc. and various organs that are grossly deformed.

Some of the occupied buildings have vacant upper floors. You can see the remains of the old operating rooms and ancient medical equipment. Windows are broken out, and pigeons fly in and out. Paint peels from the walls and old pipes leak water onto the floor.

Please don't use my name, because I still work there and I don't know if I should be talking about this stuff.–*Anonymous*

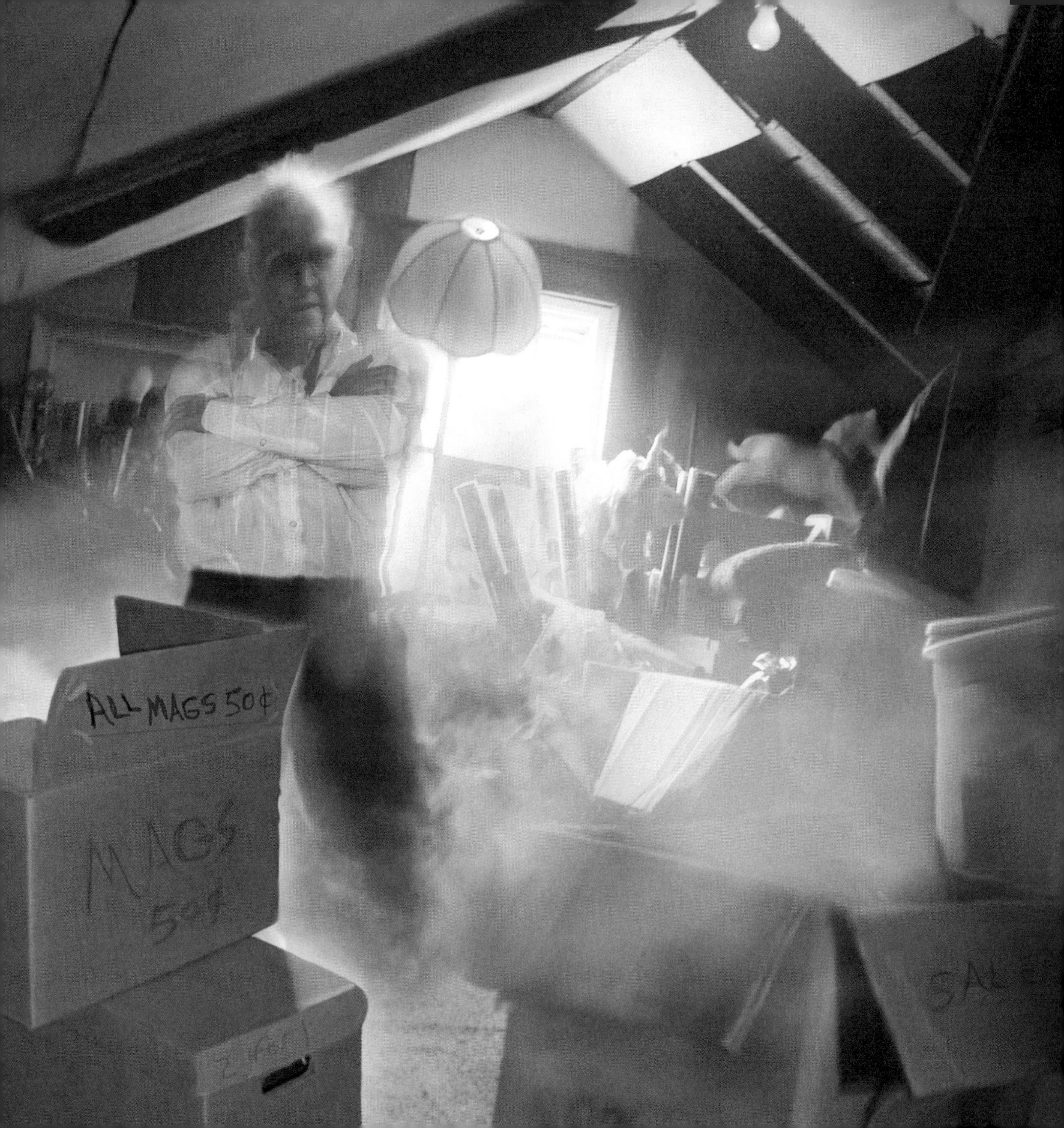
ALL MAGS 50¢
MAGS 50¢

Ghosts of the Garden State

The notion that the souls of the dead are all around us as we live our daily lives is a weird one indeed. And the thought that they inhabit our homes, schools, libraries, and theaters can be unnerving, to say the least.

At a very young age, we begin to fear certain things, such as spiders, snakes, and ghosts. We do not need to be taught to be afraid of them, we just are. They terrify us when we are awake and haunt us in our dreams when we sleep. Spiders and snakes, the poisonous ones, can kill us, so an inherent fear of them is a valuable caution to possess. But what about ghosts—why are we so afraid of them from such an early age?

As we get older, we are taught that ghosts can't harm us, because they aren't real. Outwardly we accept this as fact. Deep inside, though, most of us will secretly harbor a shadow of doubt on the subject for the rest of our lives.

There seem to be just too many convincing stories of people's encounters with ghosts for them NOT to exist, and these stories are told by people living all over this world. New Jersey is no exception. We have a long and rich history of paranormal activity, spirited spooks, and things that go bump in the night. At *Weird N.J.*, we are fortunate to hear these stories firsthand from the people who experienced them—regular citizens of the Garden State—our neighbors, friends, family, and co-workers. Are their harrowing accounts of ghostly encounters true or just fabrications of overactive imaginations?

You be the judge.

Tales from the Abandoned Orphanage

The Elizabeth Orphan Asylum was started in 1858 at the corner of Murray and Cherry streets. In 1911, Mrs. John Steward Kennedy of New York City gave the orphanage money for a new building to be built in memory of her mother, Janet Eyck Edgar. The new orphanage was given the name The Janet Memorial Home and was located between Salem and Westminster avenues. The orphanage was closed in 1962 and sat abandoned until the building was razed in 1996. But in the years prior to its demolition, the creepy old house was the site of many a hair-raising adventure, as the following stories will attest.

"Welcome to Hell"

The Janet Memorial Orphanage was the ultimate late-night thrill in our area, our local haunted house. Picture about an acre or two of land surrounded by a high fence, with a large, threatening-looking three-story building in the middle. An old abandoned schoolhouse stood next to it, which was the governor's mansion near the turn of the last century.

The Orphanage was located near Kean College, and its history has some odd quirks about it. First of all, some time in the 1970s a small private airplane crashed on the property. Then the top floor was partially destroyed by a fire a few years afterwards. This caused the building to be condemned, and that's when the weirdness began.

People ignored the NO TRESPASSING signs posted after the condemnation, and went inside the building. Stories began to circulate about mysterious sub-basements used for Satanic rituals (you were supposed to find rows of coffins down there, and if you opened one, your doppelganger would be inside). There were accounts of balls of light following people around corridors, as well as of mysterious noises, and angels on the property. Stories spread that the building's fire was started either by Satanic nuns, a psychotic pedophile janitor, assorted demons, or all of the above.

I went inside around 1990. I remember that the back gate was practically lying on the ground from so many people constantly jumping it. As we entered through the back, there was a rusty, skeletal-like chandelier. To the left was a room with a fireplace, and on the wall above the fireplace, someone had spray painted "Welcome to Hell." To the right was a big open room, perhaps a solarium. Straight ahead was a staircase. All of the walls were covered with graffiti and were cracking apart. The whole place gave you a feeling of true and unbridled dread.

I was saddened to hear that the building was demolished a couple of years back, after I'd moved out west. However, the schoolhouse supposedly still sits where it always has.–*Al Eufrasio*

Green Eyes and Bloody Walls

I lived in Elizabeth for 19 years and know all about the Orphanage. We all talked about exploring it but the farthest we ever got was the front gate. We would spook ourselves out. My mom brought us there when I was 16 on Halloween. We all got out of the car and walked up to the building. My friends and I heard faint crying and my mom noticed two greenish glows in two upstairs windows. Kind of like eyes—very creepy!

What we have heard is that when they closed the Orphanage down, they locked a girl inside and she was trying to get out for a while. The "Welcome to Hell" sign was scrawled in her blood, not spray paint.–*Donna Casteloe*

Phantom Figure and Flies

I went with my brother and a friend to the Elizabeth Orphanage during midday to test our mettle. My brother was scared (not because of the paranormal, but because he thought the police would get us), but he was determined to enter the orphanage this day. We had read newspaper clippings about how the orphanage used to house mentally challenged girls before it burned down. I don't know if anybody was hurt, but by the looks of the place, it housed tormented spirits. It was scary and I felt I would probably see something, because when you are scared your imagination plays tricks on you.

I went inside through the back entrance, which led into a big square room. The room was adjacent to another big room, which was joined at the right by a wide doorway with no door. As soon as I looked to the right, about 30 feet away I saw a body lying on the floor with a bloody blanket over the torso, but the legs were visible. I was so scared—I ran towards the body in an attempt to dispel this illusion. Thank God it was an illusion. It was some wooden beams with plastic bags over them moving gently in the breeze. The bloodstains were actually supermarket logos on the bags.

I was still pretty scared and my brother and our friend were not acting very brave, so I suggested that we leave. But first we peered into a doorway that led to the infamous basement. When we did this, we were engulfed by flies! There were flies everywhere! It was nasty.–*Marcos Granado*

Ghostly Maids Still Tidying Up

I was over at my cousin's, who lived around the corner from the old Elizabeth Orphanage. It was summer, and we decided to go for a walk to see the orphanage. Someone had cut a hole in the fence, so we went through. We looked up and noticed there were white sheets swaying from the windows. They appeared to have blood on them. We thought maybe some kids were just having fun with some paint and sheets. Then we saw a person walking out of the orphanage. We thought it was a bum or something. Then we realized it was a woman dressed in a maid's outfit, with a feather duster going around the property dusting and picking things up from the grounds. Then we saw two more maids upstairs, dusting around the windows that had the sheets on them. They weren't young looking either, so we started to get nervous and ran out the hole in the fence. When we glanced back we saw that the maids (or whatever they were) were gone.–*Javier C.*

Ghostly Grounds of Ringwood Manor

Ringwood Manor in Ringwood is a fairly infamous place around here. Edgar Cayce, the world-renowned psychic, held a séance in the house in the 1960s. I've been told of a blue light seen around the gravesite of Revolutionary War General Robert Erskine, which is on the property. I've also heard tales from the cleaning-maintenance staff about ghosts within the house, but this story happened outside.

I was about 21, and it was a warm summer day in 1991. My friends Maria, Tanya, and I had spent the afternoon walking around the park. We'd toured the landmark house and walked the grounds countless times over the years. We had heard many ghost stories involving both the house and its small cemetery.

On the grounds is a wooden gazebo, which sits on top of a series of wide, grassy "steps" framed in concrete that used to contain part of the gardens. After a full day of walking, we decided to have a seat in the gazebo. The sun was just beginning to set, and the park was quiet, except for the sound of a light breeze and some distant crickets. We sat and relaxed, chatting quietly and resting our tired feet. The sun sank lower on the horizon, until the color seemed to melt from the surrounding landscape, draping everything in varying shades of gray and black. We were discussing where to go for dinner when misty translucent forms began to appear before our eyes. There were many of them, and they seemed to be floating up to the gazebo from the lower grassy step as we sat and watched. Most were indistinct in shape, but several were in the general form of human beings. We all fell silent with slackened jaws.

As the figures came closer, we heard the whispering of words like, "Hello," and "Who are you?" We were now on edge and wildly looking around the gazebo for a logical explanation. We saw that there was no one left in the park, and the main parking lot was now completely empty.

I got up and said to Tanya and Maria, "I think maybe it's time to go!" They agreed, and we took off like shots. I had parked the car about a mile away from the house in the Greenfields parking lot, next door to the park. Unfortunately, we had to go through the cemetery to get to the car. We weren't thrilled, and kept up a very brisk pace as we walked the dirt and stone road.

Once we came to the cemetery, Tanya made the mistake of looking behind her to see if we had left the "ghosts" behind. When she suddenly gasped, Maria and I also looked back. One of the pale, misty figures was about 30 feet behind us, looking out at us from behind a tree. The form was that of a man with a Revolutionary War soldier's hat on. We began to run. It was now nearly pitch black and when we finally reached the park gate we looked back once more. The figure was still on the park property, and had not followed us past the gate. Then it simply disappeared.

When the three of us discussed what we had seen a few years later, we all agreed that it wasn't the misty figures, or the whispers, or the apparition of the soldier that we were really frightened of—it was fear from being in the middle of an experience that was unfamiliar, unknown, and inexplicable. We had not felt threatened by the figures themselves at all. I've been back to the park many times since that night, but have not seen or heard anything else.
—Leslie

Ghost of the Westfield Estate Sale

I'm from Scotch Plains and until a few years ago, I was a garage sale fanatic. One day I went to a narrow three-story house near downtown Westfield. When I entered the house the two old ladies that were running the sale were stationed near the front door. I peeked in the rooms on the first floor, and there appeared to be nothing. I climbed to the second floor, which was roped off. I then followed a sign that said TO ATTIC.

BINGO! There were old magazines, newspapers, and old junk in general—just my kind of stuff! I began to dig through the boxes, having a grand old time. Suddenly I felt as if someone was watching me. I turned around and there was this tall, old white-haired man standing with his arms folded, just staring at me.

He didn't say a word; he just stared. I wondered what his problem was and continued to dig. I then thought maybe he needed to get to a box and I was in the way. I turned around again, and no one was there. I finished looking through the boxes and headed downstairs. The steps were extremely creaky and it occurred to me that I never heard anyone coming up or going back down while I was in the attic.

When I went to the table to pay for my items I asked the ladies if the man had left yet. "What man?" they replied. I began to shake. The ladies assured me no one had come since my arrival. I can only assume that it was a ghostly visitor I saw in the attic. I must have been going through his personal items and he wasn't too pleased about it. I haven't gone to a house sale alone since.—*Gail Davis*

Little Girl Lost in the Graveyard

Late one evening in 1979, I was in a graveyard off of New Jersey Avenue in Absecon with my girlfriend when we saw a young girl about 10–12 years old. We had been sitting under a tree for about an hour and were getting ready to leave when she appeared. She was wearing a nightshirt or t-shirt and pants.

She started walking towards us slowly, saying, "Mommy, Mommy, Mommy." The whole time she was looking right into my girlfriend's eyes. She came to about three feet from us and said, "You're not my Mommy."

We were both startled, and in a split second I looked at my girlfriend and she looked at me. We then looked back at the little girl and she was gone! She had vanished in the blink of an eye. It was a bright night, and I could see in every direction. This girl had just vanished.

I've been back to the graveyard a few times to see if I could find the grave of a girl who died young, but have not been able to find anything.—*Joe Sciullo*

Little Girl in the Bathroom

In June of 1998, my wife and I purchased a cozy 3-bedroom ranch house in Bricktown. On our third night in the house my wife swore she saw a little girl in the hallway just outside the bathroom door. This girl was just standing there and never made a sound. Two days later an interior decorator stopped by to help us turn this house into a home. After five minutes of small talk, she asked how old our daughter was. I told her we didn't have any children yet, and her jaw dropped. She explained that she had seen a little girl standing in the hallway when she entered our house.

And strangely, our cat would sit facing the bathroom door making a very weird meow.

In October of 2002, on Halloween in fact, we had a baby girl. Once we brought our baby home, the sightings of the little ghost girl stopped, but our daughter loves playing in and by the bathroom. We discovered last month that the previous owners had a four-year-old daughter who slipped in the tub and sustained fatal injuries. That was the reason the owners had sold the house, but they never mentioned it to us. We've been in here five years now and are quite comfortable knowing that our daughter has a "sister" to watch over her. *–Daddy (of Two?)*

Van Wickle House Houses a Ghost

The Van Wickle House is located on Easton Ave. in Franklin Township. Built in 1722, this colonial building was saved from developers in 1976 and is now used as a community center. But in 1938, while a photographer named Nathaniel R. Ewan was documenting the house for the Historic American Buildings Survey, this image of a young child was captured at the left of the photo. Many believe it is the ghost of a Van Wickle descendant. This picture is from the Library of Congress.
–Thanks to Ann Smith,
Head of Adult Services,
Franklin Township Library

Old School Ghouls—Big Ghosts on Campus

Of all the places in New Jersey that are reported to be haunted, none are more rife with tales of ghostly infestations than our state's colleges and universities. Perhaps these campuses are no more haunted than any other locations in the state, but the general age of the student body gives them a heightened awareness of paranormal activity.

Poltergeist (noisy ghost) activity has long been associated with adolescence. Some investigators believe that teens themselves bring about these paranormal occurrences. According to the International Cultic Studies Association (ICSA), "In essentially every case in which poltergeist phenomena have been investigated . . . there have been one or more adolescents in the family. Further, the pattern is that the adolescent is frequently highly restricted and repressed. Inexperienced investigators . . . have often concluded that poltergeist phenomena are therefore not due to ghosts at all, but are the result of the frustrated adolescent channeling blocked energies into psychokineses! That is, that the adolescent creates the poltergeist phenomena by mind power, sometimes without being aware of it. More experienced investigators have simply laid a trap for the adolescent, and usually have managed to catch him or her using not the unknown powers of mind, but the well-known powers of fingers, arms or feet to achieve the 'psychic' manifestations."

Others have theorized that the ghost stories told by young adults are all part of a complex psychological development stage they undergo. According to an article published in the *Journal of American Folklore*, "Through a modified Jungian analysis of their legends, it is possible to identify patterns of self-discovery in later adolescence that are under-discussed in their literature. By telling legends about gender transformations, ghostly lovers, suicide, and violent death, college students undergo a quasi-initiatory experience that facilitates their development of a more complex sense of self."

Well, we don't know about all of that scholarly stuff, but we are well schooled when it comes to knowing a good scary story when we hear one. And there may be none more chilling than those told in the haunted halls of New Jersey's institutions of higher learning.

Kean University

Kean University

Founded in Newark in 1855, Kean College moved to Union in 1958 and became Kean University in 1997. Kean's Wilkins Theatre is rumored to be home to the ghost of a stagehand, George.

Ghosts Abound

I attended Kean University and worked at Wilkins Theatre. This building is haunted by at least two ghosts. The first one is well known for its pranks. Late at night, when the theater is dark, except for a single light called, of all things, a ghost light, and four small theater lights on a cat-walk, the ghost will walk across that cat-walk, causing the lights to shake. It has also been known to cause strange sounds from the pit and prop closets below the stage.

The second ghost, a more peaceful spirit, is of an older woman who has blonde hair and wears a blue dress. I only saw her during productions of classic plays and she would always remain in the wings, against the walls as if she knew where to stand to stay out of the way.–*Laura*

Wishing George Goodnight at Kean

There is a ghost by the name of George that haunts the Wilkins Theatre. The story goes that George was an old electrician in the theater and one night he died there. Legend has it that whoever is the last to leave the theater must say goodnight to George or the next performance will go badly.

Two years ago my best friend was performing in the campus production of "West Side Story." The night before, the last people to leave forgot to say goodnight to George, and during the performance that night there were problems. People missed cues, others fell backstage, and the "dead bodies" of Bernardo and Rif inexplicably left the stage. From that day on, all the theater people remembered to say goodnight to George.–*Lori-Ann Sciachitano*

Kean U. Ghosts Don't Like Being Disturbed

There is a small white house on the university grounds called the Townley House. It belonged to the Townley family who farmed the land before the school came to be. There have been many reports of people having supernatural experiences there. For example, about five years ago, a construction worker went inside the house to use the facilities. While he was in the bathroom, he felt a chill rush through him; then all of a sudden, the shower curtain started to open and close, and he heard a deep voice tell him to "Get out!" Needless to say, he ran out of the house screaming.

Apparently there are more encounters like this involving construction workers. However, the campus EMS squad that is headquartered in the building has never had any problems with the ghosts. I am a member, and I have heard footsteps when I was alone in the building, but I have never been scared out of the place. This is probably because I'm not doing any construction.–*Mike S.*

New Jersey City University

This urban campus opened in 1929 as the New Jersey State Normal School at Jersey City. In 1958, it changed its name to Jersey City State College, and ten years later it became a liberal arts institution. It was given its current name, New Jersey City University, in 1998.

The campus has a lovely tower at its center— but don't go there at night! (Or, if you prefer, only go there at night!) The ghost of Margaret Williams, namesake of the university's theater, is said to haunt it.

Ghosts of Jersey City College

I am a former student of Jersey City State College, and experienced ghosts there first hand. There are a few haunted areas, some located in the Irwin Library, others in the theater and the Science Building.

The elevator in the Science Building was definitely haunted. The hair on the back of my neck stood up every time I entered it. For one thing, the doors always opened on the second floor even if no one was there. The story goes that the electrician who hooked up the electricity to that particular elevator was electrocuted on the job. That elevator hasn't worked properly since.

Another haunted building on campus is Vodra Hall. I was a Resident Advisor for the fifth floor one year. I had to move into my dorm room early to undergo training for the coming fall semester. I was the only one up there. I went through all the rooms to make sure everything was in order and went back to my room at the end of the hall. I had just sat down when I heard laughing coming from the other end of the hall, near the elevator. I thought that was strange, since no students were supposed to move in for another week. I walked down the hallway, and the laughter stopped. I re-checked every room, even opening closets. No one. No sooner did I get back to my room when I heard the laughing again, and doors closing.

I ignored it, and soon the sound of a radio joined the laughing. A loud crash finally jolted me and I ran down the hall. There was no one in any of the rooms, and everything was just as I had left it. After that, I spent as much time out of my room as possible, and left my radio playing all night.

The Tower of the Margaret Williams Theatre is another haunted place. One night a friend and I walked to the tower. It was a full moon, and I thought it would make a neat picture if I could line the shot up right with the tower. The doors to the theater building were open, but there was no production that night. Curious, we went inside. My friend said that a classroom right next to the theater was supposed to be haunted. We walked in, our footsteps echoing around us, and goose bumps all over our arms.

The air felt electric. I remember trying to laugh off the creepy feeling I had. Then, all of a sudden, we heard music. We walked back to the doorway and the music was louder. It sounded like a chorus and we assumed there must be practice going on, so we peeked through the theater-door windows. The theater was dark, and no one was there.

The song was unlike any I have ever heard, and the music was like the singing of angels. It was so beautiful that it almost brought tears to my eyes. We never found the source of the sound; honestly, I didn't want to. It was too incredible, too otherworldly.—*Suzi, The Smiling Goth*

Ghostly Theatrics at Jersey City University

I am a theater major at New Jersey City University. I know about the ghost of Margaret Williams, who resides in the theater named for her. One of the directors told me that one day he went into the theater to get ready for rehearsal. The vacuum was in the corner. All of a sudden, it turned on and rolled down the side aisle. It wasn't even plugged in!

The college staged a production of *Gypsy* a few years ago. One of the leads told me she was at rehearsal and was singing her solo when the spotlight turned on and faded, right on her. The spots are worked from the balcony and no one was up there.

Another student said she was doing a show, and some people were in the dressing rooms. The rooms are equipped with speakers that transmit what is happening on stage. They were chatting and half listening when they all got quiet, listening to the fantastic performance on stage. Then they realized that the number was not in the show they were doing that evening.

I think I have seen the ghost wandering through Fries, the building connected to the theater. It was in a window, glaring at me and my friend, and then disappeared.—*DR*

Georgian Court University

The campus of Georgian Court University in Lakewood, a Catholic institution with a focus on women's education, is the former estate of George Jay Gould, son of railroad baron Jay Gould. In 1896, Gould hired architect Bruce Prince to design his estate as a second home. Gould, with his wife Edith Kingdon and their six children, enjoyed the mansion they called Georgian Court (after its Georgian-period architectural style) for many years. After Gould's death, his relatives sold the property to the Sisters of Mercy, who had founded Georgian Court University in 1908.

The estate remains much as it did when it was in the care of the Goulds. It has a casino building, a bowling alley, tennis and squash courts, a swimming pool, and a ballroom, and is surrounded by 152 acres of planned landscape and lush gardens.

Rumors suggest that underground tunnels connect Georgian Court's various buildings and were used by Gould to help him engage in secret extramarital affairs. True? Maybe. Perhaps in 1921, when Edith Kingdon Gould died on the estate's golf course, she had happened upon a tunnel entrance and couldn't recover from the shock.

Ghosts Come Out for a Tree Lighting

I am a longtime participant of a youth organization that holds a weeklong camp at Georgian Court College each year. I'm the DJ and A/V guy, and I am constantly moving the equipment around the campus, sometimes late at night. You always get that chilly feeling running down your back there, even when inside the buildings.

While a professional DJ was hosting a dance for the camp, one of my friends told me that about ten of the participants wanted to go over to a haunted tree where a woman died in the early 1900s. I was hesitant, but agreed to go. We touched the bark of the tree and scraped at the ground, but nothing happened.

Earlier that night we had held a ceremony for the kids in the field where this tree is located, but we forgot to blow out the candles that were in the field. We went

over to the candles to see if anything had happened. All of a sudden we heard a woman's muffled scream in the woods. The freaky thing is that I heard the same scream every year I was there, but just thought it was a cat or something. We all gasped, and then we started to see small balls of lights in the woods: blue, red, yellow, green, and pure white. We ruled out fireflies because they stay relatively close to the ground and are a lime green–yellow color. These were of many colors and reached up to the tops of the trees.

By this time, other people had come over to see what we were doing in the field, and they saw the orbs too. We were all mesmerized. Some adventurous people walked down to the edge of the woods. As they got closer, I noticed that the orbs intensified in the general vicinity (we are talking about 30 to 50 lights in a minute's time). Then they would calm down, but if the same person went close again, there would be no orbs, almost like the orbs "knew" that person already. All of this went on for about an hour.
—Ted

Legendary Infidelities at Georgian Court

Jay Gould was one of the robber barons of the 1920s. He owned the estate that is now Georgian Court University. His wife Edith had a rose garden, which was her prize possession. She would spend lots of time tending it because her husband was always off on "business"—with other women. When the school was built, they ripped

down her precious rose garden to make St. Joseph's Residence Hall. It is said sometimes you can smell roses in the dorm and some say they

see strange footprints. On very quiet nights, especially on the third floor, you can hear things go bump in the night.

There are other strange legends that live on campus. One tells us why there are so many flower urns all over the campus. Supposedly every time Edith caught her husband with another mistress, he gave her an urn. I counted over a hundred on campus, and I'm sure there are more.

Another story is that there are catacombs and tunnels underneath most of the campus, built so that Mr. Gould could sneak his mistresses around undetected by the Mrs. It's said that one leads to the Casino building (which is now the gym), another to the Mansion on campus, and other various places. Currently all the

passages are sealed off. Georgian Court University offers a great education and some good ghost stories to scare the freshmen.—jing0k

Drew University

The university, which sits on two hundred acres in Madison, was founded as a Methodist seminary in 1867 and is now an independent university.

The most historic building on campus is Mead Hall, which was built in 1837 but purchased by founder Daniel Drew in 1867. He renamed the building for his wife, Roxanna Mead, who subsequently became the university's most oft-sighted ghost. Was Roxanna responsible for a twenty-three-hour fire leading to the near destruction of Mead Hall in 1989? One can only guess, but no doubt she is pleased with her updated digs, since Mead Hall underwent a $13 million renovation and reopened in 1993. Perhaps that was her plan all along!

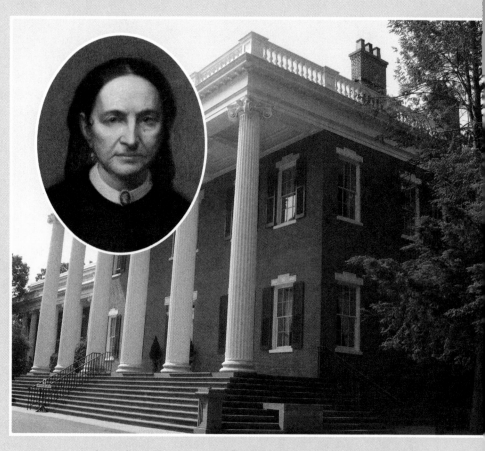

Ghostly Guardian of Drew's Girls

I am an undergrad at Drew University, which some folks claim is the third most haunted campus in America. I have heard plenty of stories, many from folks with whom I'd entrust my life.

My roommate's friend attended Drew several years ago. Late one night he was walking back to the Hoyt dorm with two friends, and as they crossed the front lawn, something appeared before them (they were sober, and even if they weren't, they wouldn't have all seen the exact same thing). Later, they agreed it was a pale man dressed in an 18th century soldier's uniform. He glared at them for a moment and then disappeared. Needless to say, the guys tore out of there, but a bad feeling followed them. This could have happened because it's rumored that when Hoyt was built, they had to move a cemetery.

Another story about Hoyt is that there is said to be a resident ghost on the fourth floor. One version claims she was assaulted and her body was tossed out of a fourth floor window. The other alleges that after her boyfriend broke her heart, the girl hung herself in her room (Room #412 or #403, depending on the storyteller) or in the attic (which might explain why the attic is kept locked all the time). The floor is now an all-girls floor and the women consider the ghost to be a protector. She hates men and causes disturbances, keeping guys from going up there after dark.

The drama students claim the Kirby Theatre on campus is haunted by "Reggie," who died several decades ago and is usually seen in jogging shorts or running pants. One night, two guys working late were locking up the place and, half-jokingly, wished Reggie a goodnight. In response, the lights inside flickered on and off (there was no one in the building this late).

I knew Mead Hall was haunted upon my first visit here. Just try walking past the paintings on the first floor, and you'll feel like you're being followed. People have claimed to see a woman wandering the halls, possibly Miss Mead herself.

Drew is an awesome place, and apparently some folks have decided to stay even after death.—*Cat*

Heavy Breathing in Drew's Chapel

I went to Drew University Theological School and spent many years working in Seminary Hall. I never heard any mention of a ghost there, but I did have one strange experience. As a seminary student I visited the chapel regularly, but usually in the evening when things were quiet and there was no one around. On this particular evening while saying my prayers, I heard something that sounded like breathing. At first I thought the radiator had sprung a leak. I got up and checked around, but could find nothing. It stopped briefly and then started again. Then I realized it was someone or something breathing, very heavily. I also felt a presence as if someone was watching me. I ran out of there. I never had that experience again in the chapel, but I did have another similar one.

Asbury Hall is the apartment complex/dormitory for seminary students. There is the story that a seminary student hung himself in the attic and his ghost still haunts the building. When I heard this story, I, of course, immediately went into the attic, but I didn't find, or feel, anything unusual. Some time later, I got up in the middle of the night and stopped at the water fountain on the second floor. At the foot of the stairs I saw a mist forming. I just stood there and watched it. I was definitely frightened.

I had that same experience years later. Again, the middle of the night, the foot of the stairs, but this time it was different. I felt a presence (for lack of a better word), but I was not frightened this time. I just stood there and then went back to what I was doing. I never experienced anything after that.

—Sandy Barker

William Paterson University (Hobart Manor)

Founded as the Paterson City Normal School in 1855, William Paterson University in Wayne is now a liberal arts institution. The university is situated on land once called Ailsa Farms, which was owned by the family of Garret Hobart, twenty-fourth Vice President of the United States, under President William McKinley. Hobart's wife, Paterson resident Jennie Tuttle Hobart, purchased the land and its mansion in 1902 after Hobart died. Her son later expanded Hobart Manor, and in 1948 his widow sold it to the state of New Jersey. It later became part of the university. Today the refurbished Hobart Manor houses the offices of the president, institutional advancement, development, and alumni relations.

However, the fact that it's home to a variety of offices doesn't keep the ghosts away. Among those spotted at Hobart Manor: Mary, a servant or maid; various Hobart family members; and even an aged Jennie Tuttle Hobart herself. Apparently, the administration doesn't dismiss the rumors offhand: ghost hunters Ed and Lorraine Warren were brought in by the campus activities office to survey the building in 1991, and they confirmed the presence of spirits—adding that building renovations such as those Hobart Manor has undergone tend to arouse long-sleeping specters.

Jennie Tuttle Hobart

Rowan University

Originally the Glassboro Normal School when it opened in 1923 and later Glassboro State College, Rowan College was so named in 1992 when industrialist Henry Rowan donated $100 million to the institution—then the largest gift ever given to a public college or university. In 1997, the college became Rowan University.

Rowan's most notorious ghost is that of Elizabeth Tohill, perhaps due to the "drama" she stirs up during theater rehearsals and performances in Bunce Hall. Tohill was a drama professor from 1930 to 1956, and Tohill Auditorium was named in her honor. Apparently, she's stuck around to ensure that the productions there meet her high expectations. She has been said to appear around—and even on—the stage in the auditorium.

Running from the Unknown at Rowan

My personal experiences in the otherworldly occurred at Rowan University. In winter, I would cut through Bunce Hall to and from an evening class. Bunce is among the oldest buildings on campus and boasts several ghost stories. My own story raises the hairs on my arms to this day eleven years later.

I was cutting through the building after class late in the evening. The building has two floors, laid out in very long hallways. I entered the outer doors and had just passed through the fire doors, which normally close slowly and quietly. I was about ten steps into the long hallway when the fire door slammed—once loudly and then again. I looked behind me and saw the windows start to fog up. I sensed a strong presence at the doors and I could feel the temperature plummet.

I turned to start walking again, figuring the wind had whipped up and the heat had shut off on a timer or something. Then the footsteps started, coming toward me. I looked both ways. I was the only one in the hall. I turned and did the only thing that made sense: I started jogging. The foot falls behind me picked up the pace. It felt as if someone was a few feet behind me, bearing down on me, and they wanted to do me harm.

As I got closer to the end of the hall, three things continued to increase: the sound of the feet behind me, the depth of the cold, and my sense of oppression. I looked back over my shoulder several times during my run. The air was getting thicker and harder to breathe too. I could see my breath by the time I reached out to slam a palm against the far fire doors. The foot falls of my spectral pursuer seemed almost on top of me as I slammed into the far fire door full steam and vaulted the stairs down to the exit door. I burst through the doors like a freight train and just stopped myself from falling face first onto the sidewalk.

I turned around and found the door stuck in the open position. I guess I hit it hard enough to push it to the sticking point. Imagine my horror when the door suddenly slammed faster than anyone human could have closed it. I stared at the window as it fogged up and then iced over. I got the feeling that the presence that chased me was contained behind the door and seething that I was not with it.

I braved the cold from then on, but the experience has stayed with me to this day. I shared the story with several other students and former students and many of them have also spoken of creepy things happening in Rowan's old buildings.
—*greatwazoo42*

The College of New Jersey

Perhaps setting a name-change record, the College of New Jersey began as the New Jersey State Normal School in 1855 and has had five subsequent names, including a long tenure as Trenton State College from 1958 to 1996, when the name changed to the College of New Jersey. The college was originally located on Clinton Street in Trenton, but moved to a large campus in Ewing in 1928.

Those who came of age in the Trenton State era are loath to let go of that moniker, which explains why you'll still hear the college referred to as such. So nowadays this New Jersey institution essentially has two names—and at least as many ghosts.

Murdered Music Major Haunts Trenton State

This is a ghost story that my grandmother and uncle have both told me on different occasions. They are both graduates of Trenton State College (I am the first in the family to get kicked out, but that's another story).

One night in the late 1930s, a music major at TSC was practicing for a recital in the basement of the music building when she was murdered. My grandmother was a freshman at the time, and she said it shook up the campus quite a bit.

The following year, stories started circulating that a piano was heard playing from time to time in the basement of the music building late at night, when no one was there. I dismissed this story at first because my grandmother also told me stories about hypnotizing chickens. Then some years later, my uncle (a TSC student in the '50s) told me a similar story. He was not the kind of man to tell tall tales.

During my year there I witnessed some strange stuff. The story of the haunted music building lived on, and if you wanted a coed in your arms late at night you would go for a romantic moonlight stroll and just happen to remember the story as you neared the building. As I write this I remember the faint sound of music in the air (scared the bejeezus out of me and my date) late one night!—*Michael J. Chaplin*

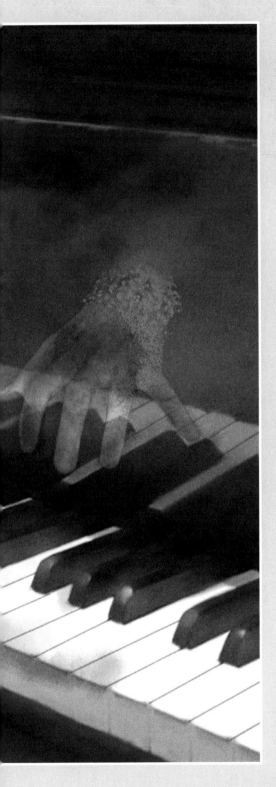

Holman Hall Is Also Haunted

I am a graphic design major at The College of New Jersey, and I spend a lot of time in the arts and sciences building known as Holman Hall. Late one night during my freshman year, my habit of working late turned into a story that I will not soon forget. It was around 11:00 PM when I entered the building to work on a painting. I walked up the main flight of stairs, and for some strange reason I exited on the 3rd floor (the painting room is on the 4th floor). The 3rd floor, which is usually packed with computer graphics students at night, was empty, and I found myself completely alone within Holman Hall. I didn't think much of it, and made my way to the 4th floor. I began painting in the back corner of the room, facing the door.

Almost immediately, I heard footsteps and the murmur of voices outside the door. The footsteps and whispers continued until I heard an extremely loud bang followed by the sound of scuffling feet, right outside the door of the room where I was working. Curious, I went to find out what had happened and see if someone needed help, but there was no one there. Not too concerned, I returned to painting. After another ten minutes, the footsteps and voices continued and once again, a bang startled me beyond belief. Beginning to get freaked out, I made my way to the hallway and began a search of every room, trying to locate the source of these noises. For safety, I had a box-cutter in my hand at this point, but I found nothing.

I had a lot of work to get done, so I returned, reluctantly, to my project. The same noises continued another one or two times and I promised myself that I would leave if I heard them again. What happened next is somewhat hard to explain. The noises that were originally scaring me were now replaced with what seemed to be the sound of splashing water, as if someone was taking buckets of water and splashing them directly in front of me. Needless to say, these bizarre noises freaked me out and I ran out of the building.

The next day I began to tell people my strange story. Everyone seemed to believe me, which was a good thing, but one person I told the story to shed an entirely new light on my story. She told me about a project she had done on the history of the college the semester before.

According to her, a book in our library documented the location of Native American graves directly underneath Holman Hall. This new information made me rethink what had happened the previous night. I began to do a little research and found that there are three Native American graves located on the ground where Holman Hall was built. During the laying of the foundation in 1973, excavators destroyed the graves, without removing or commemorating them in any way.

I think this is the key to my supernatural experience in the painting studio. The building has four floors, all immediately above one another, with the exception of the painting studio, which creates an overhang on the southern end of the building. This is exactly where the graves are located.

You can make the conclusions for yourself, but I think it's the only explanation. –Ed

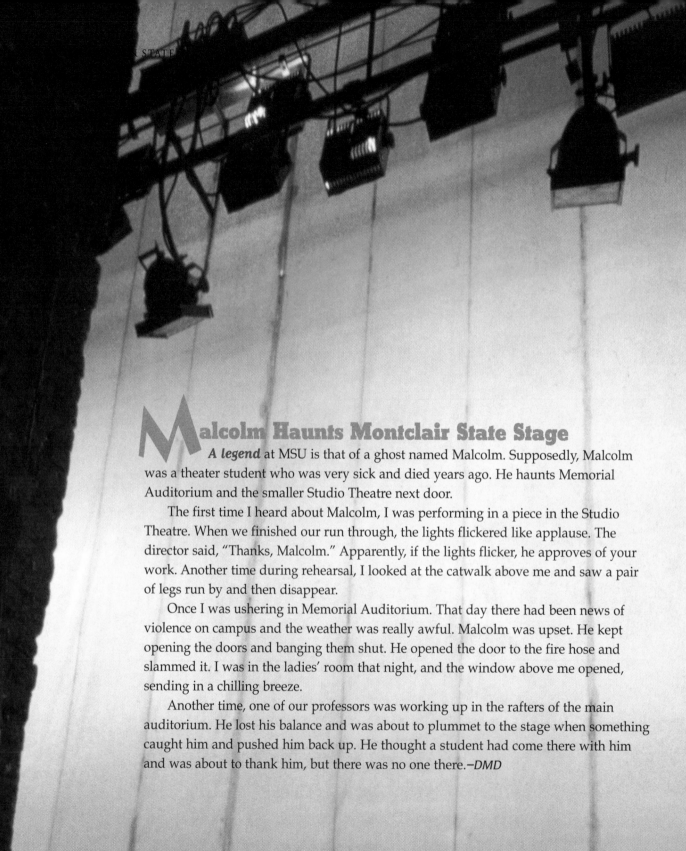

Malcolm Haunts Montclair State Stage

A legend at MSU is that of a ghost named Malcolm. Supposedly, Malcolm was a theater student who was very sick and died years ago. He haunts Memorial Auditorium and the smaller Studio Theatre next door.

The first time I heard about Malcolm, I was performing in a piece in the Studio Theatre. When we finished our run through, the lights flickered like applause. The director said, "Thanks, Malcolm." Apparently, if the lights flicker, he approves of your work. Another time during rehearsal, I looked at the catwalk above me and saw a pair of legs run by and then disappear.

Once I was ushering in Memorial Auditorium. That day there had been news of violence on campus and the weather was really awful. Malcolm was upset. He kept opening the doors and banging them shut. He opened the door to the fire hose and slammed it. I was in the ladies' room that night, and the window above me opened, sending in a chilling breeze.

Another time, one of our professors was working up in the rafters of the main auditorium. He lost his balance and was about to plummet to the stage when something caught him and pushed him back up. He thought a student had come there with him and was about to thank him, but there was no one there.–*DMD*

Centenary College

The college was founded by the Methodist Episcopal Church in 1867 as a preparatory school and women's college. It underwent several incarnations before becoming a four-year coeducational institution in 1988.

In 1886, when the school was still known as Centenary Collegiate Institute, an eighteen-year-old kitchen maid named Tillie Smith was found murdered in a field behind the school. Apparently, on the day of her death, Tillie, who boarded at the school, had asked janitor James Titus if he would let her into the building after the ten p.m. curfew, as she had plans to stay out late attending a local theater performance. But instead of letting her in upon her return, he attempted to sexually assault her and strangled her to death in the process. He was convicted of the crime and served seventeen years in prison.

A Fleeting Glimpse of Tillie

I went to Centenary College in Hackettstown and many people had Tillie encounters there. Tillie appears in a Sigma sorority picture taken a couple years after her murder, but the sorority keeps this under lock-and-key. She occasionally pulls pranks, opening doors, moving things, turning on stereos. I've witnessed stereos and CD players turn on by themselves. Some people have seen strange activities in the chapel on the third floor of the Seay building.

My own encounter with Tillie happened when my friend Eric and I were working in South Dorm one day as part of our work-study, patching holes in the walls and painting. The dorm was not in use at the time because of electrical and heating problems. You had to get a key from the dean in order to get in, so we were the only ones who could have been in there. Yet, from where we were on the first floor we kept hearing footsteps on the second floor. We decided to investigate. No one was up there, but the sound of footsteps moved to the third and last floor. We ran up the stairs to try to catch whoever it was, but all we saw was a shadowy form rush down the hall. The hall was curved, and the figure rounded the curve, disappearing into the shadows just as the hall lights went out! We ran out of there, never to return by ourselves again.–*Rick C.*

Tillie's valiant struggle to protect her virtue became the talk of the town, and locals contributed money to provide her with a proper burial (initially, she had been buried in a pauper's grave). A marble monument was erected in Union Cemetery with this simple epitaph: SHE DIED IN DEFENCE OF HER HONOR.

Tillie's reach still looms large, with frequent ghost sightings and even a play about her commissioned by the Centenary theater in 2002. Today, Centenary's on-campus grill is called Tillie's. Coincidence? We think not.

WILLIAM H. HAHN JR.
1905 — 1980
I TOLD YOU I WAS SICK

There's an old expression that says, "Dead men tell no tales." But that's just not true. Dead men and women are telling tales every day in cemeteries and church graveyards all across New Jersey. They are tales of triumph and tragedy, love and hate, happiness and sorrow. They are stories of lives lived and lost, and they are all nonfiction.

Burial places are like vast outdoor libraries where we read of the lives of those who came before us and shall not pass this way again. Try exploring just about any

Grave Matters

of our state's cemeteries, and you are almost certain to find history, mystery, and even humor waiting for you there. The words used by the authors of these works were not decided upon lightly. They were, after all, etched in stone for all to see for time immemorial.

So read what they have to say, and hang on their every word. It is not a morbid curiosity that spurs this fascination we have with the words of the dead. To the contrary, it is a curiosity of life.

Deceased of Distinction

New Jersey has more than its share of noteworthy people buried in its cemeteries—famous celebrities, history-making politicians, and world-renowned authors. But everybody knows about those folks. We want to introduce you to some other distinguished dead who reside beneath our fair state's soil.

Lincoln's NJ Roots

It is not commonly known that Abraham Lincoln had ancestors who lived in our weird state. Between 1710 and 1714, two Lincoln brothers, Mordecai and Abraham, migrated to Monmouth County from their birthplace in Hingham, Massachusetts.

After settling in New Jersey, the Lincoln brothers operated a blacksmith shop on the outskirts of the sleepy village of Imlaystown, not far from today's Six Flags Great Adventure Amusement Park. The ruins of the Lincoln blacksmith shop are still standing.

Mordecai Lincoln married a New Jersey girl named Hannah Salter, daughter of a wealthy mill owner. The Lincolns turned out to be the great-great-grandparents of "Honest Abe," sixteenth president of the United States.

Mordecai and Hannah had five children, one of whom was a little girl named Deborah. On May 15, 1720, Deborah died at the age of three. She was buried in a plot at Ye Olde Robbins Burial Place, established in 1695 by the Robbins family of Monmouth County.

Today, Ye Olde Robbins Burial Place is an overgrown, tick-infested thicket, barely visible from a country road. To visit little Debbie's grave, one has to follow a narrow path leading into a dense forest. On roughly cut, red sandstone block is an inscription that reads DEBORAH LINCON (the second L was not always used by the early Lincolns) AGED 3 YEARS 4 MONTHS MAY 15, 1720.

Years later, an iron bar was placed around the grave, honoring little Debbie as the great-grandaunt of President Lincoln.

Shortly after Deborah's death, the Lincolns moved to Berks County, Pennsylvania, and their descendants settled in Virginia, Indiana, and finally Kentucky, where our future President was born in his famous log cabin on February 12, 1809.

On a crisp November morning in 1991, when I first visited the burial site, the locals warned me not to reveal the exact location of little Debbie's grave. Over the years, some had reported hearing mournful sobs emanating from the graveyard, especially during the month of May when Debbie died. There were also tales about ghostly horse-drawn funeral processions entering the graveyard on cool spring nights.–*Stephen Conte*

Dead Giant in Franklin Township

The mysterious man known as Colonel Routh Goshen was larger than life—literally.

For fifteen years, Goshen was a resident of Amwell Road, in the small section of Franklin Township called Middlebush. Known as the Middlebush Giant, he stood seven feet five inches tall and weighed over four hundred pounds. He was one of fourteen children, and his parents were also giants.

Colonel Goshen toured with P. T. Barnum, who, in true Barnum fashion, exaggerated a bit and billed him at seven feet eleven inches and six hundred twenty pounds.

Goshen died in 1889 and was buried in a coffin eight feet four inches long. His real name wasn't discovered until 1980, when a letter to the Middlebush Reformed Church claimed that Goshen was really Arthur Caley, born on the Isle of Man in 1837. It was the master showman, Mr. Barnum, who had given him both a new name and a militaristic title.

There's even some showmanship in his burial site. Apparently, the colonel was concerned that circus enthusiasts might make a spectacle of his final resting place, and he asked to be buried in an unmarked grave. The burial plot remained that way until 1970, when local Boy Scouts erected the memorial that stands today in the Cedar Grove Cemetery on Amwell Road in Franklin Township. The giant's enormous remains are not actually located directly beneath the marker, however. His body is buried nearby underneath a patch of honeysuckle trees.

Grave of the Gypsy King

What do you see when you think of a gypsy? Bright clothing, tarot cards, vagabonds? To most people, the image of a gypsy is surrounded by an aura of mystery and mischief. So it's only natural that our weird state is home to the largest population of gypsies in the United States.

You might spot some of these gypsies around Memorial Day, making a yearly pilgrimage to Hillside Cemetery in Madison—wherein lies the so-called King of the Gypsies, Naylor Harrison.

Born in England in 1842, Harrison came to America as a child. He became a successful horse trader and eventually amassed a fortune. His horse trading headquarters were located in Madison for fifteen years, though he moved to Morristown toward the end of his life. Although he was a world traveler and owned land in many parts of the country, Harrison and his wife, "Queen Louisa" (herself a renowned palm reader), loved New Jersey. And New Jersey loved Harrison. He was well respected by the Madison community, and considered an honest businessman.

As a result of his good name and great fortune—he was said to be worth more than a million dollars—many gypsies looked to Harrison as their leader. He was called King Naylor, and for years, bands of gypsies would come to Madison each spring for an annual celebration with their "king."

When Harrison died in 1928—ironically, from injuries he received after being kicked by a horse—his funeral procession of five hundred was the longest ever seen in Madison, and to this day, his grave site remains a mecca to modern gypsies. They journey here each year to decorate the tombstone with flowers and to pay tribute to their king and queen. In fact, if you stumble upon any weird markings on trees or telephone poles in the area, following them just may lead you to the grave site. These "ideograms" are drawn by gypsies to mark the way to important places—ones where you might find medicinal herbs, semiprecious stones, or, in this case, the final resting place of the famed King Naylor.

So keep your eyes peeled for gypsy signposts and make your own pilgrimage to King Naylor's grave—if you're lucky, you just might meet a New Jersey gypsy on the way there.—*Abby Grayson*

Storied Stones

Sometimes a tombstone can tell far more of a story than just what is inscribed on its face. Around the state, we find that certain stones have become legendary. Often we discover that the mythology that grows around these graves has little or nothing to do with the person who is actually interred there. Yet the stories live on—long after the people they are about have returned to dust.

Cursed Tombstone of the Witch

A *legend* has circulated throughout the town of Edison for generations about a witch who was buried in the cemetery on Woodbridge Avenue in the 1700s. Her name was Mary Moore, and rumor had it that if you walked around her grave thirteen times at midnight, she would appear.

Her tombstone was different from others of her day. While almost all bore a skull with wings above the name of the dead, Mary Moore's stone had a skull with cross-bones.

Two friends of mine, Josh and Sam, went to the cemetery one night when they were seniors in high school. According to what Josh told me, Sam thought it would be cool to steal Mary Moore's tombstone and use it as a decoration for his room. So they dug it up and brought it back to Sam's house. About a month later, Sam was walking down his street at night and was hit by a car. He was killed instantly. They never caught the driver; it was a hit-and-run.

Sam's mother told Josh that he could take any of Sam's belongings as a reminder of their close friendship. Josh took several items, including the tombstone. Another month passed and it was Christmas Eve. Josh was walking to a party when an 80-year-old man sped through a red light and struck him, dragging his body for miles. Apparently the old man's brakes had failed.

At Josh's funeral, his older brother told me that he was getting rid of Mary Moore's tombstone as soon as possible. No one knows exactly what he did with it and no one dares ask. But it's not in the old cemetery anymore.

—Noel Stevenson

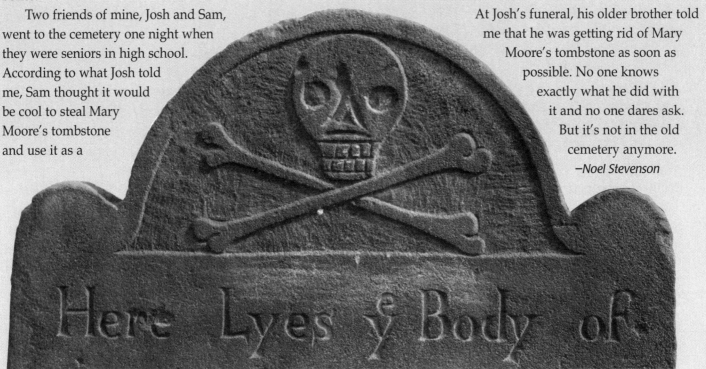

Here Lyes y^e Body of

The "Evil" Tombstone

In Cinnaminson, Burlington County, there is a cemetery that supposedly has the grave of a witch. I've seen the stone and oddly enough, the word Evil is inscribed above the name Amanda Bowen. When I was young, the older kids would make us go into the cemetery at night and leave an item (that they would supply) on her grave. Manhood wasn't easy.—*Dan McGinnis*

That Tombstone Isn't "Evil," It's Just Misunderstood

I can offer you a detailed explanation of what the tombstone inscription means. It is a phrase in Arabic that reads from right to left and signifies that the occupant of the grave was a member of the Baha'i faith. The phrase is pronounced "Ya Baha'u'llah B'ha" which means "Glory of Glories."

There is no occult involved and the person, I can assure you, was definitely not a witch. I feel like I have to stand up for the Baha'i.

Thanks, I hope that sufficeth.—*Maggie*

The Lonely Grave

Mettler Cemetery in Montague is an unassuming-looking little graveyard that's easy to miss if you blink. It is located along Old Mine Road in the remotest reaches of the northwestern part of the state.

At a lonely burial site situated close to the woods surrounding the cemetery lies the final resting place of a young child. The tiny stone that marks her grave reads MARY ANN, DAUGHTER OF THOMAS AND CLARISSA PERRIGO, DIED 1856. Nothing else is legible.

What is weird about the grave is not the little stone or the date, but what now surrounds it. Mary Ann's grave has become a shrine. It is filled with objects like rosary beads, stuffed animals, a naked Barbie Doll, money, and a mobile with angels. The strangest of perhaps some 50 items that surround the stone is a hand-written letter that starts off, "Mary Ann we were wondering . . ." the rest of which was destroyed by moisture. So the question arises, who has adorned the grave with these offerings? What is the legend or tragic story of the little child who died so long ago?—*George R. Draney and Burt Albouy*

Malpractice at Midnight

This gravestone lies flat in the grass of the Presbyterian Cemetery on Main Street, Succasunna. Its sad, angry story tells just enough to make you want more. The inscription reads:

IN MEMORY OF
CHARLES H. SALMON.
WHO WAS BORN FRIDAY
SEPT. 10TH 1858.
HE GREW, WAXED STRONG AND
DEVELOPED INTO A NOBLE SON
AND A LOVING BROTHER.

HE CAME TO HIS DEATH THE
12TH OF OCT. 1884 BY THE
HAND OF A CARELESS DRUG
CLERK AND TWO EXCITED
DOCTORS AT 12 O'CLOCK AT
NIGHT IN KANSAS CITY.

−Tom Mandrake

Welfare Is Not Quite Dead Yet . . .

In July 1978, Bordentown mayor Joseph Malone III decided to pull the town from the clutches of the state's welfare system. The local part-time welfare director had retired, and the mayor set up a new welfare commission, composed of himself and two city commission members, James F. Kelly and Joseph Bowker, who was a tombstone seller. The trio rejected aid from the state and implemented a workfare program that required recipients to earn their daily bread. The city's welfare load dropped from over thirty cases to one.

Enter the strong arm of G. Thomas Riti, the state welfare director. No upstart community was going to refuse any of his commission's handouts. A bitter battle led all the way to the state supreme court, where Judge Alexander C. Wood III ruled that only the state, not a city, could impose a work requirement on welfare recipients. It would seem that this stone monument, placed outside the main doorway of Bordentown's city hall, may have been erected prematurely. Perhaps it should have read BORDENTOWN WORKFARE R.I.P.

In memory of
NEW JERSEY
WELFARE BUREAUCRACY
− 1978 −

WHAT ARE WE DOING WRONG
_____ JAMES F. KELLY
WHATEVER THE HELL IT IS, IT'S WRONG
_____ G. THOMAS RITI
WE MAY NOT BE LEGAL, BUT WE'RE RIGHT
_____ JOSEPH R. MALONE III
NO MORE FREE MONEY
_____ JOSEPH A. BOWKER

Upright Citizens Brigade: Outstanding in Their Field

Sometimes you just can't keep a good man (or woman) down — even after the Grim Reaper has laid low their mortal bodies. Here are just a few upstanding citizens from New Jersey's graveyards, outstanding in their respective fields — literally.

Ever Get the Feeling You're Being Watched?

A walk through Holy Sepulchre Cemetery on the border of Newark and East Orange can produce some stony stares from its stoic residents. While it is commonplace to find religious iconography (such as angels or Christ) in mortuary memorials, Holy Sepulchre's upstanding citizens are unique. The cemetery offers the highest concentration of portraiture statuary of any burial ground we know. This means that the person you see is the person that's dead.

This soldier grave of Marine George Batten is located in Wenonah Cemetery in Wenonah.

St. Andrews Ukraine Cemetery in South Bound Brook.

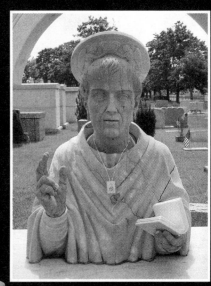

A pious pillar from the Atlantic City Cemetery community.

Pull Up a Chair and Sit Awhile

If any of these cemetery citizens ever gets the urge to pull up a seat and take a load off his stony feet, the Fowler grave would be the perfect piece of furniture. This comfy cushioned club chair can be found resting in the Eglinton Cemetery in Clarksboro.

Death: the big sleep, end of the line, eternal rest. In our society, we are taught to believe that after death we shall rest in peace, uninterrupted until the end of time. Unfortunately, things haven't always worked out that way for some of our deceased, whose sacred slumber has been disturbed in some pretty strange ways. Whether it's a natural disaster, a religious ritual, or a bunch of rowdy hooligans, it seems there's always something that's going to deny certain dearly departed of their peaceful rest.

Hillside Cemetery Spill of 1902

A torrential downpour in August 1902 caused the Spring Garden Brook in Madison to overflow, run through Hillside Cemetery on Main Street, and wash out fifty-nine graves.

The bodies were found along the course of the brook the next morning, much to the disbelief of the neighbors. Edward Dehart discovered bodies floating into his yard on Cross Street. He quickly enlisted helpers to wade through the water and collect the cadavers that had broken away from their coffins. They placed as many bodies as they could back in the coffins, but only thirty of the corpses were identifiable.

Also on that fateful day a man named Dugald MacDougall and another worker heard an "awful hair-raising noise" that seemed to be coming from a decomposing corpse caught in an upright position in the bushes. What they had heard was the wind whistling as it blew through the throat of the deceased. MacDougall was quoted as saying, "I never heard a sound like it before or since."

Fowl Remains in Newark

Someone's been playing chicken in the Mt. Pleasant Cemetery in Newark, where we found four decapitated fowl and dozens of burned candles among the gravestones— evidence of Santería rituals. Caretaker Scott Willman told us that grave robbing has also plagued the cemetery in recent years. Several corpses have been stolen from mausoleums, some dating as far back as the early 1800s.

The Ballad of Clem Turner

My father told us kids the story of Clem Turner every year, when we made our vacation trip through Tuckahoe to Cape May in the 50's. It seems that Clem put in his will that he did not want to be buried, but kept fresh, by periodic renewal of embalming chemicals, and he wanted to be placed on his porch every day from noon to 1 P.M. with a dish of clams.

We always thought our dad was just kidding. Then one day he came home with a newspaper containing an article saying that the state had Clem's will overturned and had him buried in order to reduce traffic congestion (presumably caused by disbelieving sight-seers) in this small town.

I have run into one other person who had heard the story but my kids think I'm as crazy as I thought my dad was.–*Stacy Tettemer*

The Student Body's Coming Out Party

No one ever thinks of Union as a college town. But being home to Kean College (now Kean University), every once in a while a story would surface that would surpass the old fraternity pranks of seeing how many goldfish one could swallow, or how many students could be crammed into a Volkswagen.

Sometime between 1979 and 1981, a frat party was thrown by Kean College students that was so wild and bizarre, it took the phrase "waking the dead" to whole new heights. It seems that a bunch of students wanted to make their party a little livelier, so they hatched the brilliant idea of "unearthing" some fun from a local cemetery called Hollywood Memorial Park.

The students chose their guest of honor from a mausoleum, helped him out of his compartment and chauffeured him to the party. Once there, the other rabble-rousers decorated him with proper party attire, giving the stiff a party hat, propping a smoke in his hand, and sitting him at the head of the table with a cocktail!

As the revelry drew to a close, the students realized they had to dispose of their gruesome guest. Not willing to take him back to the cemetery, they dumped him off in a local branch of the Elizabethtown River.

The Einsteins were convinced that this would be kept among themselves, honoring the code of the frat. Then the pictures were developed, and the code of silence was shattered.

"Hey, dude, check THIS out!" *— Toni Kostuk and Nick Clemente*

Life of the Party

Regarding the body snatched from Hollywood Memorial Cemetery, the group that dug him up was actually a local rowdy party bunch. Not the dregs of society, but not upstanding pillars of the community, either. I believe that night there were three guys and two or three girls out partying in Irvington.

They made a pit stop by the cemetery in Union on the way back to Springfield. Apparently one of the guys found a crypt and popped the door open. I understand the girls were horrified when the guys brought the body out to the car. They put it in the trunk and headed home. The next night they held a party in honor of the dead guy (who had been dead about 100 years and was dressed in typical 1800s style of clothes).

They propped him up in the corner (*Weekend at Bernie's* style) and put a joint in one hand and a beer in the other. I believe they had intended to return him to the crypt the following night but the guy they shared the house with came home and freaked out. So in a panic the partygoers took the corpse to the local park (Bryant's Pond) and dunked him in the lake, where he floated to the surface the next morning.

The rest is history. I don't believe there was jail time but I'm sure some of those involved had some heavy fines.
—Captain Lanidrac

Tragic Tombstone Tales

All burial grounds offer us a place where we may reflect on our own lives and mortality. And sometimes they remind us just how tragic and bittersweet this life can be. After reading some of the tales inscribed on certain stones, you can't help but feel a little more, well, glad to be alive.

A Very Bad Year for the Thorps

One day, while taking a leisurely stroll through one of my favorite cemeteries, my attention was drawn to a long row of headstones that told the sad tale of a family named Thorp. It is in the First Presbyterian Churchyard in East Hanover, amongst the beautifully carved Revolutionary War era gravestones, that the Thorp family's saga unfolds.

As if David and Mary Thorp's loss of two children, David Hatfield (age 5), and Nancy Green (age 6), during a single month in 1825 is not heart-wrenching enough, far worse luck was yet to befall their clan. The next tombstone in the row has been made illegible by time and the elements, but it too undoubtedly marked the passing of another of the Thorps' children.

The winter of 1832 ended on a somber note for the Thorps, as they suffered the loss of their son, Robert Condit (age 15), on March 5th. Spring allowed little time for mourning poor Robert's passing though, as the Grim Reaper also claimed the lives of sons Joseph Hatfield Thorp (age 24), on April 21st, and Silos Craig Thorp (age 8), on May 10. After witnessing the deaths of six of her seven children, Mary Thorp departed this life herself on August 23, 1832, at the age of 47. Just two months later, in October of that same awful year, David Thorp (age 53) would follow her to the grave, leaving their one surviving son, David Beecher Thorp, an orphan at age 3.

He would live to the ripe old age of thirty, before giving up the ghost in 1859. His, the only white head stone in the family's grassy plot, stands like an exclamation point at the end of the Thorps' column of dark and somber red sandstone markers. Today, standing in the serene environment of the old churchyard, one can only gaze upon that long, grim row of monuments and wonder at the depth of grief that must have descended upon this one family's rural household back in the year 1832. –*MM*

When the Dotterweichs Drowned

Barbara Kuhn of Wayne sent us this photo of the stone for the Dotterweich family, which is located at the Preakness Reformed Church in Wayne. The memorial tells the tragic story of the family's loss of five children on a single day, the thirteenth of December 1874. According to the inscription, the children, ages 6, 9, 13, 14, and 16, all drowned when the ice broke on a local pond.

When the Wares Were No More

In a cemetery in Bridgeton, not far from where I live, is this Ware family tombstone where five out of six family members died in 1933. I don't know anything else about it.–*Jen Williams*

When the Smiths Were Smitten

These pictures are actually the front and back of a headstone found in the Cedar Grove Cemetery on Rt. 514 in the Somerset/Franklin area. The front side is the mother and father and their children are on the back. Notice the dates of the kids' deaths. Each week, for five weeks, one of them died. I just can't imagine how their parents survived that. Unfortunately, I have no information to explain their deaths.–*Adele Baudoux*

Watch What You Eat

A large horizontal stone lies in the churchyard of St. James Episcopal Church in Edison. It covers the burial place of two young boys who died in 1693. Today the stone is cracked and the inscription is very difficult to read. This is what is written on it:

SPATATERS UNDER
NEATH THIS TOMB
LIES 2 BOYES THAT
LAY IN ONE WOMB
THE ELDEST WAS FULL
12 YEARS OLD THE YON
GEST WAS V TWICE
TOLD BY EATING
MUSHROOMS FOR
FOOD RARE IN 1 DAY
TIME THEY POYSEOND
WERE RICHARD HOOPAR
AND CHARLES HOOPAR
DESESED AUGUST ANNO
DOM 1693

Just in case you have difficulty translating this "old-fashioned" way of writing, this is my interpretation of what the epitaph means:

Spectators, beneath this tomb lies two boys that lay in one womb, the eldest was 12 and the youngest was 10. They died within one day of eating poisoned mushrooms. Their names were Richard and Charles Hoopar and they died in August 1693.–*Evelyn Williams*

What a Way to Go—Horribly

I once heard a story about a grave in Princeton that said this man died a horrible death.

Well, I think this is it. It's a pretty neat grave, but it states he died in a horrible accident.–*Jim Parris*

Mushroom Boys of Edison

As reported in *Reader's Digest,* the oldest recorded case of mushroom poisoning in the U.S. is chronicled on a tombstone in Edison, in a cemetery on Woodbridge Avenue near Middlesex County College. On a large flat slab now barely legible, there's an inscription to the effect of Here lies a set of twins . . . one was good, the other evil. And then it describes their death by mushroom poisoning. I'm not sure of the date, but the "U"s are printed as "V"s and the language is pretty cumbersome.–*Patti Tauber*

Keep Off the Poisoned Kids

The mushroom twins are buried directly across the street from where we lived in the 1950s. We were never allowed to step foot on the graves. For sure, a bony hand would reach up out of the ground and grab our feet if we did.

It's over 50 years ago, but that grave stands out vividly in my mind. The headstone is long unreadable, but it told the heartbreaking story of a brother and sister who died after eating poisonous mushrooms. They were buried together in one grave. I had some good nightmares after reading that marker.–*Carol L. Hoffman*

Graveyard Humor: Looney Tombs and Merry Memorials

Imagine that you've just been told that you are about to die and you have to come up with a few last words. What would they be? Wait, don't answer so fast! These words are going to be inscribed on your tombstone for all the world to see for the rest of time. This will be the one phrase that sums up your personality and time spent here on earth. Would you try to come up with something profound and enlightened? Would you offer some tidbit of wisdom or sage advice to the living who might happen by your grave years after you've shed this mortal coil? Or would you look the Grim Reaper dead in the eye, without fear, and try to bring a smile to his bony face?

Throughout New Jersey, we find many final epitaphs that are anything but morbid. In fact, they're quite lighthearted and humorous. In show biz, they tell you it's always good to "go out on a high note." Many of our state's former residents have taken that advice to the grave with them. Here are just a few of their killer zingers, wicked one-liners, and parting shots.

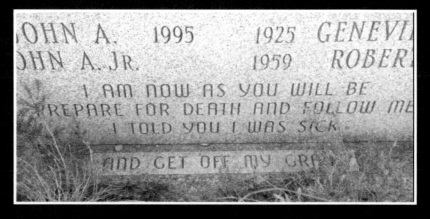

Eugene William Snyder

Have Fun... *...Will Travel*

"He died with his boots on"

SEPTEMBER 9 1944 – DECEMBER 3 1995

HER WORK IS DONE AND LIKE A
TIRED SCHOOLGIRL SHE HAS
GONE HOME FOR THE HOLIDAYS

James Joseph
Corcoran

Beloved Father
Son & Brother
May 12, 1965
September 14, 2002

Up in Smoke

DAVID COLLINS

APRIL 28, 1950

FEBRUARY 17, 2001

LIFE'LL KILL YA

ANTONUCCI

FRANK P.
MAR. 17, 1938
AUG. 8, 2000

TRUCKING THROUGH THE HEAVENS

Distraught Man Loses Head over Mother's Dead Body

It was the morning of December 7, 1996. Tom Maye, president of the board of trustees for the Hazel Wood Cemetery in Rahway, was on his way to work. It was a warm day for that time of year, and a white mist shrouded the gently rolling hills of the graveyard. Passing the main gate at about ten thirty a.m., Mr. Maye was alarmed to see what he thought to be a car on fire inside the cemetery.

"There was a lot of smoke or steam," he told *Weird N.J.*, "and the windows of the car were all fogged over."

Upon closer investigation, though, he discovered that the vehicle, a brown 1983 Olds Cutlass, was not on fire at all, but was overheating.

"As I approached it, I could hear the engine racing at top speed," Mr. Maye recalled. "The wheels were spinning furiously, kicking up mud everywhere. The car was still in gear, the only thing that stopped it was that it had run up onto a tombstone! I thought that someone was pulling some kind of a prank, so I walked over to shut off the ignition."

Looking into the driver's-side window, Mr. Maye then made a gruesome discovery.

"I saw what I thought was a mannequin sitting in the driver's seat without a head. Its foot was pressing on the accelerator, and its hands were on the steering wheel. One of the hands had its middle finger extended onto the wheel, and I thought, If this is a prank, then these guys are good!

"Then I reached in to turn off the engine and got blood on my hand. Then I saw that there was blood everywhere and realized that this was no dummy."

In fact, the decapitated driver was fifty-one-year-old Robert Brien, who had committed suicide in a most unusual way. Brien, who had reportedly been despondent since the death of his eighty-year-old mother the previous September, had decided to end it all just a few feet from her grave site. According to police, the deceased had first tied one end of a long rope around the trunk of a nearby cherry tree. Then, after snaking the cord through the rear driver's-side window of his automobile, tied the other end around his neck. Leaving enough slack in the rope (about thirty-five feet) to allow himself time to build up a good head of steam, Brien then put the pedal to the metal and headed off into the hereafter.

"At first I thought that he had blown his head off with a shotgun," Tom Maye recollected, "but then I saw his head on the back seat of the car. He had placed a flannel shirt over his face before he had taken off."

Today, years after the incident, the tree that Mr. Brien used to anchor his noose still bares a horizontal scar on its trunk as a testament to where one distraught man literally reached the end of his rope. His final resting place is located just a few yards away from where his car finally came to a stop. He shares a headstone with his beloved mother.

Buried in the Backyard

Sometimes the thing that makes a grave weird is not who is buried there or even what is written on the stone. In some cases, the weirdest part of the story is where the grave is found—like in someone's yard! Hey, this is New Jersey we're talking about, and we all know how land changes hands, gets reused, and redeveloped—and sometimes a dead body or headstone can get misplaced in the shuffle. Still, it always strikes us as a little strange anytime we hear of another tombstone turning up where you'd least expect it. And we can't help but wonder, Whatever happened to the body that it once commemorated?

Tombstone in the Backyard

There was a lot of snow on the ground during the early part of 2003 when Wendy first visited the cottage she'd be purchasing in the Indian Lake neighborhood of Denville. On closing day in May, she made a surprising discovery during her final walk-through with her realtor. Only inches from her back patio lay a granite tombstone!

Neither the seller nor the listing agent had disclosed that this peculiar item would come with the house. Apparently, no one felt it was worth mentioning when the house was put up for sale, especially since it was buried under snow. Fortunately, Wendy went ahead and bought her cozy cottage and set *Weird N.J.* on the case.

We noted that the marker's surname is McManus, with the names and dates of Patrick A. 1881–1946 and Josephine B. V. 1888–1954. Because the cottage was built in the early 1930s, this couple would have moved into the house in the later part of their lives. Curiously, the initial B in Josephine's name is not fully carved. It almost looks as if a mistake was made, since the V that follows it is completely finished, as are the rest of the letters. Did the stonecutter misread his directions and carve a B when her initial was V?

This was the first of many mysteries about the McManus couple.

Census records showed that there were no matches with this couple's names and ages in New Jersey or anywhere else in the United States. The Denville Tax Assessor's Office did not have a McManus listed as a previous owner of the cottage, and the health department held no records for the 1946 or 1954 deaths. In fact, the lack of records on Patrick and Josephine causes one to wonder whether they ever existed at all!

The discrepancy in the carving of the initials suggests there might have been an error, in which case the stone would have been replaced. When contacted, a local memorial company revealed that old stones or stones with errors were sometimes used for landfill. It's possible that the original cottage owners made an effort to level out their sloping property and somehow came into possession of the granite tombstone. Maybe over time, erosion brought the surface soil down to it.

Perhaps the only way for Wendy to know for sure whether she's got a couple of corpses in her backyard is to start digging! –*Heather Wendt Kemp*

Tombstone of Lambert Castle

While wandering around the grounds of Lambert Castle in Paterson, I came across an old headstone. It was in back of the castle, in what appeared to be an unused doorway with a huge heating vent blocking access to most of the area. Next to the

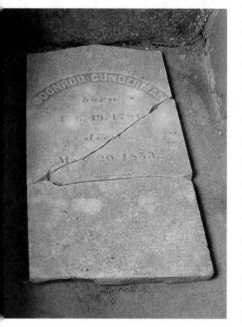

vent was a small area where the headstone is just lying on the ground. It reads COONROD GUNDERMAN, BORN FEB 19, 1786, DIED MAY 20, 1853.

The Castle is currently home to The Passaic County Historical Society. From what my brother tells me, this stone has been here for quite some time. He stumbled upon it years ago the same way I did. But why is it still in this bizarre spot? I contacted some family members via Internet searches, and found one person who believes this may be either Captain Coonrod Gunderman himself (a Revolutionary War soldier) or his son, grandson, or nephew. Still doesn't explain what the stone is doing at Lambert Castle.—*Elaine*

Weird N.J. did investigate this tombstone during a recent visit to Lambert Castle. The tour guides did not seem to know anything about the stone, but were excited enough to go outside and see it for themselves. Go see it before poor Coonrod's stone gets hidden away someplace else—like his body apparently has.

I Found Coonrod!

Referring to the whereabouts of Coonrod Gunderman's body, he's buried at the Canisteer Cemetery in Sussex County. I found his name after searching through some county records. Don't know how or why his tombstone ended up at Lambert Castle.—*Michelle Howland*

Navy Commander Sunk in Lawn

Located off Kearny Avenue on the side yard of a Whippany resident is the gravestone of Commander Michael Kearny—not the famous one-armed American general Philip Kearny (for whom the town of Kearny is named), but the Royal British Navy commander who owned a massive piece of real estate in the area.

When *Weird N.J.* paid its respects to the commander (whose wife and daughter are also interred beneath the same lawn), we asked a neighbor what his thoughts were about having a gravestone next door.

"Well, it doesn't really bother me," he said. "I've heard that there are also tunnels and wine cellars under the ground here that were once part of the old Kearny estate."

Another member of the quiet suburban neighborhood informed us that a few years ago there was a rededication of the burial site, complete with musical fanfare, and an English contingent crossed the Atlantic for the ceremony.

"The town has prohibited any building on the lot," said the neighbor. "But the owner still has to pay taxes on it. I've heard that the stones have been moved over the years, so I'm not sure whether that is the actual burial site or not."

Weird N.J. reader and local resident Mary Ann Cohen wrote to tell us, "We used to play tag there when we were kids, and used the flat gravestone as base! I don't know if the general and spouse are still there in the flesh—but their tombstones are!"

Burial Plaque at Denville Middle School

In November of 1991 my friends and I started messing around with a Ouija board (I thought it was pretty lame at the time, but I did notice some things that could not be explained). It would say things that only I knew and I wasn't touching the board! So this made me take the Ouija board somewhat for real. I decided to take it to Valley View Middle School off Diamond Spring Rd. For years we had heard unconfirmed statements that the school was built on an Indian cemetery.

We brought the board there, and it was freaking out. It told us to leave the area, but we didn't. We asked the "spirit" for a sign, and it pointed us in the direction of a tree by a bike rack. It told us to look under it. We did and we found nothing. We decided to do a little digging, and lo and behold about three inches under the dirt was a big marker made by the Educational Department of New Jersey. It stated something like "this marker is dedicated to those Denville residents buried to the south of this marker."

The school is directly south of the marker, so it turns out all the rumors of spirits in the school may be true. No one knows about it, no one! Because there is so much cover up about this I don't want to use my real name.–*Flynn*

Well, our man Flynn is right about one thing: The Ouija board did tell him the location of a little-known plaque honoring some of Denville's dead. Other than that, the Valley View Middle School has no skeletons in their cloakrooms, nor do they hide the fact that everyone has heard the legend of the Indian burial grounds. We met with the principal of the school in hopes that he could shed some light on the mystery.

"We've had a few strange things happen here, but nothing unexplained," said the principal. "A few oil leaks, some electrical problems, that's all."

The plaque is located under a juniper in the corner of the property. The reason it is buried is because a flat bronze marker gets covered with dirt and leaves over time. The plaque does indeed honor early Denville residents, but it does not specify who they were.

More Than Stones in This Driveway

I came across a pretty strange discovery in my Atlantic Highlands backyard. Buried only a little beneath the dirt driveway were a few tombstones. The engraving on one of the stones was pretty clear and I was able to figure out that the stone was for a Civil War volunteer soldier. The other stones are very faded and we were able to glean only a few clues after "rubbing" them.

My girlfriend and I are not sure if our backyard was once a burial plot. I'm sure there is a story here, though I am hesitant about drawing crowds of teenaged explorers to my neighborhood.–*Jeff*

Mattie Brown's Mysterious Marker

In Egg Harbor Township, Atlantic County, there's a tombstone at the police station. It was found many years ago, and no one could ever find out where Mattie Brown was buried. No family was ever found, nor was a stone reported missing with that name.

The tombstone is located at the foot of the radio tower facing the parking lot. But where did it come from?

Weird N.J. was alerted to this story with the message: "I have to live (and work) in this town, or I'd tell you who I am. Just call me 'Anonymous.'"

Intrigued, we visited the Egg Harbor Township police station (located off Zion Road, Route 615). We were not able to find Mattie's tombstone at first. There was some construction work going on at the site, however, and we

thought that the stone might have been removed from the area. This made it necessary for us to do the one thing that we normally try to avoid at all costs: ask the cops to help us out.

The first officer we asked about the stone was sitting in his cruiser in the parking lot. He told us that he was a rookie and was not familiar with the story. When his partner emerged from the station house, we asked him about the missing marker. This officer seemed a bit more seasoned and, after sizing us up with a suspicious gaze, began to contemplate our question. Like a man who had misplaced his car keys, the officer seemed to be racking his brain trying to remember the last place he had seen the stone. Then, suddenly, it came to him, and he pointed to an area behind the parking lot where a construction trailer was sitting.

As he walked us over to the site, he told us that the stone had been moved around the property a number of times over the twenty years that he'd been on the force. He knew nothing of the stone's origins, though he speculated that it had probably turned up on an old farm in town during development. He also said that there was no record of anybody with the name Mattie Brown ever living in the township.

When we found the tombstone, we could see that this last move had damaged it, cracking off one corner. Mattie Brown's name was evident, as were her nineteenth-century birth and death dates, but no more information was to be found. Who Mattie Brown was and where her mortal remains may lie will most likely remain a mystery.

When we asked the officer if we could have a picture of him next to Mattie, he replied in a stern voice, "Negative." We left it at that.

Mystery Tombstone

One day Louise Cooper spotted a grayish stone block that she had never noticed before, despite five years of cookouts and tending to the garden at her Fifteenth Avenue Newark home. What Louise found was a small tombstone near her rosebush, buried flat on the ground. The inscription read DAUGHTER WILMA 1908–1945.

Cooper can't find anyone to help her solve the mystery of who, if anyone, is under the stone. She called the police, who checked it out but said they really couldn't help her. Genene Morris, of the New Jersey Cemetery Board, said cases like this fall out of the jurisdiction of the state agency.

Possibly it is just a memorial stone. For now, Daughter Wilma will remain in Cooper's backyard undisturbed.

The Doctor Will See You Now— Step Right This Way

In Pompton Plains, there is a doctor's office. In the back lot, on the walkway to enter the office, there are several gravestones that match the rest of the stones in the path. It is very bizarre. –*B. Catalioto*

Jersey Sunday Herald

SUNDAY, OCTOBER 26, 1986

Action Park injuries up in '86

By EVAN SCHUMAN
Staff Writer

VERNON — More than 330 people were reported injured while visiting Action Park during its 20-week season this year, more than twice as many as last year.

But state records reveal that the number of citations for safety violations that were issued to the park this year by the state Labor Department decreased significantly, both in number and severity.

And The Herald found evidence that Action Park strictly enforced state-mandated age limits for ride attendants.

In an article in May, The Herald reported that although state law requires that ride operators and attendants be at least 16 years old, many at Action Park during the 1985 season were as young as 14.

State officials and state records point to several other changes that have taken place at Action Park that could account for the decrease in citations, including the creation by the park of a three-man, full-time seasonal park patrol which monitors safety and pre-inspects rides.

Despite repeated efforts by The Herald, Action Park officials refused to discuss any aspect of the park's safety record.

THE RIDE accounting for the most injuries this year, as in past years, was the park's most popular — the Alpine Slide — with 60. Among them were 19 head injuries, four fractured bones, two dislocated shoulders, a pinched nerve and an internal injury. Last year, 33 injuries

See PARK, Page A11

Weird Ways
We Once Were

How we choose to spend our precious leisure time says a lot about who we are as a culture. And we New Jerseyans have traditionally gone to any lengths in pursuit of a good time — from coercing horses into high dives from Atlantic City's Steel Pier to risking life and limb on a rickety old wooden roller coaster at Bertrand Island.

Our state has a long history of unique theme parks. Most of the really well-known ones like Olympic Park and Palisades Amusement Park closed down long ago. Sadly, even many of our state's smaller, family-run parks have gone out of business in recent years, victims of the changing times and people's tastes for newer and more exciting forms of entertainment. There may be no more poignant reminder that youth is fleeting than seeing an abandoned and forlorn kiddie park deteriorating in the woods somewhere — all the joy that it once provided now just a ghostly memory.

But there are theme parks still in operation, and you should visit them while you can. And ask folks to tell you what they remember about the rest. No matter what age you are, we hope this chapter will jog some fond (and in some cases, painful) memories and remind you what it feels like to be young — and weird — at heart.

Quest for El Dorado

If you are wandering around the Springfield area, you might want to check out the old El Dorado Gardens, if any of it is left. My dad, now nearly 100 years old, told me about this place, and he said it was abandoned when he was a kid.

In its heyday, El Dorado was a series of beautiful gardens and magnificent bubbling springs on the Springfield side of the Rahway River. Some of the springs were surrounded by carved stone columns and pillars, and meant to resemble Roman baths. A dam was constructed across the river and water was diverted through small bubbling creeks and under bridges. Paths connected the springs and wound through the garden. In those days, people used to go to the springs to bathe in the purifying water. (If you look in the river now though, yuck!)

Though the gardens were gone by the time my father was a boy, the place was still called El Dorado Gardens and water was still bottled from the springs. If you're ever in the area check it out, but for God's sake DON'T DRINK THE WATER!–*Captain Lanidrac*

Fairy Tale Forest by Mark Moran

Located in Oak Ridge, Passaic County, Fairy Tale Forest opened in 1957 as a twenty-acre storybook land that harkened back to a simpler time, before Xboxes, when children were entertained by Mother Goose and the nightmarish fables of the Brothers Grimm. The park was built virtually single-handedly by a German immigrant named Paul Woehle, who came to this country in 1929. Mr. Woehle, who preferred to be called Opa, maintained Fairy Tale Forest, with the help of his wife and sons, for more than thirty years. It was then operated by his granddaughter until, after several years of decline, the park finally closed its doors in 2005.

Luckily, we visited the Fairy Tale Forest in 2000, when it was still a

thriving, yet hopelessly outdated, kiddie attraction. The first thing you saw when approaching the place was an enormous boot from the "Old Woman Who Lived in a Shoe" nursery rhyme, which adorns the front gate of the park.

Once inside, you were transported to a make-believe land of brightly colored characters and cottages. As you walked the trails that led through the forest, you could look in the windows of the houses. Cinderella, Snow White and the Seven Dwarfs, Hansel and Gretel, Humpty Dumpty on his wall, and Rapunzel in her tower were all here, along with other, more obscure characters.

Several of the houses contained costumed mannequins (in various states of decomposition), and most had a loudspeaker mounted on the building to tell the accompanying tale. This was helpful, because I would have been hard-pressed to name some of the stories and can only imagine what young children thought when they gazed into those animatronic dioramas.

The most interesting displays were the ones that featured animals, like the one with the wolf at the door and the seven goat kids running to hide. The creepy part was that the kids were actually real stuffed goats! This was also the case in the schoolroom, where all the little rabbits were dressed in children's clothes and learning to read. The image looks cute enough, until you notice that protruding from each little bunny's taxidermied paws were wire ligatures that held the books.

Fairy Tale Forest had a Santa's Workshop, where robotic elves built toys for all the good little boys and girls. Two things struck me as odd about this North Pole scene. The first was the life-size robot Santa maniacally playing his pump organ—very reminiscent of the Phantom of the Opera. The second was the small walk-in chapel, complete with pews, an altar, and religious paraphernalia. I wondered if I was supposed to cross myself upon entering and then genuflect.

While my daughter loved looking at the psychedelic-colored kiosks and figures, regardless of whether she knew what story they were from, I saw the park as a look back into our not-so-distant past, to a time when these innocent, yet often disturbing, fairy tales were a part of every youngster's upbringing. Though this park is now closed, there is a similarly themed park in south Jersey on the Black Horse Pike in Cardiff, Egg Harbor Township, called Storybook Land. Its ideal location on a major thoroughfare between Philadelphia and Atlantic City has allowed this park to thrive. It's clean, well maintained, well attended, and unfortunately, not one bit weird.

Gingerbread Castle

The oldest of New Jersey's storybook parks is the Gingerbread Castle in Hamburg, Sussex County. Located just off Route 23 on Gingerbread Castle Road, this Hansel- and Gretel-esque fantasy was the brainchild of businessman F. W. Bennet. In 1930, Bennet commissioned Joseph Urban, a set designer for theatrical producer Florenz Ziegfeld, to turn an existing building into the castle that still exists today (though this park too breathed its last within the past few years).

The façade of the castle is encrusted with finely sculpted cookies, candy, and birthday-cake-like frosting. Stone owls keep vigil over the doorway, and a black tomcat hisses atop one of the building's turrets.

For many years, local children, dressed as either Hansel or Gretel, were employed as tour guides. They would walk children around the grounds to show them Prince Charming astride his prancing steed, the Old Woman Who Lived in a Shoe, and Humpty Dumpty, relating the nursery rhyme that went with each display. Children would then be taken inside the castle to see the evil witch's kitchen, where a black cauldron in the fireplace contained the bones of the unlucky little boys and girls who never completed the tour.

At one point, Gingerbread Castle closed for about ten years; then a new owner reopened it in hopes of restoring it to its former glory. This apparently did not go as planned, as the building is now closed to visitors once more.

Entering the tower of the castle, I marveled at the craftsmanship of the remaining

displays. I walked around the wishing well, where children once tossed pennies down the deep shaft. Figures of brightly colored gingerbread-cookie children wind their way up the staircase of the castle's main tower under the hungry gaze of the giant from Jack and the Bean Stalk, who is suspended on his cloud in midair. Stained-glass windows cast kaleidoscopic light on the pale pink walls as you ascend the spiral staircase to the dizzying heights of the castle's apex. At the top, a doorway leads to a balcony that offers a panoramic view of the imaginary kingdom. These days the vista includes a view of the skeletal remains of the abandoned factory next door that was once home to the Wheatsworth Mill and National Biscuit Company, better known today as Nabisco.

Back inside the tower, I wound my way back down the staircase, careful to avoid the missing

steps, and descended to the dungeon. I could imagine that a visit to this place must have had more than a few tykes screaming for Mommy. I exited below ground level through a door that on its outside featured a painting of Mother Goose riding her bird through the sky and dropping Wheatsworth Crackers to all of the happy boys and girls below.

Hopefully there will always be a little space left in our increasingly crowded state for such inspired visions as those created by Gingerbread Castle's creator F. W. Bennet and Fairytale Forest's Paul Woehle. They designed wondrously unique places for children of all ages.

The Land of Make Believe

The Land of Make Believe on Route 611 in Hope was established in 1954 as a kiddie ride and water park, not a theme park. Still, the site possesses enough quirky surprises to warrant its mention in this chapter.

The first surprise we encountered on our visit was the big red barn and accompanying silo with Santa's face painted on it. This was called (appropriately enough) Santa's Barn. Mind you, we visited here in the middle of August during a killer heat wave, so this seemed out of place. Inside the barn, visitors are encouraged to crouch down and walk through a "magic fireplace," then up the chimney to visit Santa Claus himself. My daughter was petrified and would have no part of this, so I went up the flue alone.

When I emerged on the second floor, I found myself in a dark, cavernous, winter wonderland. The loft was decked out with cotton snow, fake elves, and reindeer, Christmas trees, and candy canes. The only light came from the tiny colored Christmas bulbs, which were strung along a walkway, and the whole place was

eerily quiet. The temperature was well over 100 degrees.

As I made my way across the nightmarish North Pole landscape, I came to a full-sized log cabin and peeked around its corner. There, sitting on the front porch was Santa, all done up in his red suit, white beard, and shiny black boots. At first, I thought he was a mannequin, but then I saw the fan on the floor blowing full force to cool off the not so jolly guy. I felt really creepy being all alone in a sweltering barn loft with some guy dressed as Old St. Nick. "Hey, Santa," I said, "mind if I take your picture?"

Just then I heard the terrified screams of a small child echoing through the gloomy recesses of the barn. As it turned out, my little girl decided to come looking for me and freaked out during her journey up the chimney. "Gotta go, Santa," I said, then rushed off.

Thankful to be back outside, we wandered through the park until we came to a sign that pointed to Jenny Jump Rock. This intrigued me, for although I knew we were near Jenny Jump State Park and Jenny Jump Mountain, I had never heard of a Jenny Jump Rock. Of course, Jenny's legend is one of New Jersey's oldest and best-known folktales, but I wasn't aware that the Land of Make Believe had any kind of connection to it.

As the story goes, Jenny was the nine-year-old daughter of early settlers of the area. One day while out picking berries near a precipice, Jenny was surprised by a dastardly band of Indians, who sneaked up on her and intended to kill or abduct her. Jenny ran screaming, alarming her father who was working in his field down below. "Jump, Jenny, Jump!" he hollered, and poor Jenny leaped to her death. Whether or not any of this is true, no one can say.

At the Land of Make Believe, they not only claim to have the cliff that Jenny jumped from, but also the house that she and her family lived in. The white farmhouse, circa 1748, is located at the bottom of the ravine where Jenny took her final plunge, right beside Jenny Jump Falls. A loudspeaker mounted on the outside of the building plays a recording that recounts the tragic tale over and over again for visitors.

As we walked back down the path away from Jenny's house, we came upon a very unsettling attraction. At first, the two scarecrows standing by the side of the walk looked pleasant enough. One was supposed to be a man, dressed in a ratty old pair of overalls, a flannel shirt, and straw hat. The other was apparently his wife, wearing a weather-beaten denim dress and gingham shawl. The sign posted next to the pair read TALK TO COLONEL CORN, BUT PLEASE DON'T TOUCH HIM. Naturally I assumed that there was some sort of tape loop in the straw man that would tell an amusing story.

"Hello, Colonel Corn," I said, feeling a bit corny myself.

"Hello," he replied, "is that your little girl?"

"Yes," I said, sort of bewildered.

"She's got a pretty hat on. I'm Colonel Corn, and this is my wife, Cornelia. She doesn't talk much," he said in a voice that was somewhere between the soulless voice of Hal the computer in *2001–A Space Odyssey* and the blasé voice of Garfield the cat. What I really found disturbing was not the fact that the scarecrow could talk, but that he could see and hear me. Was there some kind of camera in Colonel Corn, and someone observing us on a video monitor somewhere? Or was there someone watching us from a darkened window and transmitting dialogue to a speaker in Mr. Corn? All of a sudden, he spoke up again.

"I'm a hundred sixty-four-years old," he said. "Cornelia here is only a hundred forty."

"Go for the younger ladies, do ya?" I said, bending down to see if his nose was really a micro-camera. Then I got out my own camera to take a picture of him.

"You're going to take my picture," he observed. "I've been told that I'm very photogenic."

"Oh, is that right. How so?" I asked.

"Well," he replied, "I'm always smiling."

"That's true," I noticed, and that too was beginning to bug me, "and you never blink, do you?" There was no answer. "Colonel Corn?" I said. "Are you still there?" Again no answer; the scarecrow had gone silent. Let me tell ya, the only thing weirder than standing in the middle of a field talking with a scarecrow is standing there talking to a scarecrow that doesn't talk back. Had the minimum-wage voice of Colonel Corn just gone on break? I had no way of knowing, but if Colonel Corn was going to give me the cold shoulder, I was leaving.

Jersey Jungle Returns to Nature

A blast from my personal past is the Jersey Jungle, a long-closed attraction that flourished when baby boomers were young and their parents were looking for ways to entertain them.

It was more or less a zoo in the woods—state-of-the-art for 1960. Visitors were promised they could see wild and exotic animals in their natural environment. (Provided of course these were bred-in-captivity creatures, accustomed to caged enclosures. . . .)

Jersey Jungle covered several acres of woodland on Route 33 East in Howell Township, and it had an extremely short life. Two years ago I made my first expedition to the place in decades. The site had been purchased long ago by the Tire Farm, which operates off an adjoining road. They have left the area pretty much untouched.

Jersey Jungle is just another one of those buried treasures, silently decomposing, on one of thousands of Jersey's wooded lanes. – *Kate Philbrick*

Bungle in the Jersey Jungle

I was one of the happy children who were driven to Jersey Jungle as a "summer event" from way up North Jersey (Woodbridge).

The billboards and signs would start early on. As you continued to drive you could see, in the distance, past the tomato and corn stands, "The Gorilla Cage," dangerously close to the edge of the road. The stuffed gorilla's raised hand was visible in a frozen wave through the gold-painted bars, under the grass roof.

At the end of the dusty parking lot was the grass-topped entrance building where we purchased our tickets. Children would receive a "rope lasso" (stiff clothesline, taped into a loop by electrical tape) and be sent into the "wild" to attempt to capture a wild boar (tame miniature pig) and get a fine plastic pig as a souvenir. We would then walk past the caged llamas and sheep, and into the petting area, where we could feed the animals. Further fun was had when Jersey Jungle "natives" would lead us on a horse ride safari. We would buy our Jersey Jungle Tom-Toms and head back to the car, which would have its badge of honor—the official Jersey Jungle bumper sticker—to display to our envious neighbors. Match this against your X-box!—*Irv Hyatt*

Way Out Wild West City

There's an Old West theme park thriving in the northern part of the state. Netcong is a bucolic Sussex County community where life is a little slower than in more populated areas of the state. The roads of Netcong are lined with antique and lawn ornament shops, hot dog joints and diners, and miles of forests. But all is not as peaceful as it may seem. You see, low-down dirty varmints roam the range and terrorize a small frontier outpost here. Lawlessness abounds, and hapless travelers are routinely set upon by ruthless gangs of bandits who rob them of their belongings at gunpoint. Bands of horse-thieving, cow-rustling outlaws square off on the dusty streets of the town center where shootouts have occurred every day (May 1 through Columbus Day) since 1956. Luckily for us greenhorns though, this is all just part of Netcong's own western-themed amusement park, Wild West City.

Located at 50 Lackawanna Drive, just off Route 206, Wild West

City has a daily schedule of the most rootinest, tootinest western-style events to be found east of the Pecos. And more grown men wearing leather chaps than you'll see anywhere this side of the badlands of New York City's wild West Village.

Kids can ride side by side with the Pony Express, shoot it out with the James Gang, and participate in the gunfight at the OK Corral, along with a host of other

violent family-oriented activities. More lily-livered kids can pan for gold, pet animals, watch Indian dances, play miniature golf, and ride ponies.

But Wild West City isn't just for the young'uns! The park also offers an authentic western-style saloon to wet the whistles of Ma and Pa. The Golden Nugget serves your alcoholic beverage needs and features costumed dancing girls. That's right pardnas, while the young'uns is off traipsin' around town, all hopped up on sarsaparilla, you can mosey on over to the saloon and throw back a red eye or two. It's one of the few places east of Pennsylvania that actually encourages the combined enjoyment of liquor and firearms in a wholesome family setting.

When I sidled up to the bar at the saloon, I asked the bartender if I was allowed to take my beer out on the porch to watch the shootout taking place on Main Street. "You can take it anywhere in the park," he replied. Now that's my kinda town!

If you're feeling like a guilty galoot after your long day gunning down hombres and ogling barroom floozies, you can stop for a quick trailside prayer at the miniature frontier chapel, conveniently located in front of the wooden tombstones of Boot Hill Cemetery. A sign posted at the entrance of the chapel states THIS IS A HOUSE OF GOD, PLEASE TREAT IT AS SO. Right outside they even have the Ten Commandments engraved on two polished marble tablets.

The park is open from ten thirty a.m. through six p.m. daily and offers a full day of cowboy-style fun right here in the wild, wild west of New Jersey. Yippie-ki-yi-yay!

Weird Adventures at Adventure Village

In Cardiff, there used to be an amusement park called Adventure Village. It was a Wild West town, complete with stagecoach rides and a miniature train ride featuring actors pretending to shoot each other.

We went there many times during the 1970s. (I think it closed in the late '70s.) In the middle of the park was the town, equipped with a saloon and a movie theatre.

Here's the weird part. Long after it closed, a large chain link fence was erected, and it was evident that the town was inhabited. Curious, my mother and I decided to investigate. We drove through the open gate onto "Main Street." The town was as I remembered it—cheap reproductions of western buildings. Suddenly people appeared at every door, and approached our car.

"This is a private town," they said. It was beginning to feel very "Night of the Living Dead"-ish, so we quickly left. I never did find out who those scary people were, or why they lived all together in tiny make-believe homes.–*Rene*

Failed Venture

I was at Adventure Village as a kid. Little Johnny from "Call for Phillip Morris" fame had money invested in this and also operated the train. He was one of the advertised attractions. They had a movie theater there showing old films and I remember seeing Laurel & Hardy's *Midnight Patrol* there. The place had a lot of conceptual problems, and you kind of wandered around wondering what you were supposed to do.

When we first got married my wife and I would go to the shore and always see lights in Adventure Village's buildings when we returned in the evening, even though it had been closed for years. One night I decided to pull in and see what was going on. I was amazed to see all the old buildings still up even with the same signs and apparently inhabited, as most had mailboxes out front. Even the old train platform was still standing with information about when the trains ran. My wife wanted to leave at this point so we took off.—*Paul Verlander*

The Village That Time Forgot

My friend Sandy and I recently headed out to Adventure Village. The property is overgrown, and hasn't been maintained in a very long time. There was no one in the town until finally, Sandy saw a car coming down the drive, and we waved and found an actual resident!

The woman was a nine year resident of the village, along with her 20 year old daughter and her boyfriend, and her young son, and all were super nice folks. They gave us a tour of the place. They said that the village is currently for sale because there is some sort of wetlands restriction, and the owner can't build or destroy any of the buildings without major legal hassles. Consequently, he has refused to put any money into the place. A little bridge over a stream was collapsed, and the pond looked like a mosquito's dream.

The woman said that she had tried to fix things up, but it was a situation with no end in sight, so she was looking to move. It's amazing to think that you're 50 yards from Rt 40, and no one knows the place exists.

All in all it was a great trip.—*Ellen Jeranek*

Spaced Out

There he stood, the twelve-foot-tall, two-thousand-pound Kodiak bear named Goliath, stuffed and dead as could be in the lobby of Space Farms Zoo and Museum—the Guinness World Record holder for world's tallest bear. The now defunct giant was brought to Space Farms as a cub and lived there for twenty-four years until his death in 1991. Ever since, he has greeted the more than one hundred thousand visitors who make pilgrimages each year to this one-of-a-kind attraction.

If you grew up anywhere in northern NJ, Space Farms Zoo and Museum in Beemerville (Sussex County) was a mandatory day trip. I mean this quite literally, as Space Farms has been the destination of countless grammar school field trips for more than a couple of generations now. But the attraction is by no means intended solely for the entertainment of bused-in grade-schoolers—not by a long shot!

Sure, Space Farm has the usual assortment of lions and tigers and bears, as well as some not so common creatures, such as South Korean elk and fallow deer from Taiwan. In all, there are some five hundred mammals and reptiles at the zoo, and the owners even have a contract with the county to pick up roadkill to help feed these carnivores. But what really

makes Space Farms Zoo and Museum a weird attraction is the museum!

In actuality, Space Farms has several museums. Spread out over the hundred-acre farm are a number of buildings that house a variety of displays, including antique cars, horse-drawn carriages and sleighs, guns, farm tools, steel-jawed leg traps, tractors, motorcycles, and Indian artifacts. The most bizarre exhibit is a room that features freaky-looking antique dolls in glass cases right alongside human skulls and large pickle jars containing the preserved embryos of a variety of animals, which float in a hazy greenish yellow fluid.

Among the more macabre items on display are the miniature horse-drawn hearse carriage—complete with tiny coffin—and a hearse sleigh. So how did this strange collection come to be? Here's what Space Farms' literature says:

Space Farms began in 1927 when Ralph & Elizabeth Space bought the first 1/4 acre at the same site of today's 100 acre complex. The Spaces were native farm people, both growing up on small family farms in Sussex County.

Ralph's mechanical expertise enticed him to open a small repair shop and gas station. Elizabeth helped by starting a small General Store carrying the few necessities the local people needed. . . . Later, to supplement the family income, Ralph was employed by the N.J. State Game Department to trap predators marauding farm animals. . . .

Most of the distress calls were from local farmers in the springtime, when bobcats, foxes and raccoons had young to feed and preyed on the plentiful farm goats, sheep, chickens and ducks. Rather than kill the animals . . . Ralph built small enclosures around his garage to save them.

Ralph's original intentions were to keep the animals until the fall when the pelts were valuable. When the time came, however, three small Space children—Loretta, Edna and Fred—cried and begged their Father to keep the animals. By the next spring, the animals had multiplied and the collection of wildlife grew.

People around the area soon heard about the Space Family's wild animal collection, and would drive by to see it. They would buy some gas, maybe some candy and soda, and visit the animal collection. Although he never intended it, Ralph Space soon had a very small zoo!

Okay, that explains the zoo part of Space Farms, but where did all of those thousands of items in the museum come from? The literature continues:

EAGLE

THIS CAST IRON EAGLE
STATUE IS THE ONLY ONE
REMAINING OF THE ORIGINAL
13 FROM THE OLD POST
OFFICE BUILDING IN N.Y.C.,
WHICH WAS DEMOLISHED IN
1930. ALL OF THE OTHERS
WERE USED AS SCRAP IRON
DURING WWII.
12 FT. HIGH   3.5 TONS
WING SPAN 13 FT.

EDUCATIONAL EXHIBIT NATIVE WILD LIFE DISPLAYED by RALPH SPACE, WILD ANIMAL FARM, BUTLER, N.J. SUSSEX, N.J.

People around the area soon heard about the Space Family's wild animal collection. . . . They would buy some gas, maybe some candy and soda, and visit the animal collection. . . . Ralph Space soon had a very small zoo!

Soon after the zoo began, the Great Depression hit the country, and the local farmers were not spared. Still needing supplies and repairs, the farmers would "pay" [the Spaces] with their family heirlooms: old firearms, dolls, wicker cradles and other items of local Americana. The antiquities were given in good faith; all agreed that the items would be given back when better days came and bills could be paid. In the meantime, they were placed on the walls of the general store. Soon, visitors would stop by to see the animals and the antiques, and this was the beginning of Space Farms Zoo and Museum.

Today, three generations of the Space family work at the zoo. Fred himself, clad in his trademark safari outfit and bushman's hat, can often be found seated in the gift shop or restaurant, greeting visitors as he has for over fifty years now.

Space Farms Zoo and Museum is located at 218 Route 519 in Beemerville, and is open from May 1 until October 31.

Weird Wheel of Food

A few years back, Keansburg Amusement Park had a very strange prize wheel. It was known as the Wheel of Food, where you could place a quarter bet on a wheel that might land on a number or a picture of an item of food. It was bizarre enough to play for food as a prize, but even more bizarre were the products they offered.

Strange medicines and cough syrups that you never heard of were next to old cookies and Band Aid boxes. Canned hams and Spam were big items, as well as no-name colas. The stand was truly a Jersey legend. Sadly, it closed up. I haven't been back to Keansburg since. It won't be the same if I can't go down there to try my luck winning some outdated groceries. *–Mike Vlkovic*

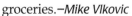

Bumper Car Psychos Love to Slam

I am always amazed at the weird people that occupy our state. I always take my daughter to Keansburg (which is just plain weird in itself).

There are interesting sites there, but the one that always catches my eye are the Bumper Car Psychos. If you go down on a Friday night you can catch them there. It is really pathetic actually but there are two guys each weighing about 400 pounds that can barely fit in the cars in the first place. They just love to slam into people and knock them around. I can sit and watch them and get a good laugh. *–Dawn*

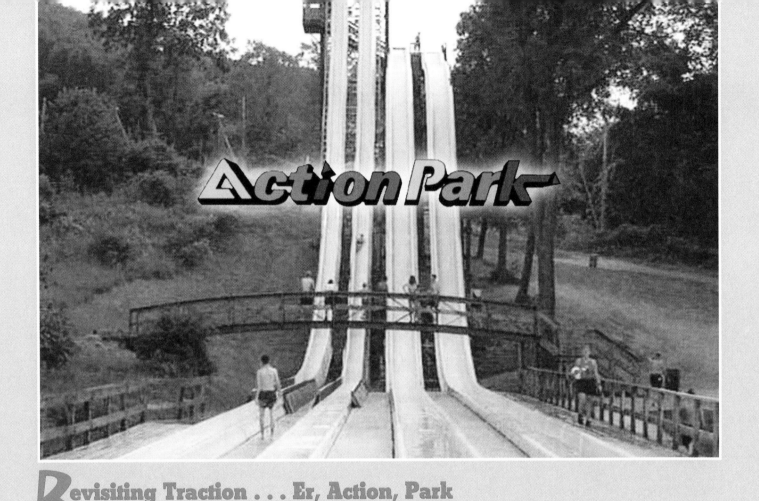

Revisiting Traction . . . Er, Action, Park

If you were compiling a list of things you might have experienced in your NJ youth, you might include knowing all the sites in the opening credits of *The Sopranos* and that a "piney" isn't a tree. One other touchstone that many New Jerseyans have in common is having been seriously injured at Vernon Valley's now defunct amusement park, Action Park. So let us now fondly reminisce and compare scars.

"The Action Never Stops . . . at Action Park . . ."

So went the jingle, played endlessly on TV and radio stations in the '80s and '90s. The commercials marketed Action Park as an essential summer experience for reckless youths. From its opening in 1978 to its closing in 1998, people came from all over to slide, swing, and drive

themselves to adrenaline-induced distraction. Some also came to inadvertently experience serious injuries. The park earned its nickname, Traction Park, on the scraped skin and broken bones—and in rare cases even the very lives—of many of its attendees. Almost any ride was capable of dealing some serious pain. You could choose your poison on the hills of Waterworld, on one side of Route 94, or in the swamps of Motorworld, on the other. For nice, safe, vicarious thrills, read on.

Losing Skin on the Alpine Slide

The Alpine Slide was called Action Park's most popular ride in a 1986 *New Jersey Herald* article. One park official declared it "the safest ride there is," noting that a ninety-year-old grandmother and mothers with babies on their

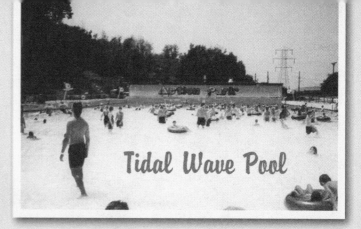

Tidal Wave Pool

laps had taken rides on it. The same article said that the slide was responsible for "more accidents, the majority of the lawsuits and 40 percent of the citations" against the park.

The concept was simple enough: You sat on a sled and descended down concrete tracks, using a hand brake to control your speed, either slowly or at a speed described by a former park employee as "death awaits." If you were lucky, your injury would consist of just some lost skin. Lose control of your sled, however, and it would crash through the hay-bale barriers, your body subject to the laws of gravity and nasty hillside rocks. Take the ride too slowly, and you would find yourself rammed by the person behind you. At least fourteen fractures and twenty-six head injuries caused by the ride were reported between 1984 and 1985.

The Alpine Slide was also responsible for Action Park's first death: that of a nineteen-year-old park employee in 1980, who was thrown from his car, hit a rock, and sustained a fatal head injury.

You'll Be Shocked on the Kayak Ride!

The Kayak Ride, which allowed people to paddle tiny boats through white water, was never very successful, because the kayaks would get stuck in their own tracks. It was particularly unlucky for one twenty-seven-year-old man during the summer of 1982. He fell or got out of his kayak, and in the process of trying to get back to it, stepped near an exposed wire that was underwater. He was taken to a nearby hospital, where he was pronounced dead. Two of his family members were also electrocuted, but lived.

The ride, drained for investigation, was never opened again.

The "Grave Pool"

The Tidal Wave Pool was a huge freshwater pool—one hundred by two hundred and fifty feet long and eight feet deep—that could hold up to one thousand people. Four large fans forced air into the pool and created waves, which could reach a height of forty inches. Two people drowned in the "Grave Pool": a fifteen-year-old boy in 1982, and an eighteen-year-old man in 1987. Many more came close, despite the fact that twelve lifeguards were stationed at the pool at all times.

One problem was that many of its users were not good swimmers. But even good swimmers would forget that the freshwater waves were not buoyant like waves in the ocean, so they would have to work harder to stay afloat. Crowded swimming conditions meant that people would bash into each other or the sides of the pool.

Former employees claim that lifeguards often made thirty "saves" a day, whereas your average lifeguard at a pool or lake might rescue one or two people in an entire summer.

Other Ways to Hurt Yourself in Waterworld

Waterworld was also home to rides like Roaring Rapids— involving several people riding a "whitewater" raft—and the

Man drowns in pool at Action Park

By MATTHEW GRECO
Staff Writer

VERNON — A Queens, N.Y., man died Sunday, apparently having drowned in the "Wave Pool" at Action Park.

Gregory Grandchamps, 18, of Jamaica, Queens, had been swimming in the deep end of the pool at about 1:30 p.m. when a lifeguard spotted him under water, dove in and pulled him from the pool, a park spokesman said.

Cardiopulmonary resuscitation was begun and Grandchamps was taken by the Vernon Township Rescue Squad to Wallkill Valley Hospital, said spokesman Vernon Merritt.

Grandchamps was dead on ar...

Sussex County Prosecutor's Office are investigating the death, said Police Dispatcher Patricia Dzikowicz.

"At the time of the incident there were 12 guards on duty around the 'Wave Pool,'" said Merritt. "The cause of death has yet to be determined."

The "Wave Pool" is a 100-foot-wide by 250-foot-long pool that produces 40-inch-high waves that are generated for periods of 20 minutes, Merritt said. The waves are turned off for 10 minutes at a time throughout the day, he said.

The waves were on when Grandchamps was ...

Tarzan Swing, which allowed you to swing over an icy-cold body of water and throw yourself into it. Roaring Rapids caused injuries such as fractured femurs, collarbones, and noses and dislocated shoulders and knees—kind of like *Deliverance* without the banjo. The Tarzan Swing was known for scraped toe knuckles and also the shock that people would experience when their bodies were immersed in the icy cold water below. The water was so cold that people would forget how to swim once they hit it.

The Legend of the Loop

It's a waterslide that never totally was. Its three-hundred-and-sixty-degree loop loomed over parkgoers as they entered Waterworld, taunting them with its improbability. It was the Cannonball Loop slide, and it was open for only about a month in 1985 before being closed by the Advisory Board on Carnival Amusement Ride Safety.

Employees who tested the ride reported that if you entered it going feet first, you'd come out head first, and vice versa. One person got stuck in the loop, necessitating the construction of a hatch that could be opened to extract people from that part of the ride. According to one employee who spoke with the *Herald*, "There were too many bloody noses and back problems" that resulted from riding the Cannonball Loop. It was eventually dismantled.

Driving Danger Across Route 94

Motorworld, located across the street from Waterworld, was also capable of injurious fun. Patrons treated the Super Go-Karts like bumper cars, which caused serious head-on collisions. While the carts didn't go too fast due to built-in speed governors, park employees knew how to override them with tennis balls, which would allow the carts to go up to fifty miles an hour.

Teen drowns

VERNON — A 15-year-old New York City youth drowned in the wave pool at Vernon Valley Action Park Saturday, police said this morning. The victim's name was not released.

Shortly after 5:30 p.m. Saturday, two unidentified females reported to lifeguards at the wave pool in the park that they believed someone was at the bottom of the pool, police said. immediate search was made by the boy was pulled

The Tank Ride was the worst assignment for park employees—not because of the people driving the tanks, but because of the tennis-ball shooting guns that surrounded the ride. Patrons could have fun shooting tennis balls at the people in the tanks—so, should a park employee need to go down into the tank "pit" when there was a crash or a stuck tank, attendees could happily fire away at them.

The Super Speedboats could go up to forty miles an hour. They were set up in a swamp, in the middle of which was a small rocky island populated by an uneasy alliance of water snakes and lifeguards. One day two park attendees driving their boats crashed into each other. One boat flipped over, its driver strapped in and stuck underneath the water. The lifeguard on duty had to dive into the swamp, where he reports that he was followed by all the snakes that were keeping him company that day. He flipped the boat over and was able to save the soggy driver.

That'll Leave a Scar

If you were injured, you were in good company. In 1986, the *Herald* cited the previous year's reported accident toll at Action Park: more than one hundred and ten, including forty-five head injuries and ten fractures. And it is important to stress "reported," because the park got into trouble with the state for not revealing all accidents.

Park officials were quick to point out that the park had over a million visitors each year—maybe twelve thousand on a busy weekend—which makes the actual injury rate statistically small. Regardless, enough injuries occurred that Action Park eventually bought the town of Vernon new ambulances to keep up with the injury volume. In 1987, the *Herald* spoke with the director of the ER at a nearby

hospital, who said five to ten people were brought there daily from the park. Injuries included "ankle sprains, cuts and contusions, and . . . a few broken bones." He also noted that many of the injured came in with alcohol on their breath—not surprising, as beer kiosks were more plentiful than ice-cream stands at Action Park.

Action Park closed rides as the lawsuits stacked up and liability insurance became more and more expensive. By the time it was bought by Intrawest in 1997, its attendance was way down. Intrawest morphed it into Mountain Creek Waterpark and reopened it in 2000, putting a family fun spin on the place by eliminating alcohol, asking patrons to cover up offensive tattoos, and building expensive condos in the swamps of Motorworld. Intrawest leased the place to a company called Palace Amusements that specializes in water parks.

Mountain Creek Waterpark sent us a letter that stated that Action Park underwent significant "cultural, operational and physical" transformations in the process of becoming the Mountain Creek Waterpark. They've won industry safety and customer satisfaction rewards since these transformations occurred and want to make it clear that this new water park is not the death trap you so fondly remember. In short, Mountain Creek is no longer worthy of inclusion on a list of unique-yet-painful Jersey experiences you survived and can get nostalgic about years later. You'll have to get your scars elsewhere.

—Joanne Austin

Action Park is charged with negligence in suit

By JEAN ZIPSER
Staff Writer

NEWTON — A Staten Island couple has sued Action Park, claiming a lifeguard hit the husband with a life preserver while attempting to rescue a swimmer in the Wave Pool in 1985.

The lawsuit, filed in state Superior Court, by the Parsippany law firm of Kanengiser & Kalish Esq., claims Michael and Kathleen Rapcavage of Riedel Avenue, Park on July 8, 1985, when his nose and life preserver thrown by a

A LIFEGUARD at the side of the pool spotted the trouble and threw a life preserver in the pair's direction. The life preserver hit Rapcavage in the face, fracturing his nose, left cheek and eye socket, according to the lawsuit.

As a result of the injury, Rapcavage suffered a dislocated eye, impaired eyesight and other neurological and orthopedic damage, the lawsuit states.

Action Park is charged with negligence for failing to employ competent, responsive and properly trained and supervised lifeguards, according to the lawsuit.

The park and its owners and operators are also charged with failing to fire incompetent lifeguards and to warn visitors about how to use the Wave Pool safely.

... 'lawsuit demands damages, court and Queens,

We Called It Accident Park!

Being a former employee of the company that owned "Accident Park," as we jokingly called it, I found the place most amusing. One of the last rides introduced there was this sort of reverse bungee jump. Riders would be placed in a harness and attached to a bungee cord between two towering poles and held to the ground as the cord was stretched. Once enough tension was attained, it would be released and the riders would be shot into the air like marbles in a slingshot and then free fall back to earth, still attached to the bungee. We often wondered how many whiplash cases came out of that ride.—*Jersey Ed*

All I Remember Was Blood

Most kids growing up know of at least one person who died in a car accident. But, if you grew up where I did, you know of at least one person who was seriously injured at Action Park.

When you entered the park, three things immediately got your attention. The first was the Alpine Slide. You'd get on a low plastic seat with wheels and a bar for "steering." Then, they'd put you on a long, cracked, downhill racetrack and send you on your way. No helmets. No brakes (none that worked anyway). No warnings about the fact that a misplaced hand could result in a chopped-off finger. No stopping the crazy kid behind you from smacking into the back of your head. What fun! They actually had the audacity to have a "slow" lane and a "fast" lane. They should have been called "injured" lane and "dead" lane.

The second thing that would catch your eye was the abandoned slide. Action Park built an enclosed water slide, like a tube, that followed all sorts of twists and turns, and then, just for fun, did a complete loop, like a roller coaster loop. Upside down! Let me remind you that riders of this would not be in a car, not on a train, not on anything but water . . . water that would, with the help of gravity and magic, supposedly propel them through a narrow tube that loops completely upside down. Needless to say, it wasn't long before some woman got caught in the top

of the loop. The ride was closed, and, just as a morbid reminder, left on display for all to see.

There was, however, a physics-defying ride that the park chose to keep open. It was a cluster of four or five short, fast water slides that ended by shooting you out into a lake. Kids would fly out at various times, landing on each other or on some misplaced sharp rock. One of these "shoots" would make an abrupt 90 degree turn, slamming you into a wall and then projecting your young, gnarled body into a gooey pond of crying kids and water snakes. It was awesome.

The third thing that would catch your attention was the first aid cart. Kind of like a golf cart, it was piloted by two teens wearing oversized EMT shirts. When you saw it, you wouldn't see a kid with a scraped knee. You'd see a kid holding a blood-soaked towel on a huge head wound, or a gash the size of a Big Gulp on someone's leg. Blood, blood, blood. All I remember was blood. All for under 25 bucks a person.—*Alison Becker*

Water rides top state hazard list

By staff and wire reports

Tomfoolery causes the most injuries on New Jersey amusement rides and those that propel thrill-seekers along a path of water account for about half of all accidents, according to a state

spokeswoman. No wiring malfunctions have been found.

Another major summertime attraction — and one of the most dangerous if not used properly — is the water slide, said Barth.

"The biggest ride with accidents

Brothers in Bloody Arms . . . and Legs

The first I ever heard of Action Park was from the altar boys at our church. They went each year as an end-of-summer trip sponsored by the parish. Each time, they came back with horrific tales, ones that made you think they returned alive only because they were attending the park on a trip sponsored by God himself. They came back with visceral evidence to prove their stories were true, usually in the form of second-degree burns suffered in collisions on the Alpine Slide. One kid came back with a sprained ankle—the story went that he was riding a park train that stopped on a bridge, then caught fire. He was forced to leap to safety from this flaming train, injuring his ankle in the process.

My only trip to Action Park came during my middle school years. I remember that harrowing day as if it were yesterday. Upon entering the park, we saw a waterslide that went in a full loop-the-loop. Even as a twelve-year-old, I understood how physics would not allow anyone to come out of that tube with anything but mangled, broken limbs.

My most terrifying experience came on a slide called the Cannonball. I started the ride at the top of a hill. There was no warning that halfway down I would be shot into a pitch-black tube. This was incredibly daunting. It became even worse when the tube opened back up only when it emerged sticking out from the face of a cliff. Unsuspecting riders were shot out of the cliff face some two stories above the water, just high enough that you had time to think and panic about your situation. Rider after rider, myself included, would scream in terror before hitting the surface of slimy green water with a sickening slap. After this, the victims of the ride would gather at the edge of the pool to watch others suffer the same fate. It was like the victims of a car wreck gathering at Dead Man's Curve to watch the next car smash into the median.

The Tarzan Swing was a real treat as well. This ride was simply a beam hanging from a twenty-foot-wire above a pool of stagnant water. One by one, people would grab the

Cannonball Falls

beam and swing out above the water, until they reached the swing's apex, when they were expected to let go and plunge into the icy depths below. Hundreds of people waited their turns, watching each person go before them. This led to an interesting phenomenon—riders realized they had a captive audience, so they would have a contest to see who could do the most lewd thing while people watched them fly through the air. People giving the finger, shouting awful things, and undressing in midair were commonplace.

The ride to rule all others was unquestionably the Alpine Slide. It was the best, yet least safe, ride ever. For one thing, the track was positioned directly below the ski lift that brought you to the top of the ride, so everyone riding down was spit at by the people above them. Second, the brakes on the sleds didn't work. You either went supersonically fast, or so slow that you

would be slammed by the supersonically fast sled behind you. People often fell off their sleds onto the stone tracks while going 40 miles per hour. You can imagine how that felt: folks wearing shorts, their bare skin sliding on a stone track. Plenty of lacerations and burns.

Action Park was a true rite of passage for any New Jersey kid of my generation. When I get to talking about it with other Jerseyans, we share stories as if we are veterans who served in combat together. I consider it a true shame that future generations will never know the terror of proving their grit at our state's most dangerous amusement park.—*Chris Gethard*

Designed to Hurt?

I remember the upside down water slide called the "Cannonball Loop." I was about 11 at the time and could have told anyone that it was a horribly bad idea. Could you imagine pushing a 250-pound whale of a kid through there a few hundred times a day? Statistically, it was bound to destroy some unlucky child.

The river rapids ride was great. Under-inflated and overloaded rafts would slam into walls of concrete. On one of these turns, my friend's mother, as the raft buckled in half like a taco, flew into her son's knee and broke her nose.

I also remember a cage in the park where you could put on a parachuting suit and fly through the air. I did not try it—I had already seen enough.—*Greg Shpunder*

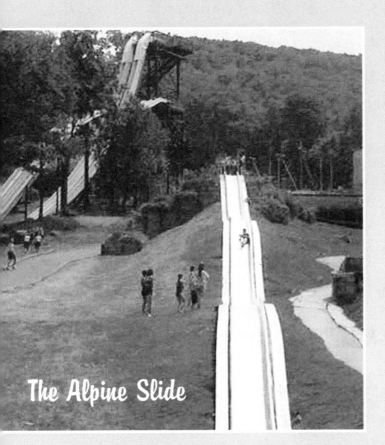

The Alpine Slide

Employee Spills His Guts

I worked at Action Park! And there was some very important craziness going on. First, the grass skiing. Yes, we used to grass ski on the mountain in the summer. That was stupid. Then they built the skateboard park—a masterpiece of design where the smooth bowls were separated by the black top pavement between them. Who thought that was a good idea? The blacktop did not even meet the cement at a smooth edge. That skate park was responsible for so many injuries that we eventually covered it up with dirt and pretended it never existed.

Now, a few points of interest:

The Alpine Slide was not cement; it was fiberglass—which explains why your skin would fall off when you fell off. The attendant would give us employees a lot more than the usual 20 seconds at the top for the poor soul in front to get a good head start. Picture croquet, at high speed.

The Cannonball Loop was the brainchild of some Swiss guy. I was one of the idiots that accepted a crisp $100 bill to test run it. That was my last ride.

All the stories about injuries are true, including the one about the idiot who jumped off the diving cliff into the 40-foot deep pool—and he could not swim. After that, they painted the pool white so they could see bodies lying on the bottom.

And let's not forget the brewery! On the Motor World side, no less! Action Park got a brewer from Germany to come over and make high-octane suds. Yeehaw! We used to steal kegs, drink the beer, ride the Indy cars down Route 94, crash the Indy cars, get the Indy cars back to the park without anybody seeing us and then go for a swim at the pools to sober up.—*Amazingly-not-wheelchair-bound Tom Fergus*

Watching the Friction

My favorite pastime at Action Park was watching people on the Alpine Slide—especially when someone would fall off the sled. A friend of mine actually melted his nylon/polyester shirt to his skin on the slide. Then there were the numerous walking wounded burn victims you'd see over the course of a day. People just wearing a bathing suit and no shirt would travel at high speeds in rough fiberglass composite slides that made for friction burns you can only describe as criminal. Ah, the good old days!—*John C.*

Abandoned Adventures

" Time here is not measured by the rhythms of occupants any longer, but by the peeling of paint, rusting of metal and the crumbling of brick."
—Shaun O'Boyle, *Modern Ruins*

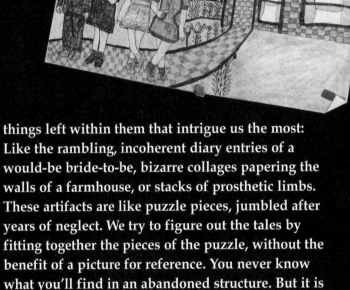

They call to us through broken windowpanes and darkened doorways—beckoning us to come inside. They whisper in our ears, "I have a story to tell you about what once happened here. Come and I will share my secrets with you." Their voices are enticing and almost impossible to resist.

So we heed their call, sometimes against our better judgment, and venture over their weathered thresholds in search of something—something mysterious, unknown, and alluring. Broken glass crunches under every footstep as we move deeper into the hollow carcass of another of New Jersey's abandoned landmarks.

Some of these places speak to us of the optimistic dreams of those who created them, poignant reminders that sometimes our aspirations just don't pan out. Seeing such structures today can be a very sobering experience—one that reminds us that even our best-laid plans and intentions might all just crumble and decay into ruins in the end. For this reason, abandoned places are both captivating and foreboding.

In many cases, it is not the abandoned structures themselves that we find most fascinating, but the things left within them that intrigue us the most: Like the rambling, incoherent diary entries of a would-be bride-to-be, bizarre collages papering the walls of a farmhouse, or stacks of prosthetic limbs. These artifacts are like puzzle pieces, jumbled after years of neglect. We try to figure out the tales by fitting together the pieces of the puzzle, without the benefit of a picture for reference. You never know what you'll find in an abandoned structure. But it is often something you never could have expected—sometimes something very very weird.

But be warned: Some abandoned buildings are located on private property, where it is illegal to trespass. Those who ignore the law may be risking more than just a fine—they may be risking their lives. And some are structurally unsound and too dangerous to enter. So sit back, read on, and let us take you on a tour of some places that are probably best experienced from a safe distance.

Collage House Creeped Me Out!

I want to tell you of two houses that were right off of Route 23 South, in Sussex, directly across from a Dodge dealership. One was pretty much right on the highway. It was an old Victorian "Addams Family" style house and was really cool and creepy.

A girlfriend of mine found the place driving home one night, and we visited it a week later. She wouldn't let me go inside because she didn't want me to leave her alone and she wasn't about to go in there with me. So I was outside with her the whole time, but that was creepy enough. We took pictures of it from different angles and left. I found a key hanging from a nail inside the back door which I still have on my key chain.

I didn't discover the second house behind it until I went back with a friend. It was a small bungalow with louvered windows and a sun porch, probably built in the 1930s or 40s. I pushed my way inside and explored the place. There were tons of old phone books and newspapers all over the floor, along with a hundred empty beer bottles. There were two little bedrooms, a kitchen, a living room, and a tiny bathroom. The bedrooms were where I got totally creeped out.

The first one had pictures of airplanes and automobiles meticulously cut out and pasted on the wall. I thought that was strange enough until I went into the second bedroom. In this one, the walls were covered with pictures of children in their underwear from Sears catalogues and such. Some had different heads cut out and pasted over the original head. I immediately felt a shudder of creepiness and thought I was being watched. It felt like Leatherface

was going to come at me (you know, the guy from *The Texas Chainsaw Massacre*).

I quickly left the building and found my friend, who was poking through some rubbish in the back of the first house. I took him to the bedroom I had just come out of. He felt the same way I had, and after about 20 minutes of more exploring, we split.

There was also an old dilapidated building adjacent to the small house. We looked in and didn't really see anything interesting so we left. Besides, bats were living there. I have not been back in years. These visits took place in the late 1980s.–*Mark Kerns*

Psycho Farmhouse

I grew up in Caldwell, and ever since I could drive I would head straight up to the abandoned house on Rt. 23 North. The house looked like something out of *Psycho*. There was a barn in the back, along with a smaller house/shack. In the smaller house, each room had a theme embodied by magazine cut-outs pasted all over the walls. One room was painted orange and had pictures of women in lingerie or underwear. I was completely creeped out. –*Renata Butera*

Inside the Collage House

Back in the late 1980s, me and some members of a small art movement called the Post Decompressionists went into the Collage House. Upstairs was empty except for some drawings on construction paper taped to the wall of one of the rooms. Two sheets depict children standing in front of psychotic checkerboard houses. One picture depicts a boy and a girl in a garden watching birds at a feeder and the other had three girls and a boy standing in front of two checkered houses. All the kids in the second picture have weird lines under their eyes that make them look like zombies.

It seems like the artist could have had some sort of obsessive-compulsive disorder because all of the drawings except one is completely filled with lines, checker patterns and color. One of the weirdest things about these pictures is that despite the obsession with filling every space, all the windows are left blank.

It seems pretty obvious to me that this was some sort of demented pervert. Hopefully these collages kept him occupied, and he didn't go out much.–*Scott Warnash*

Piecing Together Memories of the Collage House

I grew up in close proximity to the Collage House. In the late 1970s, I was in elementary school in Sussex and a family was living in that haunted-looking house. Most of the kids referred to it as the Addams Family House, but in later years I realized that it actually looked much more like Norman Bates' residence in the movie *Psycho*.

There was a very strange family that lived there at the time. I'd see them once in a while, no adults, just ragged looking children. They were about my age. I don't know if they attended school, but I know that they did not go to mine. Whenever I saw one of them, milling around the barren yard, or peering out, expressionless, through an upstairs window, my heart just sank. They seemed so alone. It made me wonder what life inside that spooky old house must be like. Still, nobody I knew ever tried to make contact with them. We were all too scared.

By the time I was a teenager in the early 80s, the house, while never in great shape to begin with, looked completely abandoned. I figured that the family must have moved on, but the house and the faces of the children still haunted my dreams. So one bleak November day I decided to go get a closer look.

All was still and quiet that chilly morning as I made my way up the hill toward the old place, except for my footsteps crunching dead leaves beneath a thin layer of icy frost. As I got closer I could see that there were other, smaller buildings on the property as well. I was sure that they were all abandoned, but still, I could not get over the feeling that I was being watched from one of the dark windows.

As unbelievable as it might seem, the door to the first house I went into was unlocked, and I strolled right in. It was dark and musty inside and I allowed my eyes a minute to adjust to the light. Then I saw them—the collages—and a chill ran from the base of my spine up to the back of my neck. The entire room was covered in these bizarre decorations. Everywhere I looked there were huge sheets of corrugated cardboard, every inch of which was festooned with magazine and catalog pictures. But it was the subject matter which really freaked me out. Thousand of images of lingerie models, pasted right next to photos of babies and toddlers. It was disturbing to say the least.

As I made my way into the other rooms I saw more of the same: walls plastered with creepy collages. At that point I was completely freaked out and just wanted to get out of there. I began to feel that I was not alone, and I wondered what made me so sure that the family had ever moved out in the first place. Perhaps they were still there and just didn't go outside anymore! Something told me to get the heck out of there—fast!

I never returned to the Collage House after that day. My family moved about a year later, so I don't know if it even still stands. If it does, I won't be revisiting it. –*Ryan L.*

Mary's Tower

I'd like to tell you about a place that I call "Mary's Tower." One warm summer day, I was traveling to work on my motorcycle down Oak Grove Road near Flemington. All of a sudden, I caught a glimpse of what looked to be a brick castle through the trees.

I stopped my bike and tried to get a better look but could only vaguely make out the strange structure. I traveled down a little farther, looking for a mailbox, or something that would indicate a house. Finally, I saw two iron posts and a chain connecting them. There was also an old rusty sign on the ground with "keep out" crudely scribbled across it. This had to be the place.

I parked my bike and made my way down the long overgrown path that must have once served as a driveway. My eyes squinted as I tried again to find the structure through the thick tree line. As I walked on, I started to think that I was mistaken, that this wasn't the driveway but just a farmer's path to one of his fields. Then, to my surprise, I saw a bridge crossing a stream. I crossed over it, then, around a sharp bend in the path, looked up, and there it stood before me—"Mary's Tower."

As soon as I saw it I was captivated by its dilapidated beauty and eeriness. But I had to get to work, so I decided I would ask around about the place and come back later.

That afternoon, I told my girlfriend about the tower. She said that she had never heard about it and she grew up only a few miles from the place. We asked her father and some of his old-timer friends too, but no one seemed to know anything. So we decided we would go back for further inspection.

The next morning, we hopped in her little white Nissan and made our way to the tower. We parked about a 1/2 mile from the path, started walking, and in no time, there it stood before us. We saw a few old cars and small out buildings on the property as we made our way to the front door.

We pushed the door open and entered the tower. The place was pretty deteriorated. Plaster from the walls and ceiling coated the floors and we could hear rats scurrying up the walls as we made our way up the staircase. There were only two rooms on each floor and there were five floors. The top of the tower was flat and you could see for miles from up there. It was the most beautiful view of Flemington that I had ever seen. We stayed up there for quite a while just taking in the beauty of it all, then decided to make our way downstairs.

I searched every room for some trace of its former inhabitants but came up with nothing. The whole time it still felt like someone was watching. My girlfriend went back up to the top floor while I searched through the out buildings.

We pushed the door open and entered the tower. The place was pretty deteriorated. Plaster from the walls and ceiling coated the floors and we could hear rats scurrying up the walls as we made our way up the staircase.

Two were empty, and the third had some old pieces of farming equipment. The fourth proved to be a different experience altogether. As soon as I walked in, the smell of something rotting almost brought me to my knees.

The first room looked to be a restaurant kitchen, complete with giant stainless steel freezers and sinks. I found nothing but utensils and rotting food so I entered the back room. It had a nightstand with a candle on it, a bed frame, and an old yellowed wedding dress. A chill went down my spine and I almost turned around and ran, but my curiosity got the best of me.

I opened the drawer of the nightstand. In it was a tattered old journal with one word scrawled across the front—it said, "Mary." I opened the book and started to read it, but none of it made any sense. It seemed like the ramblings of a lunatic! Again, I felt as though I was being watched through the holes that covered the walls. I slipped the book into my pocket and got out of there as fast as I could. I yelled to my girlfriend to hurry. I wanted out of there! We both ran down the path and back to the car.

Once we were safely in the car, I showed my girlfriend the journal but she couldn't make any sense of it either. A lot of ramblings about being alone and a baby's shoe. I put it back in my pocket and we left.

A few days later, a friend and I decided to go back there and spend the night. We packed sleeping bags and flashlights and got there just as it was getting dark. We decided that we would go to the top of the tower to sleep. We unrolled our sleeping bags and opened a couple of beers and started talking about what the place could once have been. The hours rolled on and eventually we both passed out drunk.

In the middle of the night, I was awakened by something cool dripping on my face—rain. We grabbed our stuff and made our way back inside, but before we could even roll our sleeping bags back out we heard a loud hissing coming from the woods and something banging on the wall of one of the rooms. So we ran through the pouring rain back to the car, leaving our camping gear behind, and took off.

In the years since that incident, I have gone back to the property but never again entered the tower. Things seemed pretty much the same there every time I went back and I'm sure my camping gear is still in the house. The reason for the tower and who Mary is still remains a mystery.

Mary, if you are reading this, don't worry—I have your journal and keep it dear to my heart. Your secret is safe with me.–*Johnny K.*

On the Trail of Mary's Tower

by Mark Moran

After hearing the story of Mary's haunted tower, I couldn't wait to check it out for myself. Problem was, I just could not find the elusive edifice. Mark Sceurman and I had been back and forth on the country roads to which the author had directed us, but we could not find the tower.

We were convinced that Mary's Tower existed, because Johnny K. had written other stories for *Weird N.J.* magazine in the past and had never tried to put one over on us. Unfortunately, at the time, Johnny was doing a stint in the county lock-up and was not at liberty to give us a guided tour. It seemed that Mary would have her secret tower all to herself forever.

Then we received an e-mail from a local guy named Bob Z. He told me that he knew where the tower was and offered to show me around the place. I jumped at the opportunity, and the following weekend we met in Flemington. As we drove the back roads to the tower, I kept thinking, This is exactly where I was looking for the tower on my previous trips! As we pulled over to the side of the road, I could not believe it—concrete pillars and a driveway leading over a small bridge to the tower. How could I have missed this? But there it was, like the "now you see it, now you don't" land of Brigadoon.

As Bob and I made our way down the path, the building began to slowly emerge from the forest. Though it was not as tall as I had expected, its decrepit, vine-covered façade did give the tower an ominous presence. Smashed cars and trucks and collapsing outbuildings lay strewn around the property.

Bob grabbed a flashlight and led the way into the tower. The first room we entered had once been a large kitchen-laundry room. All of the appliances were still there: refrigerator, dishwasher, washer, and dryer. We made our way through a pantry and up to the main floor, which consisted of a bathroom and a fully furnished living room. The chairs and couches seemed to be of 1950s vintage and in poor shape.

On the second floor there was a bathroom and two bedrooms. The beds and dressers indicated that they once belonged to young girls. The next two floors had the exact same layout as the first, two bedrooms and a bath.

A Tall Tale of Mary's Tower

I live a few miles from Mary's Tower. A woman named Mary lived there many years ago and went insane and killed herself in a third story bedroom.

Me and my friends decided to go there one night. On the way there, they told me they had been there the night before and were chased out by a red-eyed specter. When we got there, we went inside and started walking up the staircases. When we got to the third floor we went into Mary's room and on the floor was a single rose. About three feet to the right of that was a puddle of blood that was being dripped on from some unknown source. I looked up and there was nothing it could be coming from, which still gives me the creeps. –*James Brown*

One more staircase, and we had reached the top—or so we thought. Actually, once you step out onto the flat tar roof, you find that there's a ladder there, which you can use to get still higher. Bob and I enjoyed the view for a few minutes, pondering who might have lived here and why they chose such an unusual house. Was the tower really haunted, and was there ever really a Mary here? Johnny K. believes there was, and says he has her diary to prove it.

As we made our way back down the stairs, I noticed evidence that at least one person may remember the former occupants of this bewildering tower. There, on the second-floor landing right outside the door of one of the girls' bedrooms, lay a single long-stemmed rose. It hadn't been there very long, just long enough for the flower's petals to turn a deep shade of red, almost black, like the color of dried blood. Maybe it was left as a memento or perhaps a loving tribute. I don't know, but something about it lying there made me think that this place was somehow sacred to somebody.

Mary's Soul Is Not at Rest

I lived in a house behind Mary's Tower as a child. The story is that she was hit by a car and died on the road. Her soul could not rest because they never found the car that hit her. If you drive down the road late at night she will stand in the road and wave at you. I have seen her with my own eyes and so have many others like my mother and sisters. At the house we lived in, a man would carry buckets of water past our kitchen windows towards the tower every night. He was a ghost. –*Samantha H.*

Prosthetic Leg House

Rumors of an abandoned house deep in the woods of Zion Mountain in Hillsborough Township had circulated my high school for years. The house was supposedly home to many prosthetic limbs and other oddities. But the directions were vague and the story so unbelievable, I assumed it was just a story. Until one day a few friends and I decided to take a trek down the back roads of Zion Mountain to search for it. Within minutes, we were standing at the overgrown pathway that led down to the property.

The house was old and decaying, but the land and architecture were impressive. Stone walkways and walls were built around a river bordering the yard, complete with small man-made waterfalls. Immediately my friend Gary spotted a prosthetic leg sitting in front of an entryway to the house. This was just a hint of what was waiting for us inside.

We traveled through the dark corridors as the rotting floor boards bowed beneath our feet. The kitchen was destroyed; burn marks were going up every wall, dishes smashed in the sink, and old fashioned leather shoes were thrown about. No legs were found inside the house, but there were two small bungalows, which we had yet to investigate. Sure enough, piles of prosthetics of all shapes and sizes were pouring out of the doors. Not to mention one of the rooms had a floor made completely of broken glass, and contained several large drums filled with oil. What the hell had the people who lived here been doing?

The sun was beginning to set and we decided to call it a day, but not before I snagged a souvenir—the obviously used prosthetic leg of a woman! The leather strap was worn down, the shoe it was wearing was scuffed up, and it even sported a lacy sock, which creeps me out to this day.

The leg has provided endless entertainment for my friends and family. I even used it as a prop for my old grind-core band! I still cannot get over that house, and that it's within minutes of my front door. I guess that is the beauty of living in the great state of NJ!–*Daniel Santoro*

Dam Me, Damn You Blues

In 1962, the army Corps of Engineers began planning the building of a massive dam six miles upriver from the Delaware Water Gap, near Tocks Island. Aimed at controlling floods in surrounding areas, the dam was to have the added benefits of producing hydroelectric power and expansion of the recreational portions of the Water Gap area. In the long run, however, all the project created was a lot of tension, fighting, and quaint little ghost towns.

From the first days of the project, homeowners on both the New Jersey and Pennsylvania sides of the river opposed it. Many of these people were members of families who had inhabited the area for generations. When they voiced their displeasure, the army Corps of Engineers began bullying them into giving up their property, threatening that the maintenance of local roads would be abandoned and emergency vehicles would be unable to get to their homes. Many residents were frightened enough to leave the area, and they were given submarket values for their property. Others stayed despite the corps' quasi-terroristic tactics.

The outcry against the dam brought the project to the attention of environmentalists, who realized that there were inherent problems with the plan. Not only would salmonella build up in area reservoirs due to the dam, but the structure itself was going to be built upon unstable glacial land deposits, which increased the chance of its breaking. This in turn would lead to a devastating flood, far worse than any natural disaster the dam might prevent. The environmentalists managed to gain national press coverage, scoring hard-hitting victories in articles in *The New York Times* and even *Playboy* magazine.

More protests ensued when the army corps decided to fund their project by renting out the now abandoned homes. After they ran an ad for "houses for rent" in (of all places) *The Village Voice*, the area was descended upon by hippies. In his book *Delaware Diary* (Rutgers University Press, 1996), author Frank Dale describes the scene that followed:

Interstate 80 took on a *Grapes of Wrath* ambience with old cars, motorcycles, and hikers with blanket rolls, all heading west. Communes and "families" were soon established in the dam area, especially on the Jersey side of the river. These flower children, intent on creating a self-sufficient farming society based on love and togetherness, settled first in an encampment that they called Cloud Farm. Others followed and, with or without leases, soon occupied all of the vacant buildings on the Jersey side. The overflow crossed to Pennsylvania and moved in to vacated houses there. These new residents referred to themselves as river people; everyone else called them squatters.

Local residents were outraged that their neighbors had been forced out of homes that were then rented to people who collected welfare from the local community.

Tension between the locals and hippies rose, and soon there was a lot of property damage, vandalism, and harassment reported by both sides. The only thing that everyone agreed upon was that the bad situation was the responsibility of the army Corps of Engineers.

The corps decided to take action. In 1974, a veritable army of federal marshals and state troopers armed with shotguns and tear gas canisters descended upon the area. Close to two hundred hippies, including one woman who had given birth ten hours prior to the raid, were forcibly driven from the land. Their belongings were set out in the streets, and the corps drove bulldozers into the area and began demolishing buildings, many of them with historic value.

Needless to say, this didn't go over well with anyone. More problems occurred when the project lost its support

from both New Jersey and Delaware because of the effect it would have on the quality of their water.

By the late 1970s, pretty much everyone was against the project, and the plan was killed by Congress in 1978.

To this day, abandoned communities with churches, cemeteries, homes, and shops can still be found scattered throughout the lush hills and valleys north of the Delaware Water Gap.

The Last Exit in New Jersey

Twenty-five years ago, on the way to a barbecue in Bushkill, PA, I noticed my gas gauge dipping dangerously low as I cruised along Route 80 west toward the Delaware Water Gap. Just before I hit the bridge into Pennsylvania, I jumped off the interstate at the last exit in New Jersey. I should have noticed at the time that the road was unnamed and that no food/fuel/ lodging signs were in place.

I had just entered the "Twilight Zone."

I must have driven for a half hour, passing nothing but abandoned homes and farms. I began to feel really weird—inexplicably frightened. What if I ran out of gas in such a desolate area? Finally I sighted a town up ahead. Relieved, I pulled onto the main street, only to slam on the brakes in surprise. The entire town—post office, homes, town hall, church—was abandoned, and also oddly enough, painted the same eerie shade of white.

I made a U-turn, and with smoking tires screamed out of that ghostly town. I made it across the bridge into PA on fumes, eventually pushing the car the last 100 yards into a gas station.

When I finally reached the barbecue and related my harrowing experience, someone there gave me an explanation for the abandoned town. They told me that the government had purchased all the land north of the Water Gap because they planned to build a gigantic dam and flood the entire river all the way back to Port Jervis, creating an immense man-made lake the size of Lake Michigan.

Recently, I retraced my journey of a quarter century ago. I found the road still littered with abandoned homes, still unmarked by signs. The town was just as it had been when I first saw it. If you decide to visit, make sure that you have a full tank of gas!—*Steve Petrella*

The following is an excerpt from *Spanning the Gap, The Newsletter of Delaware Water Gap National Recreation Area* (Vol. 11, No. 2, Summer 1989). It offers a good historical record of how the tiny village of Walpack Center became abandoned, and what's being done today to preserve this modern-day New Jersey ghost town.

Around the middle of the 19th century, Walpack Valley was relatively isolated by Kittatinny Ridge to the west and the highlands of New Jersey to the north. The valley had many small farms with Peter's Valley (or Bevans), Walpack Center, and Flatbrookville serving as village centers for the farms. . . .

Located near the center of the valley, Walpack Center was more isolated than the other villages, which at least were on the major crossroads or near the river ferries. People passed their lives quietly, tending fields, gardens, animals, and shops.

By the early part of the 20th century, however, the industrial revolution caught up with Walpack Center. . . . Mechanization . . . meant that small farms could not compete with larger farms of the

Midwest. The lure of high pay in the factories and big cities proved too much for the young to resist. The population in Walpack Center began to decline, and with it went a way of life.

In 1965, Walpack Center became part of Delaware Water Gap National Recreation Area. The National Park Service is taking a number of steps to preserve Walpack Center. Some of the buildings are being used as employee residences. The Walpack Historical Society is using one building as their museum and headquarters. Other buildings, including the church, await further restoration.

Today Walpack Center is listed as a Historic District on the National Register of Historic Places.

The Fish Factory of the Great Bay by Mark Moran

Like the hollowed-out carcass of a long-dead giant beast, a lonely fish-processing plant stands on an island in Ocean County's Great Bay. It is known locally simply as the Fish Factory. Its original name was the Crab Island Fish Factory, though the marsh island on which it is located is officially known as Fish Island. In its heyday, the plant was used to process menhaden, or mossbunker, a small oily fish in the herring family. Considered unfit for human consumption, bunker are netted by the ton along the Atlantic coast. They are then ground up to make products such as fish meal, fish oil, fertilizer, bait, and pet food. The facility has stood abandoned since the collapse of the local fishery sometime around 1972.

Though we had known about the Fish Factory for some time, it was not until one steamy July day a couple of years ago that Mark Sceurman and I finally visited the abandoned site. Our guide for the trip was longtime *Weird N.J.* contributor Gary Z., who had originally told us about the place. He had made his first excursion to the island some twenty years prior, in the middle of February in a canoe. We waited until a less hostile season to make our crossing.

Mark and I accepted the invitation of Gary and his friend Joe to cross the waters of the Great Bay for an up-close look at the Fish Factory. Fortunately for us, Gary had upgraded from a canoe to an outboard motorboat.

The island is on the outskirts of Tuckerton, off Great Bay Boulevard, which is also known as Seven Bridges

Road. It is a long, desolate stretch of pavement that extends over the wind-swept marsh and sees little traffic. The only nearby building of note is a former coast guard station, which is now used as an environmental outpost by Rutgers University.

As we drove across the vast expanse of the Great Bay Wildlife Management Area, we could see the hulking shell of the Fish Factory off in the distance. We slathered on our bug repellent and headed out across the shallow bay. There was a strong headwind blowing, and the dark gray clouds of a distant storm loomed on the horizon. Though the wind was enough to blow our hats away, it was no match for the ever-present flock of biting green flies that buzzed around us like a squadron of biplanes pestering King Kong.

As we approached our quarry, we could see that thirty years of abandonment had taken their toll on the old factory. There were gaping holes in the walls and roofs of the buildings, and the piers surrounding the island were twisted skeletons of rusted steel beams, jagged wooden pilings, and crumbling concrete bulkheads. It was apparent that not only nature, but also fire had played a hand in the deteriorated state of the site. Much of the remaining piers surrounding the island were charred black and falling into the water.

As we attempted to land, the wind was fierce and constant. This made docking a tricky affair, but like the Sirens did to Ulysses, the cavernous ruins of the old Fish Factory beckoned us to come ashore.

We made our way to the back of the factory, where we found a safe harbor out of the wind to dock our vessel. Once we were ashore, the going was difficult, as the dilapidated piers were weakened to the point of being life-threatening. There was no telling which timber or concrete block we stepped on might give way and tumble into the bay at any given moment. Once we made it safely off the pier, the vegetation was all but impenetrable, even with the aid of the twenty-four-inch machete I'd brought along to hack it down.

All along the beach, we found shards of dishes, china, and crockery, some bearing the names of hotels on the bottom. There were also old bottles and silverware of unknown origin strewn about the flotsam and jetsam.

Among the hundreds of dead horseshoe crabs that littered the rocky beach were old fishing nets, still in surprisingly good condition. The rank stench of the hot summer sun beating down on the overturned crabs made me wonder what this place must have smelled like thirty years ago when the fleet of bunker boats came in, their nets were laid out to dry, and their catch was being rendered into useful products inside the factory. Ah, the smell of it!

After some time spent picking through the bones of the old Fish Factory, we pulled out our rods and reels and drifted around the bay for a while to see what fish the waters might still have to offer. Mark S. came up with the only catch of the day—one small and scrawny sea robin. All in all, though, exploring abandoned industrial ruins and lazily drifting around the bay in search of fluke is not a bad way to spend a hot summer New Jersey day.

Remembering the Stink

I've been to the old Fish Factory many times, and last time I walked through it, about six years ago, there were large boilers still there, along with pallets of empty unused paper sacks, just awaiting some fish fertilizer. All the locals refer to the Fish Factory as "The Stink House." The smell off of there in the summer when the plant was still operational was definitely not pleasant.
—Rolf Demmerle

Lambertville School

Three years ago an art student friend of mine, Casey, overheard a classmate talking of weird ghost-like paintings inside an abandoned school. So Casey, our friend Jess, and I decided to pay a visit to the school.

The brick and stone high school is located in Lambertville, just across the river from New Hope, PA. The structure sits on top of a hill and it closed, from what I hear, in the 1950s. A fire destroyed a portion of the roof in the 70s.

A short dirt road leads to the school, and we parked in front of the entrance. Near the door is a stone monument shaped like a tombstone. It reads LAMBERTVILLE HIGH SCHOOL— ERECTED A.D. 1854, REMODELED A.D. 1926. PRESENTED BY THE CLASS OF 1927. For over 70 years old, the monument was in perfect condition.

We opened the front door, and saw two large staircases. One led to the second and third floors and the other went down to the basement. The steps were covered with soot, plaster, and broken glass. A toilet lay at the bottom of the basement staircase, and it reminded me of a picture taken of the debris near the *Titanic*.

The building seemed to be in pretty good shape. We walked down into the basement, which was a mess. Light fixtures hung by their wiring, and the numerous cabinets were open and off their hinges. It was your typical deserted basement, so we went upstairs.

On the second floor, we opened two huge oak doors,

took a left and carefully walked down the halls. There were broken desks and chairs lining the corridor. It was totally fabulous. How many times have we dreamed of our dreaded schools being wrecked? Here it actually happened. Three rooms down we found the paintings.

Etched into a blackboard that surrounded three-quarters of the room were faces of children. We speculated that the room once held art classes. However, these figures covered the entire board (about twenty-five feet in length). How could a teacher or students draw on the board if there were already permanent sketches on it? It is possible that someone did this after the school was closed.

None of the children are smiling. They all have pained faces, and many have their arms clutched to their chests. They all seem to be looking to the right of the room, near the windows except for one girl, however, who looked directly to the center of the room, both arms crossed like she was in a coffin.

We took a lot of pictures, and although my description seems lengthy, we were on site for only ten minutes. There are several houses adjacent to the school, and someone had called the police. The policewoman was nice and told us that we didn't belong there. So we left, but often I find myself wondering how those etchings got there, or if one day I'll walk into a Lambertville antique store and find a portion for sale.
—*Seth Brahler*

The Children of the Chalkboard

Some years ago, my friends and I went to Lambertville High School. We went there to explore and found those pictures on the chalkboard. I took pictures before some jerk marked it up with graffiti.

In one picture the kids appear to be saying the Pledge of Allegiance. In the other picture it looks like a scene of a class in progress.

Whoever the artist is, the detail is fantastic. All of the little faces just looking so thrilled to be there. All that's missing is somebody staring at the clock waiting for the bell to ring.

I had visited the school last year when I heard rumors of it being torn down, but to my relief it was still there. You can tell it has become a hang out for the local riff-raff, so I didn't hang out. –*Andrea Nonnemacher*

Lambertville High Is Abandoned and Haunted!

The old high school is haunted. I know this for a fact because I spent the night there myself . . . alone! It was around 1987–88 and I was sneaking out during the middle of the night to bring a blanket to some friends who were going to sleep outside in a friend's yard. We were to meet up at the old jail in Lambertville.

When they didn't show up I went back to my grandmother's house where I was staying, only to find out that I had locked myself out. Rather than get caught, I decided to sleep in the old high school. I had been there so many times I wasn't afraid to be in there by myself.

I let myself in and walked up to the second floor where there was a small office. I curled up under a desk with the blanket and pulled a big board in front of the desk so you couldn't see me, and promptly fell asleep.

I woke up in the middle of the night when I heard what sounded like a door being shut quietly downstairs. All was quiet for a while and I almost fell back asleep, when a few minutes later I heard what sounded like broken glass breaking under the weight of someone's foot. It seemed like it came from the bottom of the stairwell. I froze, and a cold sweat broke out all over my body as I strained to listen for any noises. I heard something slowly shuffling up the stairwell, as though trying not to alert me to its presence.

Finally, it reached the top of the stairs and stood there for what seemed like an eternity before I heard it quietly walk down the hallway and stop before each and every classroom. Then it came to the room I was in! It was listening, hoping maybe that it could flush me out of where I was hiding. Finally, I heard it shuffle away and I laid there all night petrified with fear, afraid to even move for fear that it would hear me and rush in and get me.

I lay there until the sun rose up and then I tore out of there. I don't know who or what was in there with me that night, but I guarantee you it wasn't a cop, as even they only go into the school two at a time!

—Richard Scurti

Screams and Growls at Lambertville High

I am writing about the evils of school.

It all started when my friends John, Walter, Steve, and I decided to visit Lambertville School for the third time. All the other times we visited, either bums chased us out or nothing happened at all. But this night proved to be different.

We piled in to my friend's Camaro and set off. It was about 90 degrees that night under a full moon. We arrived and parked in our normal spot.

We trekked up the road to the school and went to a side entrance. Once inside, we decided to go up to the second floor.

Once up the stairs, we saw a mini hallway with 3 or 4 classrooms on each side. One classroom looked like a science room. As we entered, we got the chills. The room had to be about 30 degrees, considering we could see our breath and we were all freezing. That confused us because the school has no roof and it was 90 degrees outside.

After exploring that room we went up to the third floor. A couple of my friends peered into a room where the bums once chased them. After discovering nobody was there, we all started to relax, and went back down.

As soon as we were in the second floor hallway again, we heard a little girl scream from the third level we'd just been on. We looked at each other and brushed it off saying it was a breeze or a car going by. Then we heard it again, louder. She screamed at the top of her lungs, as if she was in pain. Then we heard the most terrifying, meanest, and loudest growl. It felt as if a man that was on the verge of death got up and moaned and growled right in my ear.

We shoved and pushed each other to get out the door. None of us could explain what happened to us that night. We also got very few people to believe us. All I know is, after going to a million different *Weird N.J.* places, I have never heard a more horrific sound in my life. —Jim

Industrial Strength: The Hudson & Manhattan Powerhouse

To come of age among the silent industrial ruins of Jersey City's waterfront was truly a singular phenomenon. The ransacked remnants of two centuries stood before us like an urban Acropolis.

Kids back then, including myself, sprained many an ankle running across endless acres of rail beds. Rusted pikes poked out of the tracks like sprouting stalagmites. Slouched rail cars sat forlorn and forgotten. Capsized tugboats and fishing vessels held vaguely onto moorings, their thick ropes and colossal chains limp. The corporations that created this river-edged row of industrial monuments had packed up, expired into bankruptcies.

In the mid –to –late '80s, the Newport development transformed all this overnight, opening the door to the current frenzied boom sweeping Jersey City's waterfront. Today there is almost nothing to remind us of the rail yards and terminals. Yet one reminder

still stands. Somehow it was overlooked—The Hudson & Manhattan Railroad Powerhouse.

Known to neighborhood kids as Frankenstein's Castle, the Powerhouse was the ultimate playground— the perfect place for an all-day game of manhunt. I never would have guessed in 1982, at the age of fourteen, that nearly twenty years later I'd be leading a preservation campaign to save it from demolition.

While nostalgia plays an important part in my preservation intentions, I cannot ignore the simple fact that this structure is an architectural wonder, a supreme industrial structure that stands like a stone and steel sentinel among a rising canyon of green-glass condominium complexes, office towers, and hotels.

The Powerhouse's design and architectural elements, particularly its intricate brickwork, are highly regarded by architects and historians. Christopher Gray, the architectural history columnist of *The New York Times*, called the Powerhouse a "cathedral," a "masterpiece of brickwork."

The coal-powered, steam generating Powerhouse energized the Hudson & Manhattan Railroad Company's three Hudson Tunnels, an underwater and above-ground rapid transit system that connected New Jersey to New York. It provided power to tunnel lines, trolleys, stations, and terminals on both sides of the Hudson River, including the Hudson Terminal in New York City. The Hudson Tunnels, now part of the PATH system, were begun in 1874 when DeWitt Clinton Haskins sank a deep shaft at the foot of 15th Street in Jersey City. The entrance to this shaft still exists, a few feet away from the Newport residential area.

Over thirty years later, William G. McAdoo unveiled a state-of-the-art trolley system that promised to bring convenience to commuters and economic

prosperity to Hudson County merchants and real estate entrepreneurs. Then, on February 25th, 1908, President Theodore Roosevelt sent a telegram to the Powerhouse instructing engineers to activate it, thereby lighting a subway system that continues to this day.

The Powerhouse was the product of a team of visionary engineers, architects, and businessmen. Its quick construction (October 1906–February 1908), pushed ahead by teams of hundreds of men, must have been a spectacular sight in its day. When it went into around-the-clock operation, the mechanical sounds that bellowed from its hulking boilers and turbines must have been ethereal, otherworldly.

Designed by John Oakman, the Powerhouse is a monumental yet elegant Romanesque Revival industrial building. Several architectural styles are evident: slender arched windows wrap around the sweeping façade; Greek crosses cap an enormous cornice-crown of dark brick, brilliantly woven into a cloistral arcade; a Medieval coal tower rises above the balustraded roof; and massive slanting Egyptian walls lean against the sky. There are three enormous smokestacks (there used to be four before

Thanks to the tireless efforts of John Gomez and the Jersey City Landmarks Conservancy, the Powerhouse was listed on the National Register of Historic Places in December 2001, a distinction that all but guarantees it will not be demolished. But the building's future is uncertain. To learn more about the Conservancy's campaign, please visit www.jerseycityhistory.net.

one was struck down by lightning) circled by steel catwalks.

Oakman was a master architect at a young age. An elder relative of his, Walter Oakman, was president of the Hudson & Manhattan Railroad Company, which was busy building the trolley tunnels under the Hudson River. He handed the lucrative commission of designing the H&MRR's stations and industrial buildings to John Oakman's firm, Robins & Oakman. The commission included the building of the Powerhouse, which had to be mighty enough to electrify an enormous subway system.

Oakman made it more than mighty—he made it spiritual, as beautiful as any train or ferry terminal in the metropolitan area. His Powerhouse was a perfect example of organic architecture: It relied on raw coal, river water, and sunlight to function; in return it emitted pure energy. If Beethoven had been an architect, the Powerhouse would have been his Fifth Symphony.

Today, the Powerhouse stands majestically among rising skyscrapers as the sole survivor of a remarkable era. It is the last great architectural monument on the Jersey City waterfront. But it has been unused and unprotected for decades. As a result it has fallen into a distressing state of deterioration.

The grand structure, however, a city block in length and width, remains sound and as solid as ever. Perhaps like Frankenstein's monster, the Powerhouse is just waiting for the little live current that it needs to bring it surging back to life.—*John K.*

Last Call for Newark's Pabst Brewery

We are now ascending the six-story stairwell of the old Pabst Blue Ribbon brewery in Newark to get up close and personal with a NJ icon that for many years has overlooked the city.

Stepping over broken glass, squatters' clothing, and many, many beer bottles, we reach the roof . . . and there it stands.

Now, seeing the Big Bottle from the distance of the Garden State Parkway, one can only think, Man, that's a BIG bottle. Standing on the roof of the brewery's bottling plant, the enormity of the structure almost makes you dizzy. Gazing up at it, you can almost feel yourself falling backward. And being six stories up, this is not a pleasant sensation, especially for those of us with a fear of heights!

Once the icon of the Pabst Brewing Company on South Orange Avenue, the sixty-foot water tower was constructed in 1930 by the Hoffman Beverage Company and advertised their famous Pale Dry Ginger Ale. The bottle is 185 feet above street level and can accommodate six men standing on top of its crimped bottle cap. It has a capacity of fifty-five-thousand gallons of water.

In 1930, when the Hoffman Company opened, the bottle was the largest in the world. It was made of one-quarter-inch copper-plated steel and had a diameter of seventeen and one-half feet at its base. The Pabst Brewing Company purchased the building and bottle in 1945.

These days the bottle looms over vast cemeteries, as if beckoning the dead to one more drink for the road. Now a faded brownish shade of rust, it seems to perfectly reflect the dilapidated neighborhood that surrounds it and the ominous abandoned factory that once produced millions of gallons of beer.

Our tour guide, contractor, and *Weird N.J.* reporter Nick DeBenedetto had gotten permission for us to photograph the grand old building just weeks before the wrecking ball was scheduled to demolish it. Local neighborhood associations have mixed feelings about the fate of the bottle. Some think it reflects the trouble the area has seen over the years and don't mind being rid of it, while others feel it is a genuine New Jersey treasure.

Nick is also involved with the Web site oldnewark.com run by Glen Geisheimer. The site has

many images and remembrances of Newark when the city was a bustling metropolis.

Nick never worked in the brewery but did a few small jobs there as a contractor around 1982, a few years before the plant shut down production for good.

Together we explored the cavernous rooms of the long-abandoned buildings and discovered a plethora of remnants still scattered around from the Pabst days, including the bottling machinery, beer vats, thousands of boxes, bottles, and even cancelled pay checks.

As we crossed the bridge over Grove Street to the brewing facility, things got a little stinky. The stench of the rotten yeast and hops permeated the building, even though it's been years since the last batch of beer was

brewed. There were huge holes in the floor where the beer tanks once stood, over three stories tall.

Workers were removing all the scrap metal and asbestos while we made our way through the cafeteria and into the darkness of the two floors below ground level.

"The cafeteria actually had a beer tap in it for the workers on break," Nick told us. "How many places do you know that would do that for their employees?" At one point, we got lost in the dank passageways, with every stairwell beginning to look the same. The darkness of the enormous building was a bit unnerving, considering it has been closed for a decade with little or no security to keep out vagrants and God knows who else. We breathed a little easier when we managed to get back to a familiar hallway and recrossed the bridge into the bottling facility.

We found the main offices had been completely cleaned out, but the loading dock still had a beer tanker sitting in one of its bays, waiting for one last refill that would never come.

The property is being razed for retail stores and housing, in hopes of bringing the Fairmount section of Newark some much needed revenue. The era of Newark's proud beer-making heritage is long gone. Once names like Krueger, Ballantine, Hensler, Anheuser-Busch, Feigenspan, and Pabst employed thousands of residents. Today only Anheuser-Busch, on Routes 1 and 9, remains. We'd love to see the Big Bottle saved as a symbol of all these once great Newark beers and the community that brewed, bottled, and breathed the beers that made the city famous.

Throughout 2005, demolition continued on the grand old brewery, and by early 2006 almost nothing was still

standing—nothing, that is, except that big brown bottle. It still stood tall somehow above the rubble of twisted steel girders and smashed concrete. It stood there, as if by sheer force of will, seeming to defy not only those who would seek to destroy it, but the laws of gravity itself. It was almost as if the building beneath it was never really supporting it at all, as if there was a spirit there that bolstered this venerable old New Jersey roadside icon. Alas, the big bottle was finally dismantled and gingerly hoisted down from its rooftop perch in sections on June 26, 2006. At the time of this writing, its future is uncertain.

When we last visited, we noticed an old locker with a bumper sticker on it that featured the Pabst Blue Ribbon logo and the words Pour It With Pride Newark emblazoned on it. For a city that may be on the verge of a comeback, taking pride in its beer-making history by saving this landmark should be worth raising a bottle in celebration, rather than discarding this bottle in the name of progress. We'd like to think that there will always be a place somewhere on the New Jersey landscape for odd and abandoned sights such as this, even if they are recycled.

INDEX

Page numbers in **bold** refer to photos and illustrations.

WEiRD N.J. VOL.2

by

Mark Moran and Mark Sceurman

ACKNOWLEDGMENTS

This book would not have been possible without our dedicated staff and faithful contributors. While we couldn't possibly name all the folks who have shared their talents and stories with us over the years, we would be remiss if we did not mention certain people whose contributions were particularly invaluable to this book: Abby Grayson, Joanne Austin, Ryan Doan, Chris Gethard, Heather Wendt-Kemp, William Angus, Michael Launay, and James Pontolillo.

We'd also like to thank our pit crew at *Weird* headquarters who help keep this strange train on the tracks while we are out lost somewhere in the swamps of Jersey: Susan Roselli, Rich Moran, Shirley Sceurman, and Barbara Moran.

And last, but certainly not least, we'd like to thank our publisher, editors, and designer, Barbara Morgan, Emily Seese, Gina Graham, and Richard Berenson, who took all the weirdness we could throw at them and somehow managed to pull it all together and squeeze it between the covers of this book.

Publisher: Barbara J. Morgan

Managing Editor: Emily Seese

Editor: Marjorie Palmer

Production: Della R. Mancuso
        Mancuso Associates, Inc.
        North Salem, NY

PICTURE CREDITS

SHOW US YOUR WEIRD!

Do you know of a weird site found somewhere in the United States, or can you tell us about a strange experience you've had? If so, we'd like to hear about it! We believe that every town has at least one great tale to tell, and we're listening. It could be a cursed road, haunted abandoned site, odd local character, or bizarre historic event. In most cases these tales are told only in the towns in which they originated. But why keep them to yourself when you could share them with all of America? So come on and fill us in on all the weirdness that's lurking in your backyard!

You can e-mail us at: Editor@WeirdUS.com,
or write to us at:
Weird U.S., P.O. Box 1346, Bloomfield, NJ 07003.

www.weirdus.com